THE HISTORY OF THE
NME

For Kat, who I first met in the lifts at King's Reach Tower.

First published in the United Kingdom in 2012 by
Portico Books
10 Southcombe Street
London
W14 0RA

An imprint of Anova Books Company Ltd

ISBN 9781907554483

A CIP catalogue record for this book is available from the British Library.

10 9 8 7 6 5 4 3 2 1

Printed and bound by Toppan Leefung Printing Ltd, China

This book can be ordered direct from the publisher at
www.anovabooks.com

For more details, please visit www.historyofnme.com

THE HISTORY OF THE

NME

HIGH TIMES AND LOW LIVES AT THE WORLD'S MOST FAMOUS MUSIC MAGAZINE

PAT LONG

PORTICO

Contents

Introduction

Friday afternoons at *NME* were always the best. Most of the copy would have been dispatched to the printer's by lunchtime and, barring any cataclysmic news event, the following week's newspaper would be complete. In the 1970s the staff of the paper would've celebrated with a bottle of chilled champagne and a joint the size of a small canoe. During my time working there in the noughties we made do with the ritual weekly plate of fish and chips in the work canteen and a couple of cans of whatever warm lager had been sent to the office by one of the magazine's commercial sponsors. The volume of the conversation and the music on the stereo would grow. A few members of staff would start listlessly kicking a football around. Others would be ringing press officers and record companies to get themselves on the guestlist for the weekend's gigs. Expenses claims would be constructed, often applying greater levels of attention to detail and imagination than had previously been spent writing the three-page cover interview with The Libertines or Kasabian. Freelance photographers would float in to huddle around the lightbox, proudly displaying the contact sheets of their latest shoot with Black Rebel Motorcycle Club or The Coral. While my colleagues were busy, I would sneak off downstairs to the windowless basement room where the huge bound volumes of *NME* back issues were kept. Just accessing the IPC archive felt like being in a Bond film. The basement could only be accessed by a special lift; once inside you moved a set of towering mobile bookcases by rotating a huge metal wheel like that of a Swiss bank's bullion safe. But once inside, what riches there were within those yellowing pages. I'd marvel at ancient live ads featuring the strange and exotic names of moderately successful but now forgotten bands – Hatfield and the North! The Close Lobsters! Atomic Rooster! – or features that went on for thousands of words before the band was even mentioned. But mostly I'd just feel jealous.

In my time at the *NME* we'd got jaded and cynical. Hardened music fans, we were disillusioned at how rock music had become just another cog in an industrial entertainment process, a leisure option like going to Center Parcs or buying a Chelsea season ticket. Our forebears wouldn't even countenance such thoughts. For them rock music was an elemental life force that had to be nurtured and protected with well-spun words and the occasional snarky, punning headline. For *NME* journalists, writing passionately about rock music was a way of making sure that it was always more than just a commodity: sacrifices of health, sanity and very occasionally even life were made in the *NME* journalists' noble yet quixotic pursuit of rock myth. There they were in the IPC archive, like the Dallas bystanders captured in Abraham Zapruder's 18-second Super 8 footage of the Kennedy assassination: watching, slack-jawed and occasionally aghast as pop-cult history was made. Kurt Cobain OD'ing. Richey Manic disappearing. The first-ever Led Zeppelin gig. Hendrix setting fire to his guitar onstage at the Finsbury Park Astoria. Excitable early interviews with The Rolling Stones or Blur. The Smiths splitting. Bowie making a fascist salute at Victoria station. Smoking dope with the Happy Mondays or Bob Marley. Reviews of forgotten groups at extinct pub venues. A treasure trove of myth and memory.

No other country in the world has anything like the weekly music press, but then no other country in the world takes music as seriously as we do. Every morning at *NME* you'd open your post with a mixture of glee (free CDs!) and trepidation (abusive letters written in green biro!). In 2003 I had threatening voicemails from a man with a West Country accent left on my office ansaphone every day for a month. My crime? Writing a small but dismissive review of a new single by the Stereophonics. I didn't mind, really: for four generations the weekly *NME* has provided a crucial cultural lifeline to the bored and disaffected around the world. If one man was driven to a sexual-sounding Cornish rage by my casual cruelty towards Kelly Jones then that was clearly a price worth paying.

There aren't many people who read the *New Musical Express* regularly for any length of time that have ever truly shaken off its grip. Once, on the way back from reviewing a late-night gig, a Clash-loving London taxi driver asked me what I did for a living. When I told him, he almost crashed the cab with envy and amazement, before telling me a story about losing his money and shoes at a Sham 69 gig in 1980 and having to walk home eight miles, barefoot but content.

Music is such an inescapable part of the British cultural landscape that it's strange to think of a time when it wasn't ghettoised in a weekly newspaper, when families didn't spend their summer attending well-provisioned inter-generational rock festivals, when parents didn't swap music with their teenage children. Once the pages of *NME* were literally the only place in the world where you could find out where Red Lorry Yellow Lorry or Kingmaker or the Groundhogs were next playing in your town. Now, of course, we all know everything instantly. It's a fact that, thanks to digital technology, the soundtrack to our lives is richer and more varied than at any point previously, but it's also meant that *NME* has suffered the same loss of readership, advertising revenue and influence as all print media. You don't need to be a romantic to think that, somehow, that's a shame.

The history covered in this book ends roughly about the year 2000, two years before I started working at the *NME*. This is partly because the digital media revolution that has occurred since the start of the 21st century would merit a whole book in itself, and partly because I wanted to avoid having to make predictions about the future of the paper. The *NME* of today is never as good as the one we grew up reading, of course, but despite the naysayers, it's proved resilient enough to be the last of what was once a handful of weekly music papers still appearing on newsstands.

But that's today. That's now. This book is about then. It's about how a Tin Pan Alley trade rag became one of the most important and influential magazines on the planet, despite being staffed by people who could often barely function in the real world. It's about how the weekly music press developed an influence on British culture out of all proportion with the size of its readership, about how the values and ideals of the underground were sneaked into the mainstream via a weekly music paper published by a vast multinational publishing company. It's about the British love affair with rock'n'roll music and the strange, talented, obsessive, wonderful characters that chronicled a whole culture. Inside are brand new interviews with all of these people. But mainly it's about fights and drugs and breakdowns and strikes and rock and reggae and punk and ska and acid house and Britpop, about the Sex Pistols and David Bowie and Public Enemy and Oasis and The Smiths. It's about the *New Musical Express*: wonderful and occasionally misguided repository of our 60-year love affair with pop music, the magazine that changed the nation's cultural DNA forever.

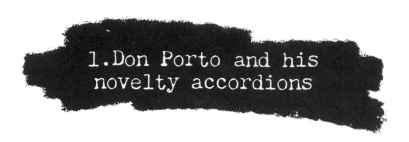

1. Don Porto and his novelty accordions

'They were on their knees — within 15 minutes the receivers were going to be called in...'

The past is a foreign country, one where people are inordinately fond of polka music. Yes, despite its iconoclastic later reputation, the most culturally important British magazine of the second half of the 20th century had its roots in... the accordion.

At the beginning of the 1930s, Britain found itself in the grip of an absolute mania for accordion music. At an accordion convention organised by instrument manufacturers Hohner in 1932, almost 40,000 people turned up to hear bands called things like Don Porto and his Novelty Accordions, causing a minor sensation when the crowd all tried to cram into the 2,000-capacity Westminster Central Hall just around the corner from the Houses of Parliament.

It was an austere time, but the flamboyance of these acts – who often dressed in 'exotic' gyspy costumes to disguise the fact that they were jobbing musicians from the Home Counties – was a welcome distraction from the drabness and poverty of a time when the National Debt was at its second highest point in the 20th century. Indeed, so popular was this movement that it had its own magazine, *Accordion Times*, established in 1935 and catering entirely for the manifold requirements of the professional and amateur squeezebox aficionado.

Sadly, though, the boom didn't last. The accordion bands struggled on, but by the end of the Second World War life was getting tough for the publishers and staff of *Accordion Times*. They were on the brink of closure when salvation came in the form of a merger with a brand new weekly paper, and so it was that on the first Friday in October 1946, professional musicians nationwide were able to pay fourpence for a four-page black and white tabloid aimed directly at their needs and interests. Inside that first issue was a hot-blooded editorial about Musicians' Union toothlessness, adverts for instrument manufacturers, a letters page soliciting contributions, a cartoon strip and stories about the most popular crooners, bandleaders and jazzmen of the day ('Paul Robeson indicts Britain!'). And there on the masthead, next to a woodcut illustration of a metronome, proud gothic script proclaimed the name of this new venture: *Musical Express*, with the slightly smaller subtitle 'Incorporating *Accordion Times*'.

From its offices at 33 King Street, just down the road from Covent Garden fruit and veg market and the recently reopened Royal Opera House, *Musical Express* exuded a raffishness and Bohemianism that is still striking today. Specialising in news aimed at professional musicians, rather than music fans, it was a cosmopolitan and glamorous paper that transcended the mood of the threadbare, gloomy Britain of bombsites and ration cards. *Musical Express* dealt with music like it was the most important thing in the world, and that the people who played it were an elect group, apart from everyday society, regardless of their instrument or nationality. Many of the conventions established in those first issues of the paper – the tour news ('Band swap rumour – whose band is going to play in America?'), the classified ads, the outraged letters from readers – would still be in place over half a century later. Indeed, one early issue ran an outraged editorial expressing shock at the fact that a rival paper, the *Melody Maker*, had fixed its annual readers' poll. It was a rivalry that would only grow in rancour over the next 50 years.

With the end of wartime paper rationing, *Musical Express* doubled in size, although its accordion coverage suffered, trimmed back first to a column and then dropped entirely. The readers didn't seem to mind – by the end of the decade, *Musical Express* had become the biggest-selling weekly music paper in the country, leaving *Melody Maker* to cover the more serious end of jazz while it wrote about the more populist Big Band craze. For the *Musical Express*, like the people of Britain emerging from the ordeal of the Second World War, the future must have seemed glowing.

Maurice Irving Kinn belonged to a breed of men that had become a showbusiness archetype by the early 1950s: the working-class East End Jewish impresario. Born in Poplar in 1924, he started his career on Fleet Street as a teenage tea boy for the *Irish Times*, leaving to move into showbusiness. Kinn overcame a natural shyness and stammer to make a healthy amount of money managing Cyril Stapleton and Joe Loss, the most successful British big band leaders of the post-war period, before becoming a promoter of high-profile dance band concerts. Perhaps unusually for someone in his line of work, Kinn was regarded as fair and trustworthy in a business populated by sharks and hustlers, which is why he received a phone call out of the blue from one of his debtors, the advertising director of the *Musical Express*, late one Friday afternoon in 1952. Far from being a success, the paper was losing money hand over fist. 'The paper had lost so much money that it was going to close down if they couldn't find a buyer by the following Monday,' said Kinn in an interview with the writer Paul Gorman in 2001. 'I went in there to talk to them because they owed me money and got caught up with this idea of running the paper. They were on their knees – within 15 minutes the receivers were going to be called in.'[1]

Maurice Kinn was nothing if not a shrewd businessman, and could see the immense value of running his own music paper. He'd be able to use it as a promotional tool for the concerts that he was staging, while the prospect of receiving regular advertising revenue from his competitors must've been appealing. He paid the thousand pounds[2] *Musical Express*' owners were asking for the title and duly found himself the proprietor of an ailing and unpopular weekly paper with a disgruntled staff, a low readership of 20,000 a week and no knowledge of how newspaper publishing actually worked.

What he needed was an expert, so Kinn recruited his old friend Percy Dickins to help out. Dickins was a former jazz saxophonist who had ended up on the staff of *Melody Maker* as advertising manager and was tempted to defect by Kinn with a promise of shares in the new title should it prove successful. Kinn and Dickins now needed an office, and, really, there was only one place they could consider: Denmark Street. Named after Prince George of Denmark, the husband of Queen Anne, since the late 19th century Denmark Street in London's West End had been a hub for the capital's music publishers, earning itself the nickname Tin Pan Alley in tribute to its New York counterpart.[3] Just as the film companies colonised nearby Wardour Street across the Charing Cross road in Soho, this narrow row of shops and offices was synonymous with the music business: nicknamed the '200 Yards of Hope', Tin Pan Alley was where aspirant songwriters or musicians would come to try and peddle their latest wares to cigar-chewing publishers in camel-hair coats, or where band leaders would raid the cafes and coffeeshops for new musicians for one-night stands and tours.

Don Black was later to become an Oscar-winning lyricist for songs as diverse as 'Diamonds are Forever', 'Born Free' and Michael Jackson's hit 'Ben', but in 1952 he was a showbiz-obsessed teenager who would bunk off from his job polishing the brass on the banisters at the London Palladium to mooch about in central London. He was naturally drawn to Denmark Street. 'There was just music everywhere,' he remembers. 'There were two cafes next door to each other – Julia's and The Suffolk Dairy – where everyone would kill time: musicians, comedians, publishers, managers, agents. Someone like Frankie Vaughan or Dicky Valentine would come down to Denmark Street to find his new song and there'd be a ripple of excitement all up and down the street.'

Melody Maker had started out at number 19 Denmark Street after music publisher Lawrence Wright founded it in 1926, but it was at number 5 that Kinn and Dickins began to dismantle the ailing *Musical Express*. They set to work by immediately recruiting a new staff; Kinn and Dickins coaxed the seasoned writer Ray Sonin out of an early retirement to be their editor. A former *Melody Maker* staffer who had written successful songs for Vera Lynn and BBC radio comedy scripts for Noël Coward and the popular wartime comic Tommy Handley, Sonin had been a music journalist since the late 1930s, until a substantial pools win enabled him to retire to write crime and science fiction novels with titles like *Murder in Print* and *The Adventures of Space Kingsley*. Kinn, Dickins and Sonin decided to rip up the magazine's tired template and start again from scratch. The front cover of issue number 268 of *Musical Express* duly featured a bold promise, written by Kinn, of what the dwindling readership could expect when the paper was relaunched after a fortnight's break:

'The presentation and contents will be fresh and stimulating because the *New Musical Express* will be produced by a brand new, hand-picked staff of editorial experts with long experience in musical journalism.'

Kinn was true to his word. On Friday 7 March 1952, a few weeks after the death of King George VI and the accession of his daughter Elizabeth, the same month that British wartime citizens' identity cards were finally abolished, the first-ever issue of the New Musical Express was born.

Fittingly, Kinn's magazine felt far more modern than the old *Musical Express*. Readers parted with sixpence and received a magazine with The Goons, Big Bill Broonzy and bandleader Ted Heath on the front cover, inside which the magazine was laid out more clearly and written in a new, hipper style which suddenly made the old era of dance bands seem hopelessly formal and desiccated. In 1952, the leading music paper was *Melody Maker* once again, but it was still a serious trade journal, reporting stories about the minutiae of which drummer was leaving which big band for another. The *New Musical Express* focused on showbusiness and popular music in a way that was fresh and entertaining: establishing a tradition that would typify the magazine for the rest of its life; the subeditors, the people on the paper responsible for foring text submitted by the journalists, as well as adding headlines and picture captions, were clearly spending a lot of time in the smoky subs' room thinking up punning headlines, of which 'Vocal Boy Makes Good' was by far the best. There was news and gossip, fashion tips for female readers ('have you tried wearing one shade of lipstick over another?') and a reviews column written by jazz saxophonist Johnny Dankworth, as well as three anonymous columns: 'Ad Lib', written by 'The Slider', 'The Sunny Side' by 'Glissando' and, at the back of the magazine, 'Tail-Pieces' by 'The Alley Cat'. The Alley Cat, although redolent of a nocturnal prowler slinking through the city's jazz scene and listening at club doorways for the latest gossip, was actually written by the portly Kinn. He wasted no time in settling scores, pursuing his own agenda and currying favour with acts that he could promote, clearly enjoying his new role as press baron. 'My tip for the London Palladium and a cert success is a sexy singer from America,' wrote The Alley Cat in his first column, 'Tony Bennett'.

With Dickins' *Melody Maker* advertising contacts, Sonin's editorial experience and Kinn's business instinct, the *New Musical Express* should've been an immediate success. But to Kinn's chagrin, his new venture continued to fail. 'I kept the [booking] agency going, which I had to, because the paper... kept on losing money hand over fist. Two months later I had to borrow money from my mother-in-law to keep the *NME* afloat and I felt like an idiot, like I'd really made a mistake.'[4]

What the *New Musical Express* needed if it was to see out 1952 was what marketing men today call a USP: a gimmick, something to set it apart from the competition other than just its lightness of tone and insider gossip. Inspiration came from a feature of the weekly American trade magazine *Billboard*, which by 1952 had already been around for almost half a century. *Billboard* started out as the journal of the bill posting industry, becoming the paper of record for circuses, cinemas, carnies, vaudeville, fairs and amusement parks. By the 1930s *Billboard* was publishing a weekly list of the most played songs on jukeboxes in America, a chart called the Hit Parade.

**The proud proprietor: Maurice Kinn inspects the latest copy
of the New Musical Express, 1954**

In the UK the popularity of a song was still measured by the sales of
its printed sheet music, but Kinn was a visionary: he believed that sales
of records would one day outstrip those of sheet music, as more and more
households bought record players. To reflect this, he ordered Dickins to
phone 20 record shops and find out which discs they'd been selling to
the public throughout the week.

After gaining the support of his contacts in the industry, on 14
November 1952 Kinn published the first-ever UK singles chart, a novelty
that was to change the way the British music business worked forever.
Number one in what *NME* called its 'authentic weekly survey of the best-
selling pop records' was a ballad, 'Here In My Heart', sung by former
bricklayer Al Martino, subsequently known for his role as the singer
Johnny Fontane in the first of Francis Ford Coppola's *Godfather* films.
Martino, who was later forced to move to the UK when real-life Mafioso
attempted to buy him out of his American management contract,

headed up a list of 12 songs that also included recordings by Nat 'King' Cole, Vera Lynn, Bing Crosby and Max Bygraves. Crucially, this new list reflected *NME's* shift in emphasis from covering the writer of a song to its performer, simultaneously opening up a new market for the music press: instead of solely selling papers to musicians or Tin Pan Alley insiders, the *New Musical Express* connected with record buyers and fans. Within a few weeks the paper's circulation leapt up: first by 20 and then 50 per cent.

The charts grew in size and scope: Dickins' original list of 20 shops was increased to 53, mainly in London and the Home Counties, but also in the bigger urban hubs like Manchester and Liverpool. To meet the paper's deadline and get it to its printer in Walthamstow on time, each member of the paper's staff was allocated a list of shops to call each Monday morning. The results of these calls were passed on to *NME's* staff accountant, who took time from his duties on the payroll to collate and process the week's research.

The *NME* charts were an instant phenomenon. Dickins was a man of great charm and persuasiveness who used the introduction of the charts to increase the paper's advertising revenue by encouraging record companies to pay for adverts for forthcoming releases that they hoped would eventually make the Hit Parade. Don Black, who had been sacked from his job at the Palladium after being discovered watching one of the performances when he was supposed to be working, was recruited by Kinn as the *NME's* office boy as a favour to Black's older brother, and remembers Percy Dickins as an imposing figure on Tin Pan Alley:

'Percy had a slightly rarified air about him – his nickname was "Sir Percy". He used to take me to this Chinese restaurant on Denmark Street called The Universal, which was really exciting to me because I was this Jewish boy from Hackney and I'd never eaten Chinese food before, never seen anything like it.'

While Dickins was dining on spring rolls and chow mein, Kinn and Sonin were using the charts to determine methodically which artists they would cover in the paper's editorial pages: looking down the list they realised that there were names selling huge amounts of records that were simply not being covered by *Melody Maker* but were obviously hugely popular among music fans. Almost overnight the old swing bands were phased out in favour of hot new American stars like Frank Sinatra and Johnnie Ray.

A further circulation boost came courtesy of Radio Luxembourg. In order to circumvent the BBC's broadcast monopoly in Britain, in the 1920s a 100-watt transmitter had been constructed in the small central

European Grand Duchy of Luxembourg, from which English and French language programmes were broadcast across the continent. During the Second World War the transmitter was commandeered by the Third Reich and used to broadcast Nazi propaganda, including that of Lord Haw-Haw[5], across the channel. But by 1952 millions of Britons were tuning in to the commercial station Radio Luxembourg on 208 medium wave every evening to hear religious programmes, along with secular fare like science fiction serial *The Adventures of Dan Dare, Pilot of the Future* or the cockney Leslie Welch, nicknamed 'the Memory Man', a former vaudeville performer who would amaze listeners by correctly answering questions concerning obscure and forgotten pieces of sports trivia.

Derek Johnson was the programme administrator on Radio Luxembourg, and would pass *NME*'s chart to DJs in the Duchy, who started a regular weekly chart run-down presented by DJ Pete Murray, which listed all of the songs in reverse order from 12th place to the number one slot. This gave *NME*'s chart a new credence and Dickins responded by taking out on-air adverts, giving further credibility to the paper, even if passers-by could be forgiven for overlooking the *New Musical Express*' Denmark Street offices. 'You'd walk up this shabby flight of stone steps,' remembers Don Black. 'It didn't look like anything at all. But then you'd open this door and get this whiff of the newsroom, this real sense of excitement and energy in the air.' Kinn also used Radio Luxembourg as a marketing tool, giving away free copies of unsold back issues of the *New Musical Express* to any listeners who sent in a stamped addressed envelope.

Derek Johnson became a freelancer reporter for *NME*, eventually joining the staff as News Editor in 1957, along with the magazine's movie critic, future film director Michael Winner. Another crucial appointment was the photographer Harry Hammond. A successful East End showbusiness photographer-about-town a decade before Terence Donovan or David Bailey, Hammond was recruited by Kinn while taking portrait shots for sheet music covers. Hammond's style, which comprised artfully composed portraits or seemingly miraculous live shots of artists performing, pioneered the form of rock photography, becoming much imitated for the rest of the century.

Within a year, Maurice Kinn and Percy Dickins' blend of vision, charm, chutzpah, business sense and talent meant that the *New Musical Express* was thriving. In 1953 Kinn organized the first *NME* awards ceremony at the Royal Albert Hall to celebrate – the Readers' Poll Winners' Concert featured the leading lights of British jazz, including Chris Barber and Eddie Calvert – and before long the paper's circulation had nudged ahead of its rival *Melody Maker*[6] and even inspired a new imitator. Record Mirror was launched in June 1954 to try and poach some of the *New Musical Express'* advertising revenue, upping the ante by printing their own albums chart as well as a singles rundown. *Record Mirror* was followed four years later by *Disc* and suddenly British pop and jazz fans would have the choice of four music papers to buy every week. But what happened next was a remarkable, once-in-a-century concomitance of events that would have seismic consequences reaching far beyond the 200 yards of Tin Pan Alley, consequences that not even the savvy Kinn and Dickins could have foreseen.

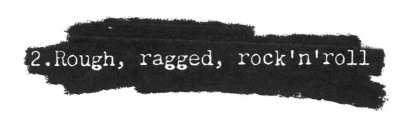

2.Rough, ragged, rock'n'roll

'This fifth-rate music can pierce through the thin shell of civilisation
and turn people into wild dervishes...'

On 21 March 1952, two weeks after the first issue of the *New Musical Express* was published and a week before Sam Phillips founded his new record label, Sun, in Memphis, American radio DJ Alan Freed hosted the first of his Moondog Coronation Balls at Ohio's Cleveland Arena. Intended as a promotional tie-in with his regular Moondog Show on Cleveland's AM radio station WJW, the event featured headliners Paul Williams and his Hucklebuckers and a black instrumental group, Tiny Grimes and the Rocking Highlanders, who performed wearing Tam o' Shanters, sporrans and kilts. Tickets for the show, priced $1.50, were widely counterfeited, so that in the end an estimated 20,000 music fans attempted to gain entry to an arena with a maximum capacity of half that number. Police were forced to stop the gig and fans were trampled and crushed as the weight of their numbers destroyed the arena's perimeter fence. The Moondog Coronation Ball was the first major concert showcasing a bill made up entirely of artists playing a new kind of music, the name for which Freed himself had coined: rock'n'roll.

At around the same time as Freed's disastrous first foray into promotion, the *NME* was carrying a breathless news feature about the instrument that it would from now on forever be associated with. 'Guitars are news!' it read, 'but what is it about this instrument which is stealing so much radio time?'

The trigger for this investigation was a new record that had recently made the number four slot on *NME*'s chart, Bill Haley and The Comets' 'Shake, Rattle and Roll'. By the following year Haley would have four records on *NME*'s chart, all rock'n'roll discs, and in his wake a new kind of star would emerge from America. This new act was young and wild, typified by the immortal description in Wolf Mankowitz's play *Expresso Bongo*, made into a film starring Cliff Richard in 1959: 'a chip on your shoulder and an H-Bomb in your pants. A sneer, a twitch – and hell in your head'.

The rise of the rock'n'rollers coincided with the move from fragile and costly shellac 78s to cheaper vinyl 45s, opening up a new market for record consumption: the teenager. According to groundbreaking research into teenage spending and consumer patterns carried out in the second half of the 1950s, British teenagers were responsible for buying 40 per cent of all records – and what the teenagers wanted was what *NME* called 'rough, ragged, rock'n'roll',[7] made by the kind of people the jazzman George Melly described as 'heroes with whom the young were able to identify in the immediate rather than the 'when I grow up' sense'.[8] For the first time, teenagers were buying records written, played, sung and even produced by people barely much older than themselves.

NME was the first of the weeklies to cover rock'n'roll comprehensively, although they retained the services of jazz critic Humphrey Lyttelton, and by the autumn of 1956 the paper was full of pieces on Fats Domino, Elvis, Bill Haley, Carl Perkins, Gene Vincent and the 13-year-old Frankie Lymon. Reading these interviews with wonder were hundreds of the children – among them John Lennon, Malcolm McLaren and Marc Bolan – who would later shape British pop music.

It helped that the serious-minded jazz magazine *Melody Maker* viewed rock'n'roll as the enemy, 'the antithesis of all that jazz has been striving for over the years' as one editorial put it. Reviewing Elvis Presley's latest single for *Melody Maker* in October 1956, former *NME* writer Steve Race wrote: 'Lo, many times I have heard bad records, but for sheer repulsiveness coupled with the monotony of incoherence, "Hound Dog" hit a new low in my experience.'

But the squares and the jazzers at *Melody Maker* were fighting a losing battle. The 100,000 people who now bought *NME* every week, or the ten million who tuned in to the BBC's rock'n'roll television show *Six-Five Special*, produced by Jack Good, wanted rock'n'roll, or at least some of them did: across the *New Musical Express* readers' letters section, 'Talking Points', the rock'n'roll evangelists clashed with the jazz fans on a weekly basis. 'Rock'n'roll provides an excellent beat for dancing and the honking sax provides excitement – what better music for young cats to jump to?' asked one reader. 'What trash this rock'n'roll stuff is,' thundered another. 'Soon it will be forgotten and the music of Goodman and Miller will still live on.'

Ten years later rock'n'roll would be regarded as the premier musical mode of communication by the counter-culture. But in 1956 the avant-garde dismissed it as purely proletarian teenage music. One of the year's most controversial cultural events was the first staging of John Osborne's play *Look Back In Anger*, which premiered at the Royal Court theatre in May 1956. Its central character, the alienated and vituperative Jimmy Porter, was a jazz trumpeter, and Osborne and the other playwrights and novelists who came to be known as the 'Angry Young Men' were far more likely to have listened to jazz or folk than anything so tawdry and elemental as a Gene Vincent disc. Outside of the pop press only the middle-aged journalist Colin MacInnes tried to write about rock'n'roll culture in a way that was at all serious or sympathetic, attempting to dissect the appeal of it as a cultural phenomenon in essays like 'Young England, Half English', rather than dismiss it out of hand as evidence of a decline in standards, as the panelists on an episode of Radio 4's *Any Questions* thought fit to do: '[this] fifth-rate music,' opined Liberal MP Jeremy Thorpe, 'can pierce through the thin shell of civilisation and turn people into wild dervishes'.

Rock'n'roll's outsider status was further confirmed in September 1956 when the film *Rock Around the Clock* was released. Featuring appearances from Bill Haley and Alan Freed, the film was associated with public disturbances across the country: in Manchester, *The Times* newspaper reported that a 'noisy and unruly mob of 200 youths ... terrorized pedestrians, obstructed traffic and were jigging to 'Rock and Roll' rhythm.' [9] As the mob passed down Oxford Street in London, one member of the crowd is reported to have shouted 'the police can't touch us. There are too many of us.' In South London, crowds of Teddy Boys rampaged through the streets, breaking windows and turning over cars. The result was widespread bans on rock'n'roll music in Birmingham, Bristol, Belfast, Liverpool, Carlisle, Preston, Blackpool and Brighton. Maurice Kinn knew where his money lay and took the side of the fans, sternly accusing the national press of 'exaggerating and distorting the situation, instead of recognizing the riots as the hooliganism of an undisciplined minority'.[10] Kinn's editorial in defence of rock'n'roll might've been prompted by commercial reasons, but the *NME*'s stance cemented rock'n'roll as a tribal identity set in opposition to the rest of mainstream society, a notion that defined the tone of the paper through punk, acid house and beyond. A large part of the hostility towards rock'n'roll lay in the fear of a kind of creeping Americanisation of British culture. It wasn't until the first domestic rock'n'roll stars started to appear that the controversy cooled. Most of these artists, like Tommy Steele, born Thomas Hicks in Bermondsey, Willesden's Johnny Kidd or Adam Faith from Acton got their first break from playing at the 2i's Coffee Bar at number 59 Old Compton Street in Soho. Here, future Led Zeppelin manager Peter Grant was the bouncer, the acts were paid in Cokes rather than cash and the impresario Larry Parnes looked for new acts to manage amid the cigarette smoke and steam from the cappuccino machine. Yet the bulk of the 2i's crowd mimicked American artists, singing in an approximation of Elvis or Carl Perkins rather than their natural accents. Few of them had much success outside of Britain; the exception was skiffle artist Lonnie Donegan, who was the first British singer to have two top ten hits in the US.

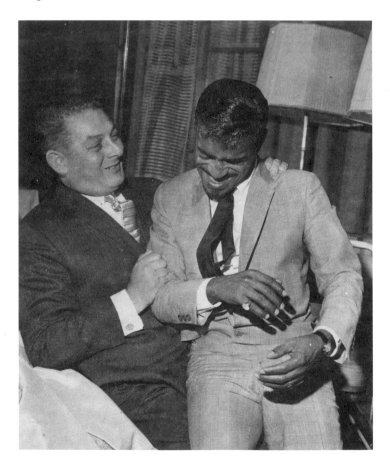

Kinn at home with Sammy Davis Jr. 'He was starstruck – he'd be talking to Sammy Davis or someone and you could see he'd be really relishing it...'

It was a vibrant, homemade scene: in a small classified ad at the back of a 1957 issue of *New Musical Express*, among the notices for dance band agencies and pin-ups ('photographs of lovely Cabaret and figure models in attractive poses'), one Bill Haley fan took out an advert to promote her new fan club. 'At last!' it read, 'Bill Haley and his Comets have a fan club! Send SAE to 2 Grove Mill, Hitchin, Herts.'

In the face of this kind of grassroots enthusiasm, the music business struggled to keep pace. As the poet, activist, small magazine editor (and jazz fan) Jeff Nuttall noted: 'The established business world, the square commercial world, the promoters, were completely out-distanced. All that they could do was run to keep up.' [11]

Maurice Kinn seemed to be doing quite well out of the rock'n'roll boom, however. In May 1958 he expanded operations, opening another office at number 23 Denmark Street where the magazine's editorial team, under new editor, a Canadian ex-pat called Andy Gray ,[12] were housed. Kinn also bought the first of several Rolls-Royces and began hosting showbizzy cocktail parties and receptions with his wife Berenice at their well-appointed flat on Mayfair's Upper Grosvenor Street. He struck up friendships with visiting American performers like Sammy Davis, Jr., and Frank Sinatra, whose 1953 UK tour had been so ill-attended that he'd considered quitting the business until a Kinn editorial in *New Musical Express* lauding him persuaded the Chairman of the Board to change his mind.

'Maurice seemed very authoritarian,' remembers Don Black, 'but I think that was because he was a very shy man. He was starstruck – he'd be talking to Sammy Davis, Jr., or someone on the telephone and you could see he'd be really relishing it. He was a fan, really.'

For someone who'd spent most of his working life around musicians, Kinn also had a surprisingly old-fashioned and prudish side. He particularly disliked any stars that he saw as unwholesome or lascivious, and would use the influence of his anonymous Alley Cat persona to make a point of singling out the worst offenders: one piece complaining about Cliff Richard was picked up by national newspaper *The Daily Sketch*, who forced Jack Good – then working on *Six-Five Special*'s successor, *Oh Boy!* – to ask Richard to tone down his routine. A later Kinn piece complained about another British rocker, Billy Fury, and his 'revolting mannerisms' in a television appearance: 'early evening viewers,' believed Kinn, 'should be catered for, not offended'.

By the turn of the decade, the Fleet Street moralists and MPs had won their battle to control rock'n'roll. The incredible burst of wild energy that made stars of Elvis and Little Richard and Buddy Holly had burned itself out. Presley had joined the army, while the most popular homegrown rock'n'roll singer, Cliff Richard, was moving into syrupy AOR ballads. It was also a time of turmoil in the publishing business: 1960 saw the launch of the first new national paper for 40 years, the *Sunday Telegraph*, but also the closure of *The News Chronicle*, *The Star* and two Sunday papers. Meanwhile, Cecil Harmsworth King's Mirror Group continued to rapaciously hoover up smaller competitors, taking over the Associated Press and the magazine publishers Odhams and Newnes, to become the largest media company in the world.

Sales of the *New Musical Express* were beginning to flag after their mid-decade peak, and advertising revenue was falling off accordingly. As 1960 became 1961, Kinn looked around him at what was going on with rock'n'roll and took stock of his business interests. His prognosis was pessimistic: this pop music lark's over, he thought. Time to get out while the going's good.

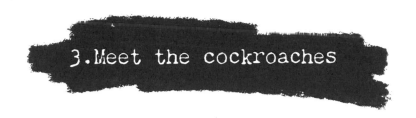

3.Meet the cockroaches

'Ringo tripped and his tray of cakes went everywhere, followed by the other three landing in a heap on top of him like a Marx Brothers routine...'

Something urgent needed to be done. Fewer people reading the *New Musical Express* made it harder for Percy Dickins to drum up advertising revenue, while the thing that'd made *NME* unique – its weekly chart – was now being copied everywhere. With fewer adverts the magazine slimmed down to 40 pages, which meant that readers got less for their sixpence when the paper was published on a Friday. Dickins resorted to selling record companies advertising space on the magazine's front cover, which meant that the editor Andy Gray had to find new ways to promote the artists being interviewed inside. The result was a kind of vicious downwards sales spiral and Maurice Kinn was faced with a set of problems that *NME* publishers would encounter over again throughout the paper's history: it's hard enough to maintain readers' attention when competition is tough or they get older and stop reading a paper for teenagers, but when the current music scene isn't exciting enough to sustain a weekly music paper it becomes almost impossible.

A new staffer recruited from a Birkenhead local paper had the answer to Kinn and Dickins' problems, although no one at the *NME* quite realised it at the time. Alan Smith had been a freelance contributor to the paper while living up in Liverpool and had got to know a hot new local group from his trips to the Cavern Club, in between writing stories about cats stuck up trees, pools winners and the other noble staples of local newspaper journalism.

Being a regional stringer, the lowliest foot soldier in the music press, Smith wasn't taken seriously. The centre of the music industry in Britain was London and there was a distinct snobbery about the role of the regions. 'I'd be talking in the *NME* office about this great band,' Smith remembers, 'but they were just regarded as a joke because they didn't have a record deal at the time. "Ere, 'ow's your mates the Cockroaches?" all that stuff.'

At the end of 1962, around the same time that The Beatles were putting the finishing touches to their debut single, 'Love Me Do', Maurice Kinn was approached by Cecil King of the Mirror Group in an attempt to persuade him to sell the paper. Kinn had had offers before, but decided that the time was right to offload it; although low overheads meant that the magazine was still making money, profits were diminishing with the decline in sales. In late 1962 he accepted King's offer and sold the *New Musical Express* business for £500,000 to the newly created International Publishing Company.

Known informally as IPC, the International Publishing Company was the result of a process of rationalisation of the Mirror Group and its various recent acquisitions. The new company was a behemoth: from their head office in Fleetway House in Farringdon, IPC presided over an empire of holdings that included 12 British newspapers, 11 overseas titles, 75 consumer magazines, 132 trade and theatrical journals, plus interests in book publishing, printing and television.[13] Their flagship title, *The Daily Mirror*, had become the best-selling paper in the country under editor Hugh Cudlipp, selling five million copies daily by the end of the year.

Perhaps naturally considering he'd built it up from nothing, Kinn sold the paper he'd revived to IPC with several strings attached. One of the conditions of sale was that Kinn would be allowed to stay on as the paper's executive director and columnist, continuing to slink around Soho as The Alley Cat and retaining a generous expense account to host his showbiz parties. But the sale to IPC, which was completed in 1963, involved a symbolic move as well as physical one: the *New Musical Express* and its staff were transferred from their shabby offices on Tin Pan Alley and installed in the IPC Magazines building on the Strand, next door to the Savoy hotel, where they joined magazines from Newnes and Odhams like *New Scientist, Horse & Hound, Ideal Home* and *Woman's Weekly*, as well as a suite of teenage mags with names like *Marilyn, Valentine, Roxy* and *Honey*. Overnight the *New Musical Express* moved from being an independently produced publication run by a music business impresario to part of a portfolio of specialist interest magazines owned by the largest media conglomerate in the world.

IPC might've been a monster, but innovation in newspaper publishing was happening elsewhere on Fleet Street. On 4 February 1962 the *Sunday Times* colour supplement was launched by editor Ray Thompson, setting the tone for the decade with an ultra-modern, ultra-mod blend of fashion and style. On the front cover of the first magazine was Jean Shrimpton in a grey flannel Mary Quant dress photographed by David Bailey, with an Ian Fleming James Bond short story inside. It was a mix of colour, flash and danger that would set the cultural tone for the next five years at least, but one crucial element was absent: pop music.

Maurice Kinn and neighbour Brian Epstein, Miami, February 1964

Alan Smith's friends the Cockroaches would provide the missing ingredient. The Beatles' second single, 'Please Please Me', reached the number one slot on the *NME* chart in February 1963, less than a fortnight after it was released. Kinn already had an entrée with the new band, having been introduced to them six weeks earlier at a Christmas party thrown by EMI at Abbey Road. The Beatles' manager, Brian Epstein, was also a school friend of Berenice Kinn's brother and the Kinns were later to become neighbours with Epstein. Kinn was impressed by The Beatles' manners and wholesomeness and the first article on the band, written by Alan Smith, ran in *NME* in February 1963. 'Things are beginning to move for The Beatles,' it promised, with Paul McCartney assuring readers that despite the success of 'Please Please Me' the band had yet to exhaust their supply of compositions: the title of their next single, 'From Me To You', was inspired by the title of *NME*'s letters page, 'From You To Us'.

But despite Kinn's networking efforts, the magazine to really capitalise on the sudden success of The Beatles was one of IPC's new teen papers, *Fabulous*. With a Beatles cover, the first issue also boasted a pull-out colour poster section when *NME* was still printed on black and white newsprint. It sold almost a million copies. Keith Altham was a journalist on the paper, becoming known in print as 'Fab's Keith'. 'They used me as a sort of figurehead,' he says. '"Fab's Keith goes on holiday with Adam Faith to Tangier", stuff like that. Or I'd be ghosting columns for pop stars like Marty Wilde and Cliff Richard. You wrote a fairly innocuous column about the discs of the week, then you had to call up the artist's manager and read the copy over the phone to them to get approval before it could be printed. All pretty tame stuff.'

Transferred by IPC to work on *NME*, Altham found that things there were little different. 'I joined in '63 and it was just a fan paper. The journalistic scope was limited. You were just confined to being enthusiastic. Every article you wrote had to start with '"things are really beginning to move for..."' and then you put in the name of the artist. But there was a very gradual progression in terms of literary ability, if you can call it that. As the music got more serious, so we were allowed more freedom to write about the context in which it was made – although Andy Gray would put "just joking readers!" in big square brackets whenever I'd make a joke in a piece.'

With the defiantly old school Kinn still in charge, the *NME* office was still a very formal place. Suits, collars and ties were mandatory, although journalists were allowed to undo their top button as the decade wore on. 'Maurice was a rather shy man,' recalls Altham. 'Formal. On my second day in the job I referred to him as Maurice. Later on in the day I got a call from his secretary saying "please be aware that Mr. Kinn would like you to refer to him as Mr. Kinn".'

Nevertheless, the incredible lightning bolt of talent and events that led to the success of The Beatles also gave new life to the sales of *NME*. At the start of the 1960s there were more than five million teenagers in Britain, spending £800 million a year[14] on records, clothes and magazines. *Fabulous* regularly sold 900,000 copies a week. Newnes' monthly colour music title, *Rave*, was the magazine of choice for the mods thanks to its Small Faces covers, and sold a quarter of a million copies every issue. *Beat Instrumental*, a magazine for musicians launched in 1963 in an attempt to corner the advertising market for instruments, made it harder for *NME* to get adverts from Selmer, Vox or any of the other big instrument manufacturers, so the editorial team was forced to move further away from writing for musicians and deal exclusively with teenage pop fans. The shift was a boon for IPC: *NME*'s sales, tethered to the insatiable thirst for Beatles news, rose and rose. Even Fleet Street started to try and get in on the act: the *Daily Telegraph* began to print the weekly Top Ten chart in March 1964. The Beatles' success also triggered an immense appetite for new music that was barely catered for by the BBC, leading to the rise of the pirate radio stations: Radio Caroline started broadcasting in March 1964 from an old passenger ferry moored off the Harwich coast. It was followed by Radio London, Radio Invicta, Radio Scotland and Radio City, which broadcasted from an old Napoleonic War-era fort on the Thames Estuary.

Following in the slipstream of The Beatles came the Rolling Stones, whose manager, Andrew Loog Oldham, counted Percy Dickins as a confidant, Dickins advising him that he should dress down a little if he was to maintain credibility as the group's manager. The Stones' first *NME* interview appeared in August 1963, with a 19-year-old Mick Jagger explaining how fond he was of money and how he spent it: 'on clothes, Chinese food and Bo Diddley records'.[15] By April 1964 when *NME*'s Richard Green reviewed the Rolling Stones' first album, he was able to report with amazement that 'Decca plan to release the record in a sleeve with only a colour picture of the Stones and no writing on the front',[16] so recognisable had the group become that their image alone was enough to sell the LP, which went straight to number one.

As *NME*'s sales doubled from their '50s peak, reaching a record 306,881 copies in the first half of 1964,[17] Maurice Kinn realised that he'd made a mistake selling the paper. His solution was to go behind IPC's back and launch a monthly magazine called *Hit Parade*. 'I only ever saw it around the West End of London,' remembers Alan Smith. 'It was very cheaply printed. Maurice would get us all to write for it on the side. He'd come in and say, "Right, this month you are Elvis Presley. Write me a thousand words on what you've been up to recently" and you'd have to go away and pretend to be Elvis. "Hello there fans…". Just totally unscrupulous.'

Hit Parade didn't last long, but Kinn's real money-spinner came with the revival of the annual *New Musical Express* Poll Winners' Party, the first of which happened in April 1963 at the 10,000-capacity Wembley Empire Pool. Using his contacts as a promoter, Kinn was able to assemble a bill containing the hottest acts of the day – and it was his name at the top of the bill and his bank account being filled, not IPC's. In a particularly far-sighted move, Kinn signed a lucrative deal with ABC TV so that from 1964 onwards the concerts were filmed and broadcast on British television within two weeks of taking place.

For the first *NME* Poll Winners' Party of the 1960s, Kinn used his Epstein connection to secure the services of The Beatles, along with Adam Faith, Billy Fury and The Shadows, on a bill headlined by Cliff Richard. But if the bill for 1963's concert seemed like the changing of the guard between musical generations, successive Poll Winners' concerts were a crucial part of the 1960s new wave: 1964 saw the debut appearances of compère Jimmy Savile, a fixture for the rest of the decade, and The Rolling Stones ('a fantastic sight with hip hip movements, and wear-what-you-like clothes'[18]) on a bill that was made up exclusively of beat bands from around the country, including Tottenham's Dave Clark Five, The Merseybeats, Manfred Mann and headliners The Beatles, who were pelted with jelly babies by fans.

Each band played a short set of between 5 and 15 minutes, depending on their position on the bill, while backstage at the concerts the musicians shared dressing rooms, leading to an occasionally fractious and competitive atmosphere – at the 1965 show, The Kinks' Ray Davies stormed offstage after hearing that his group had been beaten to the best newcomer award by the Rolling Stones.

The Beatles collect their awards from Maurice Kinn and Cheyenne star Clint Walker shortly before their last-ever British gig at the NME Poll Winner's Party, May 1966

The 1966 awards, held on 1 May, were by far the most momentous. *The New Musical Express'* reputation was such that Kinn was able to put together a bill featuring The Beatles and The Rolling Stones alongside The Yardbirds, The Walker Brothers, the Small Faces, Roy Orbison and Dusty Springfield. For The Beatles, then in the middle of recording and mixing their groundbreaking *Revolver* album, the day started with high farce when the group, forced to adopt disguises to even get into the Empire Pool undisturbed, arrived dressed as pastry cooks, complete with aprons, chef's toques and trays of cream cakes. Derek Johnson was waiting to greet them at the venue's back door: 'They got in without being spotted and were running across the kitchen when Ringo tripped and his tray of cakes went everywhere, followed by the other three landing in a heap on top of him like a Marx Brothers routine.'[19]

The first half of the concert went off without further hitches, until the arrival of The Who. Amid the screams of the assembled fans, the band did their best to upstage the night's two headliners, utilising their full pop-art panoply: feedback, smoke bombs, Pete Townshend smashing his guitar and drummer Keith Moon trashing his kit. 'Anyone who has ever seen a demolition gang smashing down a building will know what it's like when The Who get up steam,' wrote Alan Smith in one of the band's first *NME* pieces. 'Their music rolls and crashes and throbs like a berserk thunderstorm.'[20]

'Keith made a huge mess,' remembers Who manager Chris Stamp. 'He did it… to make The Who's presence felt, make sure The Stones and The Beatles had to follow this.'[21]

Backstage The Beatles and the Stones were too preoccupied with their own problems to notice The Who's grandstanding antics. Due to a contractual dispute with ABC TV the last band to play at the concert – the headliners – were not to be filmed that year. Andrew Loog Oldham and Brian Epstein were faced with a dilemma: either choose the money and status afforded by headlining the show, or the wider promotion to a television audience that taking the second slot on the bill would afford. When Lennon heard about the choice he exploded, berating the prudish and formal Kinn in a corridor backstage at the Empire Pool as the crowd, unaware of the drama unfolding backstage, cheered and stamped their feet in anticipation. In the end Epstein caved and The Beatles closed the show, after first receiving their awards from *Cheyenne* TV star Clint Walker and the staff of the *NME*: suited and respectable, Andy Gray, Percy Dickins and Maurice Kinn looked like a group of undertakers or prosperous middle-aged publicans next to The Beatles, whose hair hung way over their collars and wore polo neck sweaters instead of collars and ties.

The Beatles played four songs. As the last chord of 'I'm Down' rang out across the Empire Pool, the band threw their trophies into the hands of roadies Mal Evans and Neil Aspinall and rushed from the stage into a waiting limo. It was to be The Beatles' last-ever British concert appearance.

Maurice Kinn's relationship with The Beatles had already been put under serious strain when an Alley Cat piece he wrote in July 1963 revealed that John Lennon was married with a young son. This went against the express wishes of Kinn's neighbour Brian Epstein, who had struggled to keep the information secret, fearing that it would affect the band's commercial appeal among its fanbase of teenage girls. Then, following The Beatles' American tour in August 1965, Alley Cat ran a piece entitled 'Did The Beatles leave their tarts in San Francisco?', alleging that the band, two of whom were married, had taken up with American girlfriends while on the two-week run of dates. 'The Alley Cat could be pretty vicious,' remembers Alan Smith. 'There were a few libel writs served against it.'

The main problem seemed to be that Kinn – already somewhat cast adrift by rock'n'roll in the 1950s – had even less understanding of this new beat music. 'Maurice thought that Mel Tormé was the greatest singer in the world,' says Keith Altham. 'He didn't really have any empathy with rock'n'roll. His generation was the swing and big band generation. Once I asked him what Elvis was like and all Maurice could think of to say was "vulgar".'

Kinn wasn't alone. Derek Johnson had become friendly with Elvis and in the 1950s was one of the staunchest defenders of rock'n'roll on the paper at the time of the nationwide bans and tabloid outrage. But in an editorial in March 1965, Johnson, then aged 37, railed against the latest youth craze:[22]

'Every teenager goes through a phase of trying to make himself look conspicuous. In my day it was flashy American silk ties. [But] I am opposed to ultra-long hair on young men – and this isn't just sour grapes because I have a bald spot! I reckon it looks effeminate and often downright ridiculous… it is also unsanitary. Long hair on boys is unnatural. It can also be highly dangerous and several accidents in factories and machine shops have already been caused by this craze.'

Even *NME*'s editor was out of touch with the interests and tastes of the paper's audience. Andy Gray was a tubby middle-aged man who smoked a pipe and was known to his staff as the paper's golfing correspondent because he spent more time on the course than in the office. His editorial formula was simple: the *New Musical Express* charts were the first and best in the country, and anyone who featured in them was worth writing about from week to week. This was a method that frustrated the younger staffers.

'Andy Gray would come in to the newsroom on a Wednesday morning and just read through the charts,' says Keith Altham. '"The Animals are in at 28, who knows The Animals?' And one of the writers would put their hand up. "Who knows The Yardbirds?" One week he actually said 'here's a newie: Otis Redding, who knows her?"

'It filled us all with rage,' remembers Alan Smith. 'That was his only formula. You couldn't write about any bands unless they were in the charts. Then you'd go and write your piece: "this week it's all happening for..." and then put in the name of whoever had charted that week.'

Derek Johnson had patented the *New Musical Express* house style in the 1950s. It consisted of a straight description of whatever new disc was being discussed aimed at being understood by the broadest possible audience: so 'I Want to Hold Your Hand' was 'a bouncy finger snapper with a pounding beat and a catchy melody'[23] or the Rolling Stones' 'It's All Over Now' combined a 'jog-trotting pace with rattling tambourine and pungent guitar work'.[24]

This shallow showbizzy approach to describing pop music was typical of all the mid-decade music press, but also at odds with some of things bubbling away in the culture. In the pre-hippy period of the mid-'60s there was a great sense of a repressed frustration seeping out in whatever form possible, of a collective psychosis stemming, perhaps, from the still-fresh scars of the Second World War. At Easter 1964, almost 100 arrests were made when fighting between pilled-up gangs of mods and rockers on the beach at Clacton ended in a near-riot in a more deadly amplification of the '50s rock'n'roll riots. The violence reoccurred in Margate and Brighton six weeks later over the Whitsun bank holiday weekend, when another 100 young people were arrested.

This psychosis was there in the violence and sadism of the James Bond books. It was there in the surrealism and kinkiness of ABC TV's popular show *The Avengers*, whose costumes were made at the studio of the designer John Sutcliffe, whose firm also produced rubber and PVC fetish wear. The same thread of perversity was carried on by a new band from North London called The Kinks, whose early press shots saw them dressed in PVC macs and brandishing whips, and whose lead singer Ray Davies told *NME*'s Keith Altham that his band's new single, 'See My Friend', was explicitly about bisexuality.

By 1964 the British public were buying 100 million records a year,[25] many of them made by young groups who rejected the mainstream showbusiness ambitions of their predecessors by choosing band names that were alternately macabre (The Zombies, Screaming Lord Sutch), aggressive (The Riot Squad, The Wild Ones, The Untamed), Neanderthal (The Troggs, The Primitives), ironic (The Pretty Things, The Birds), transgressive (The Fairies, The Others) or exclusive (The Clique, The In-Crowd). In the first interview with The Who in *NME*, Alan Smith noted that 'there's a sort of vicious strangeness about these four beatsters from Shepherd's Bush'.[26]

Much of this strangeness might've been derived from the mod drug of choice: Dexamyl – which Prime Minister Anthony Eden had been addicted to during the Suez crisis – had found favour among both touring musicians and their audiences as a way of sustaining energy for all-night dances. In June 1965, when Who drummer Keith Moon was asked what his favourite food was in an *NME* interview, he replied 'blues' after the nickname for the rhomboid-shaped bright blue Dexy's pills that allowed the mods to extend their leisure time by keeping them up all night on a Friday and Saturday, before slumping during the working week in an act of subversion further masked by their fastidiously respectable and besuited appearance.

All of this aggression and oddness was played out against a backdrop of a gradually worsening economic crisis. Between 1947 and 1971 Britain borrowed more from the International Monetary Fund than any other country, partly to pay off debts resulting from the Second World War, while during the same period the country's share of world manufacturing exports shrank from one quarter to barely one tenth.[27] The answer to this manifest decline in Britain's status as a world power was a kind of pop jingoism, designed both to attract tourists from overseas and promote the export of cultural goods, but also as a way of reassuring Britons that, despite the loss of Empire, they were still a world power. The National Front was formed in 1966, while the triumphalism of the 1966 football World Cup win and the invention of the myth of Swinging London were twin prongs of this self-deception. 'We may be regarded as a second-class power in politics,' wrote a correspondent to the *NME*'s letters page in 1965, 'but at any rate we now lead the world in pop music!'[28]

But as pop music grew in complexity, scope and sophistication, a new way of writing about it was called for. The *NME*, along with the rest of the media, struggled to keep up. The first hint in the paper's pages that something was going on came in an interview in May 1964 with a hot new young American folk singer. *New Musical Express* features writer Max

Jones was dispatched to interview Bob Dylan, the 'guitarist, harmonica player and writer of songs which go a few fathoms deeper than the 'yeah, yeah, yeah' stage'.[29] Jones found the singer to be obliging, explaining that making music did not mark the limit of his ambition: rather, Dylan was in the process of writing a play to add to the two others that he'd already completed but wasn't happy with. He also complained of the fact that he was unable to get into any restaurants in London without a tie and went some way towards explaining the creative process ('the words come first, then I fit a chorus').

Exactly two years later, Dylan's patience with the shallowness of the pop process, with which the press was complicit, had expired. Annoyed at speculation in *New Musical Express* as to the true meaning of the lyrics of his song 'Mr. Tambourine Man' (was it about LSD?), Dylan held a bad-tempered press conference in a ballroom at the Mayfair hotel in central London. Resplendent in white striped hipster trousers and Ray-Ban sunglasses underneath his frizzy afro, Dylan responded with monosyllabic answers to the increasingly banal questions from the assembled national media. Sent to cover the conference for *NME*, a perplexed Keith Altham took one of Dylan's management team to one side to ask why the singer had bothered even holding the conference in the first place. 'Dylan just wanted to come along and record a press reception so that we could hear how ridiculous and infantile all reporters are' was the terse response. A week later, Dylan would be greeted with boos and catcalls during the plugged-in segment of his gigs in Sheffield and Newcastle upon Tyne. In Manchester an audience member called Keith Butler would be moved to shout 'Judas!' at the singer's perceived betrayal of his folk roots.

If there was a sense in the mid-'60s of a rift developing between the concerns and influences of the musicians that *NME* was writing about – many of whom came from art school backgrounds and were interested in modern art, experimental cinema, philosophy – and the way that the paper approached covering them, it didn't often show. The paper's younger reporters – Keith Altham, Alan Smith, Richard Green and the Glaswegian Norrie Drummond – were becoming increasingly frustrated with the limits put on them by Kinn and Andy Gray, but they were the unassailable conventions of the day. However much common ground *NME* journalists had with the acts that they were covering, they were also writing for a young teenage audience who, Kinn and Gray believed, were interested in nothing more than finding out about what The Monkees liked to eat for breakfast or how tall the Small Faces really were ('the smallest group on the pop scene – they're all less that 5ft 6ins!'[30]).

'Hip hip movements, and wear-what-you-like clothes...'
Keith Altham interviews Rolling Stone Brian Jones, 1964

Many of the groups featured in the magazine would pop into the office if they were near the Strand, attracted partly by the fact that Derek Johnson split his time as an *NME* staffer with running a model agency, so there would always be a constant stream of beautiful women coming through the office doors. Photo shoots were often taken on the roof of the building, while interviews with bands took place in nearby pubs.

'The relationship between the press and the artists we were writing about was much cosier in those days,' remembers Keith Altham. 'Later on the writing got more critical and analytical and sometimes more scathing so it meant that your relationship with the artists couldn't be as close. But back then I could just ring up all of the bands that I wanted to talk to. The Who, the Stones, The Kinks, The Animals, The Yardbirds: we were all pretty much the same age and had the same interests – sport, women, drinking. The only difference was that they had guitars and I didn't.'

Not everyone belonged to the coterie of London-based R&B bands. Sent to interview new Belfast group Them, Altham arrived at the group's rehearsal studios and spotted their lead singer, a slightly chubby redheaded 20-year-old called Van Morrison, leaning against a wall outside reading a newspaper. Altham approached him to introduce himself. 'Fuck off,' came the response. 'Can't you see I'm busy?'

'The actual interview wasn't much better,' claims Altham. 'Their guitarist was a chap called Billy Harrison who just stared at me and cleaned his fingernails with a flicknife while I was talking to them.'

Them, it seems, were the exception. The mid-'60s music business was small enough for everyone involved to know each other and *NME* journalists were a core part of the scene. 'I used to play football for a showbiz soccer team organised by Ed Stewart,' says Altham. 'It was a team of radio DJs, along with the occasional musician. Ray Davies was a useful player, elegant and well balanced. Rod Stewart was very good indeed. Keith Moon turned up once and played, but only managed the first half. It was an amphetamine-assisted performance. He tore around for 45 minutes and then just collapsed in a heap.'

For the staff of the paper, most lunchtimes would be spent at The Brewmaster off Leicester Square or the famous De Hems Dutch bar near Chinatown where Peter Jones, the editor of *Record Mirror*, would hold court. In the evenings, Kinn, Dickins and Gray would head back to their families and, if it were a Friday, the younger journalists would rush off to the *Ready Steady Go!* studios. On other nights they'd head to The Ship pub on Wardour Street, followed by one of the many new nightclubs frequented by bands: the Cromwellian, a Georgian townhouse on the Cromwell Road in West London ('the list of people who are there frequently is endless. The Who… The Kinks… Paul McCartney, George Harrison… Jimmy Tarbuck'[31]) or the Scotch of St. James', underneath Eric Burdon from the Animals' London flat.[32] Then there was The Bag O' Nails in Kingly Street, off Carnaby Street ('unlike many other London discotheques, the Bag is open on Sunday'[33]), The Ad-Lib in a penthouse overlooking Leicester Square, or the Speakeasy, tucked away behind Oxford Street and done out in Prohibition-era kitsch ('the entrance is through the mirrored door of a wardrobe and the cash desk is a coffin'[34]). Doing the rounds on an average night, *NME* journalists might bump into any number of pop stars: 'You were regarded as a conduit to getting coverage,' remembers Alan Smith. 'So people wanted to know you. You'd go to the Speakeasy and there'd be Hendrix in one corner and a Beatle in the other.'

Drugs were a part of this scene, particularly speed or uppers, with a small amount of cocaine and pot consumed. The Ad-Lib club was where John Lennon and George Harrison ended up on the evening that they first took LSD after being spiked by celebrity dentist John Riley. But for journalists allowed entry to the clubs where they could meet singers and musicians there was a tacit understanding that it was on a strictly non-professional basis. People went to these places to unwind and escape rather than be noticed and written about: most of them were members-only and barely advertised themselves, while the owner of the Scotch, Rod Harrod, once ejected someone from his club for asking George Harrison for an autograph.[35] The era of the gossip journalist, the shock exclusive or the paparazzi photographer was still a way off.

'It was understood that you wouldn't write about certain things,' says Keith Altham, 'and there was really no necessity to write about them: as long as you got the occasional interview and a bit of information about new releases that was all that was expected. Anybody's private life remained private.'

Conforming to the rites of Fleet Street, these long nights in the clubs and long lunch breaks in the pubs were augmented by the immense variety of press receptions and conferences, at which there was always free alcohol. Richard Green rapidly earned himself the nickname 'the Beast', owing to the inhuman amount of alcohol he would consume throughout the day and his habit of removing his trousers after a few drinks. His great claim to notoriety was falling asleep while interviewing the young and rather earnest Cat Stevens after a particularly heavy lunch and being shaken awake by Cat enquiring if he was quite getting everything down. Green was later sacked from the paper after attempting to enliven one particularly slow afternoon in an unusual way.

'The office boy, who later became the opera critic on the *Daily Mail*, was a guy called Dave Gillard,' recalls Keith Altham. 'Dave had a new vented sports jacket of which he was quite proud. Richard came in from the pub after one long lunch and saw the vent of this jacket sticking out from Dave's chair and just couldn't resist. The next thing we saw was this plume of smoke billowing up and Dave rushing around the room trying to put this fire out. At which point Maurice – who was a somewhat laconic individual and didn't waste words – walked in. He just said "Richard. You're responsible. Six minutes to get your stuff and leave".'

It was a cosy, boozy little world. Competition from other papers was dealt with in a sporting fashion and *NME*'s sales comfortably outstripped them all anyway. The national dailies had initially been favourable to The Beatles as a er of commercial expediency, but treated pop music with caution after the first flurry of Beatlemania had caused some of the more serious broadsheet music critics to completely lose their heads: the *Sunday Times* had called Lennon and McCartney 'the greatest composers since Beethoven'[36]. Elsewhere *The Times*' music critic, William Mann, struggled manfully to adapt his critical apparatus to the demands of the new sounds he was writing about, declaring in December 1963 that: 'the outstanding composers of 1963 must seem to have been John Lennon and Paul McCartney... the slow sad song about That Boy... is expressively unusual for its lugubrious music, but harmonically it is one of their most interesting, with its chains of pandiatonic clusters... so firmly are the major tonic sevenths and ninths built into their tunes, and the flat sub-mediant key switches, so natural is the Aeolian cadence at the end of Not A Second Time...'[37]

...and so on. So while the nationals failed to get to grips with pop, and despite competition from *Record Mirror*, *Rave*, *Disc* and *Melody Maker*, *NME* was the market leader, keeping a tight grip on its virtual monopoly on music news thanks both to the efforts of its journalists to mingle with the latest groups, and its news editor, Chris Hutchins.

'Chris was rather a Stalinistic figure,' claims Altham. 'Not well liked. He'd got one of the office boys sacked and as revenge the guy pissed in Chris' tea. He was strutting around the newsroom in a Napoleonic style sipping his tea, saying "That lad was a useless little clot, but at least he could make a good cup of tea".'

It was rare that the *New Musical Express* was scooped, as it was when *Disc* printed, in full colour, a picture from The Beatles' notorious withdrawn 'Butcher' photoshoot. The image, taken by photographer Robert Whitaker in early 1966 as part of a conceptual art piece entitled *A Somnambulant Adventure*, showed the band wearing bloodstained aprons and draped with pieces of meat and parts of dismembered plastic children's dolls.

Despite its success, however, *NME* was beginning to actively struggle with the more adventurous end of the music it was committed to covering. Maurice Kinn was an occasional guest on BBC television's *Juke Box Jury*, despite his dour manner and stammer. In order to appear knowledgeable, he would commission Derek Johnson to find out which records were set to be reviewed on the show, information that was supposed to be classified until the moment that the programme was broadcast. But under the stewardship of a middle-aged businessman, the *New Musical Express* was unlikely ever to evolve beyond its showbusiness roots. Reviewing The Beatles' landmark album *Revolver*, the paper struggled in its attempts to fit this new wild experimental music into its journalistic template, claiming both that the song 'Dr. Robert' was 'John's tribute to the medical profession' and complaining that the closing track, 'Tomorrow Never Knows' 'tells you to "turn off your mind relax and float downstream". But how can you relax with the electronic outerspace noises, often sounding like seagulls?'[38]

As the sounds being broadcast by Radio London or Radio Caroline evolved at quantum speed, *NME* was out of touch and ill-equipped to deal with the pace at which the music it covered was developing. As long as the readers had no alternative sources of information, however, the paper was in an unassailable position. It wasn't long before that position was to change completely.

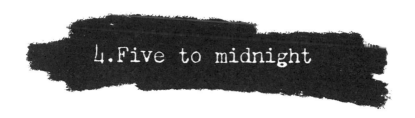

4.Five to midnight

'Why don't you ever set fire to your typewriter, man?'

For four decades from the late 1920s onwards, the mimeograph machine formed the bedrock of a small revolution in home publishing. An unassuming metal contraption that could fit onto a tabletop, the machine gave anyone with a typewriter and a modest budget the ability to start their own publishing empire by simply filling the mimeo's cylindrical metal drum with ink and turning a crank handle to reproduce whatever was on the carbon paper stencil inside.

It was a boon for community newsletters, church bulletins and harassed schoolteachers needing to mass-produce homework assignments. But the cheapness and availability of the mimeograph also led to the growth of small-press science fiction fan magazines which started to appear in the early 1930s. Dubbed 'fanzines', these hand-stapled newsletters were produced in limited print runs of a few thousand and distributed by mail through a network of readers with a shared passion: flying saucer stories and H.P. Lovecraft, speculative fiction and space travel, Martians and moon men. The best of these magazines, like *The Acolyte* or *Sky Hook*, contained short stories, poems, essays and hand-drawn illustrations, providing a whole generation of future science fiction authors with their first opportunity to get into print: a young Harlan Ellison started off editing the *Science Fantasy Bulletin* before becoming a professional writer of weird and fantastic stories and TV shows.

The boom in science fiction 'zines soon inspired a thriving underground of homemade fan papers covering everything from DC Comics superheroes to horror movies and poetry. Distinguished variously by their opinionated writing, bad spelling, odd obsessions and crackpot theories, they were a gloriously energetic and unfettered burst of creativity that existed on an entirely subterranean level: you couldn't buy these 'zines anywhere except through the postal system and once you'd bought one you gained an entrée into a whole network of home publishing.

One science fiction fanzine editor who spent much of his free time turning the mimeo's crank until his arms ached was Paul Williams. A student at Pennsylvania's liberal arts school Swarthmore College, in early 1966 Williams decided to take the sci-fi template and create a 'zine dedicated entirely to rock'n'roll music. Called *Crawdaddy!*, the first issue described itself as 'a magazine of rock'n'roll criticisms'. Meanwhile on the West Coast, San Franciscan Greg Shaw, a Tolkien fanzine editor immersed in the science fiction fan world, had a similar idea – the first issue of his *Mojo Navigator Rock and Roll News* appeared in record stores and at concerts in August 1966. Featuring interviews with hot new local bands like the Grateful Dead, as well as record reviews and gossip from the burgeoning hippy underground, the short-lived *Mojo* wrote about music in a conversational, street-level way and soon grew in size to the point where Shaw was selling copies all over the San Francisco Bay Area, setting up a long-haired distribution service in the process.

In the UK the music 'zine scene didn't get going until the second half of the 1960s. A different kind of revolution came in October 1961, when former public schoolfriends Peter Usborne, Christopher Brooker and Richard Ingrams published the first issue of their new satirical magazine, *Private Eye*. Being vastly more professional, *Private Eye*'s approach was a world away from the American sci-fi 'zine publishers, but no less groundbreaking: pasted up by amateurs with a letraset, set on a typewriter and printed using cheap new photo-litho offset techniques, within a year *Private Eye*'s blend of sixth-form humour, cartoons and scandal was selling 35,000 copies a month. Its success inspired a group of Australian university students to start their own paper: the first issue of *Oz* was published in Sydney on April Fool's Day 1963 as a self-declared 'magazine of dissent'[39] satirising politicians and challenging repressive conservatism in an early strike in the war against the establishment that would intensify as the decade wore on.

Following the success of *Private Eye*, there was an incredible flowering of small press magazines who took the ethos of the science fiction 'zine and, catering to a new rock'n'roll-loving readership, provided a sub-cultural support network of events listings, concert reviews, music reviews, articles on drugs and radical politics, 'how to' guides, polemic and poetry. One of these magazines was *IT*, started by Barry Miles and John 'Hoppy' Hopkins from the basement of counter-cultural bookshop and gallery Indica books with a loan of £500 at the end of 1966.

Miles and Hopkins were already well-established counter-cultural figures: Indica was part-owned by Peter Asher, the brother of Paul McCartney's then-girlfriend Jane Asher, and the Beatle had helped out building the shop's shelves when it opened. The shop, which contained a gallery space along with imports of books by Beat writers, was where John Lennon first met Yoko Ono at an exhibition of her work.

Published fortnightly, the first issue of *IT* contained poems, pieces on Vietnam and contributions from Timothy Leary and Ono but, a small mention of Frank Zappa's Mothers of Invention in issue one aside, nothing about music. The magazine's launch party, held at a former railway turntable in Camden called the Roundhouse, was a different er: attended by Paul McCartney in traditional Arab costume, it featured performances by the cream of London's underground, including Pink Floyd and The Soft Machine, a band from Canterbury.

Over in America, *IT*'s counterparts were the *East Village Other*, *Berkeley Barb* and *Los Angeles Free Press*, all relatively long-established underground newspapers which combined radical politics with mischief making – in early 1967, the *Barb* had run an editorial claiming that smoking banana skins led to an LSD-like psychotropic high in an attempt to force the government to ban the fruit. None of these magazines was available in the UK, but in March 1968 copies of a new magazine began to appear in bookshops and newsagents. Jann Wenner in San Francisco had established *Rolling Stone* in 1967 using a loan of $7,500 from a family friend. Originally a folded-over tabloid with cover printed A4 size on the fold, Wenner envisaged *Rolling Stone* to be a more commercial take on the underground newspaper: more rigorous journalistic standards, less controversial content and a design, perhaps unusually for a paper aimed at rock'n'roll fans, which eschewed the often illegible psychedelic typefaces and coloured inks of its peers for a more sober black and white layout inspired, oddly, by the British *Sunday Times*. Milking *Crawdaddy!*'s Paul Williams for information on how to run a newspaper, Wenner launched his new magazine with a statement of intent, claiming that *Rolling Stone* needed to exist because 'the trade papers have become so inaccurate and irrelevant and because the fan magazines are an anachronism'.[40]

From their office in a run-down warehouse, *Rolling Stone* treated San Francisco – not London, not Los Angeles, not New York – as the capital of the music world at a time when cultural commentator Marshall McLuhan's idea of the Global Village – that the world had been contracted by new developments in media and communications – was gaining more currency. In the late 1960s attempts were made by various of the underground papers to establish a sort of hairier, freakier Reuters, called the Underground Press Syndicate and Liberation News Service, which would share news on a global basis throughout the new underground press, who shared common ideals, interests and values regardless of where they were published or what language they were written in.

'The man for whom the words "Wild One" were invented...' Keith Altham watches Jimi Hendrix tune up backstage, Zurich, May 1968

Rolling Stone's rapid commercial success lay in the nimble way that Wenner navigated the dichotomies of his magazine's approach – was it an underground paper or a mainstream one? Did their readers only care about rock'n'roll or social issues too? – achieving conventional industry acclaim in the way that the anarchic likes of the *Barb* never would: in 1970, *Rolling Stone* writers David Dalton and David Felton won the prestigious Columbia School of Journalism Award for their interview with Charles Manson.

While *San Francisco Chronicle* jazz critic Ralph Gleason dealt intelligently with his city's new psychedelic rock scene, even having a hand in the launch of *Rolling Stone*, in Britain, the broadsheet journalists were still only on the cusp of getting to grips with rock and pop music. 'Pop journalism may be divided into two sections,' wrote George Melly in 1969. 'A few journalists, notably the *Observer*'s Tony Palmer and the *Guardian*'s Geoffrey Cannon, feel that their job is to press the claims of pop as a serious art form on the straights, to establish a critical apparatus, in fact.'[41]

Over at IPC magazines, the staff of the *New Musical Express* were struggling to cope with both the new competition from the underground papers and the limits that the format and style of the paper imposed when writing about the more serious end of psychedelia. The 1967 Poll Winners' Concert had been headlined by The Beach Boys and Small Faces, with former Yardbird Eric Clapton's new group Cream halfway down the bill, while in January 1967 the paper heralded the arrival of a new guitarist, Jimi Hendrix, billed as 'the man for whom the words "Wild One" were invented!'[42]

Keith Altham was friendly with Jimi's manager, former Animals bassist Chas Chandler, and got to know the American star during his stay in London. One night at the end of March 1967 they were sitting backstage in a dressing room with roadie Gerry Stickells at the Finsbury Park Astoria in North London ahead of the Jimi Hendrix Experience's headline gig there. 'Chas and Jimi were asking me about what they could do to make the headlines at this gig,' says Altham, 'and I said "Well, Townshend smashes up his guitar onstage and The Move smash up a television set with a fire axe at the end of their set". Jimi mumbled 'Maybe I could smash up an elephant", to which I replied "It's a pity you can't set fire to your guitar" There was silence for a moment, then Chas said "Gerry, go out and get some lighter fluid". I was only joking.'

Wary of it becoming too much of a gimmick, Hendrix only set fire to his guitar onstage four times in his career, yet it became a defining image of his stagecraft. 'We were backstage at the Monterey festival with

Janis Joplin, who was listening to Jimi tune up,' remembers Altham, 'and he turned to me and said "Why don't you ever set fire to your typewriter, man?"

Despite his Wild Man billing and guitar pyrotechnics, Altham remembers Hendrix as 'shy and a little distant. He'd sit drumming his fingers on his lips and when he spoke his sentences would often trail off into 'etc. etc. etc...' He loved science fiction. I remember flying out to Monterey with him and he was reading Isaac Asimov and *Stranger in a Strange Land* by Robert Heinlein. "Purple Haze" came from a science fiction novel, not drugs.'

Science fiction, drugs, pop art, radical politics, sex, the environment: the concerns of the hippy movement were nowhere to be seen in the *New Musical Express* of the late 1960s. New recruit Nick Logan, an ex-Mod from Ilford and former pop correspondent for the *West Essex Gazette,* found himself covering the commercial end of the new underground rock scene, interviewing velvet-trousered hippy troubadours like Donovan or Marc Bolan ('Marc has a fascination for woods and open air. He is a prolific writer who can turn out a new song in 20 minutes'[43]). Logan also wrote about the first British excursions by the West Coast rock bands that *Rolling Stone* claimed as their own, writing early *NME* pieces on The Doors ('The Doors appeal to those who want more from their pop than mere musical candyfloss'[44]) and Jefferson Airplane, who featured a female lead singer, 'the attractive Miss [Grace] Slick'.[45]

But the underground bands survived on a new currency that was alien to *NME*'s chart-led approach. Even though the charts were now compiled by a team of six led by researcher Fiona Foulgar, who called 150 shops weekly to get their chart returns, credibility was the key to their continued success, and credibility was one thing that *NME*, as an establishment paper published by the biggest publishing corporation in the world, couldn't provide. The mainstream press had also proved itself to be directly antagonistic towards rock'n'roll culture: the coverage of the bust at Keith Richards' Redlands mansion[46] was followed by an attack by the *News of the World* on the UFO club, set up by *IT*'s Hoppy Hopkins. The hub of hippydom in London, the UFO featured performances by The Soft Machine, Pink Floyd, Procol Harem and The Move against a backdrop of psychedelic oil wheels and strawberry-scented dry ice, but was forced to close following a *News of the World* editorial painting it as a 'Hippy Vice den'. Meanwhile *IT* itself had started to thrive – despite a police raid in 1967, the magazine was regularly selling out its 40,000 print run and employed a full-time staff of 15 people, whose wages fluctuated according to the success of the paper.

IT made the link between rock'n'roll and revolution, running articles about music alongside pieces on drugs, black power, sex and – a throwback to the sci-fi 'zines – UFOs. In a November 1967 interview for Dutch television with the DJ John Peel, newly installed at the BBC on its new channel, Radio 1, *IT* writer Mick Farren explained the ethos of the underground press:

'The policies behind the newspaper are to provide a forum for people who are excluded from mass media… if you want to be a journalist, normally you went along with some sort of training at Beaverbrook newspaper and you worked your way up. Now it's possible to start your own newspaper and do your own thing immediately.'

Peel himself wrote a regular column, The Perfumed Garden, for *IT*, named after his late-night show on Radio London, shortly before the 1967 Marine Broadcasting (Offences) Act took the pirate stations off the air.

The Act was the first strike by the government against the counter-culture. In 1967 the offices of *IT* were raided by the Vice Squad on an obscene publications warrant. The police confiscated files and accounts, but things got harder for the magazine as the decade wore on: in January 1969 Home Secretary James Callaghan told the commons that he wanted to 'call a halt on the rising tide of permissiveness' in a House of Commons debate on cannabis. The war on the underground duly intensified. In March 1970, *IT* was busted again and the police removed small ads files and advertisers contacts, effectively cutting off the magazine's income. Pressure was put on printers not to publish the magazine, while the staff were divided by in-fighting and factionalism. In May 1970, *Oz* published an issue featuring contributions from schoolchildren among the usual lysergiana, covering drugs, sex, corporal punishment and the failures of the exam system. One item was a collage made by a 15-year-old schoolboy, Vivien Berger, which juxtaposed a comic by the subversive American illustrator Robert Crumb with images cut from a *Daily Express* strip featuring popular children's comic character Rupert the Bear. The effect was to make it appear that Rupert, *sans* yellow check trousers, was rushing around waving a huge and non-bearlike erect penis. The result was a long-running and high-profile obscenity case, after which *Oz*'s publishers were sentenced to custodial sentences, threatened with deportation and ordered to pay thousands of pounds in costs.

Although Labour MPs led by Tony Benn tabled a motion in the House of Commons expressing shock at the severity of the sentences and 18 Scotland Yard officers serving on the Obscene Publications Squad were imprisoned for a variety of offences including launching repeated raids on underground papers and magazines to cover up for the fact that they were on the payroll of the Soho pornographers, the damage had been done: the most successful outposts of the hippy press were crippled, although the size and scope of the underground press was still vast. In November 1969 when Rupert Murdoch relaunched the *Sun* as a mass-market tabloid, in London alone one could buy Felix Dennis' *Ink, Black Dwarf, Red Mole, 7 Days, Idiot International* and comics compendia like *Street Comix* or Mick Farren's *Nasty Tales*, itself the subject of an obscenity trial in the spring of 1971. Then there were anarchist magazines *Heatwave* and the short-lived *Cuddon's Cosmopolitan Review*, feminist magazine *Women's Newsletter* or magazines covering ecology and science fiction like Gandalf's Garden, published from the head shop of the same name in World's End, Chelsea.

The effect of all this activity on the sales of the *New Musical Express* was minimal. However, in March 1969, Jann Wenner announced his plan to produce a UK version of *Rolling Stone*, in part funded by Mick Jagger. By the late 1960s, *RS* was selling 25,000 copies in Britain (compared to a quarter of a million in the US) and Wenner noticed a gap in the market that he could exploit further, rightly seeing the format and style of the British music weeklies as anachronistic and tired compared to *Rolling Stone's* hip and informed approach. 'Look at how awful *Melody Maker* is,' he complained. 'You just don't want to read that shit. It probably comes from the writers having to write the same thing over and over again.'[47]

Melody Maker was itself undergoing a crisis. Positioning itself as 'the thinking fan's paper', the weekly had dedicated itself to covering the more serious end of psychedelia, as well as maintaining its well-regarded jazz and folk coverage, but in 1970 long-term editor Jack Hutton defected with some of the staff, including the tea lady, to set up a rival paper, *Sounds,* for the regional newspaper publisher United Newspapers.

As well as the new *Rolling Stone*, British rock fans based in London were able to trek to Camden Town's legendary alternative bookshop Compendium and buy copies of another American magazine, based well away from the tanned and sunkissed San Francisco hippy aristocracy. *Creem*, which billed itself as 'America's Only Rock'n'Roll Magazine', was produced from a communal farmhouse in the countryside outside of Detroit by a group of aggrieved misfits for whom the Age of Aquarius would never dawn. *Creem's* totem was a broken typewriter that had been destroyed in an argument in the office and mounted on a pedestal, summing up their attitude to writing about music: dispensing with the liberal pontificating and rock-as-art ethos of *Rolling Stone, Creem* was the home of passionate, gutsy, emotive writing about rock. '*Creem* is a raspberry in the face of culture,' explained the magazine's star writer Lester Bangs to a visiting reporter.[48] At *Creem* Bangs pioneered a style of writing about music – bluff and macho but equally heartfelt and sensitive, ramming together words and creating neologisms – that set the template for the whole corpus of music criticism for the following 40 years.

Even with the underground in disarray, *NME* faced competition from underground-minded music magazines like *Sounds*, Pete Frame's *Zigzag* or *Cream*, edited by former *Melody Maker* production editor Bob Houston and adopting a more orthodox spelling than its American cousin. Competition for record company advertising money intensified and *NME* was forced to rely more and more on its small ads and classified for revenue – the Carnaby Street boutiques selling hippy beads and various shades of ethnic tat.

Competition for access to the bands also intensified as more and more music papers arrived on the scene. In December 1969, John Lennon had given an exclusive interview to Alan Smith that was published under the headline 'Beatles are on the Brink of Splitting'.[49] But for his first solo interview, Lennon chose to speak to *Rolling Stone*, in a 40,000 word piece spread across two issues.

It didn't help that when the *New Musical Express* did manage to bag big scoops, the misadventures of the journalists got in the way. 'At the Isle of Wight festival,' says Keith Altham, 'Richard Green got an interview with Bob Dylan, which no one else could. God knows how he did it. Anyway, Richard got this big exclusive on the first day and decided that was his entire responsibility done for the weekend. Of course, after three days on the piss at the Isle of Wight festival, by the time that he came back to the newspaper on the Monday morning he couldn't remember a word of this Dylan interview. It'd been wiped from the memory banks.'

As both the British student population and amount of money spent on music in Britain rose in 1971–72,[50] its rivals seriously outclassed *NME*. Roy Carr was a freelancer who'd recently been appointed staff features writer after abandoning a career as a professional jazz musician. 'A lot of people who were reading the music press were at university or technical college,' he explains, 'and they were into the music, but the music was changing, it was getting more serious.' *NME*'s approach, virtually unchanged since the 1950s, simply wasn't working. 'We used to laugh at the *NME*,' remembers *Melody Maker* staffer Chris Welch. 'They had these terrible front pages with headlines like "Controversy! Beach Boys Never to Tour England Again!", really weak stories, whereas we had powerful stuff, interviews with John Lennon or Led Zeppelin...

we'd look at the *NME* in disbelief. One week we cut out an entire issue and stuck it up on the wall as an example of poor layout and terrible coverage.'[51]

While Melody Maker's sales reached 200,000 copies a week, those of its old rival diminished rapidly. 'IPC used to keep the sales figures a secret from us,' claims Alan Smith, 'but I had it in my head it had got as low as 130,000.[52] IPC were getting a bit desperate. Andy Gray was an old duffer and IPC were an old school corporation. They'd bought a magazine that was part of the fabric of young Britain and they wanted to do something about it to increase sales but they just didn't know what.'

This approach was entirely at odds with that of Jann Wenner, who built *Rolling Stone* through an almost forensic knowledge and analysis of the interests, behaviours and spending patterns of his readers. 'The average *Rolling Stone* reader is twenty-two years old,' he said in 1971, 'seventy per cent of them are male. About fifty per cent are in college... we reckon that they account for half the record sales in America. Twenty-two per cent of them own Volkswagens...'[53]

Fortunately for the publishers of *New Musical Express*, Wenner's approach came to nothing in Britain. The original idea – a uniquely British edition of *Rolling Stone*, filled with domestic news stories and interviews that were different to the main American edition, was swiftly revised: the plan became instead to produce the usual *Rolling Stone*, but with eight pages of British content in the centre. At a launch party for the paper in their plush offices in Hanover Square, the punch was spiked with LSD. A week later the paper's staff arrived at work to find that the locks had been changed by their financial backers, leaving them unemployed. Using the magazine's advertising contacts and what little credit remained with the printers, *Rolling Stone* UK's news editor set up *Friends*, based in an office on the Portobello Road in West London. The paper changed its name to the more hip-sounding *Frendz* in May 1971.

At IPC, senior management finally decided to do something about the dire situation. The magazine was moved from the IPC building on the Strand to its own office at 128 Long Acre, a short walk from where *Musical Express* had been launched a quarter of a century before. The paper's publisher was sacked and a new one, Colin Shepherd, installed. 'Colin was a fine publisher who actually listened to the paper's staff,' remembers Roy Carr. 'As with so many people in the publishing industry, he had a fondness for an early morning tincture – gin and tonic in this case – but it didn't cloud his judgement.'

Then, one afternoon at the end of 1971, Alan Smith was pulled out of the *New Musical Express* writers' room and sent for a crisis meeting with senior IPC staff at Fleetway House. 'Percy Dickins always used to joke about how bad it was,' remembers Smith. 'He was supposed to be the advertising director, but just couldn't sell the adverts because the editorial was so bad. He realised that I'd been the deputy editor of a local paper and knew how to put a paper together and must've made a note of me. When I got to Farringdon I was sent to see this guy sitting behind a desk in a huge office while I had to balance on the edge of a little sofa feeling very uncomfortable but trying to appear cool. He told me that the hands of the *NME* clock were at five to midnight, and unless something was done within months to arrest the decline in sales, the magazine would be shut down.'

Smith was given three months to reverse the decline. No one was quite expecting what was going to happen next.

5.Bugging the decent folk

'It was the charm-offensive equivalent of invading Poland.'

'The story of the seventies,' wrote cultural commentator Peter York as the decade drew to a close, 'was the story of everyone getting in on what a minority within a minority got in the sixties because they were in the right place at the right time.'[54]

Certainly in the first part of the new decade there was a sense that the interests and obsessions of the metropolitan hippy underground – the *IT* readers, the people who'd attended the UFO club or shopped at Indica – were beginning to percolate more widely around the country, as underground papers like *Styng* in Leeds or *Grass Eye* in Manchester began to spring up to cover their local scenes.

Meanwhile the festival movement, which had begun in its modern form in Britain with a bill including Fleetwood Mac and Cream at the seventh annual National Jazz and Blues Festival at Windsor Racecourse in 1967, began to grow larger. At the 1969 Isle of Wight festival, a quarter of a million hippies endured medieval conditions to enjoy sets by The Who, The Band and Bob Dylan's first gig in three years since his almost fatal motorcycle accident. *NME*'s reviewer had other things on his mind, however, complaining that some food vendors had asked 'seven-and-six for hamburger and chips'.[55]

In 1970, inspired by his experience gatecrashing Led Zeppelin's headline gig at the Bath Festival of Blues and Progressive Music, a young Somerset farmer decided to hold his own rock festival. Fifteen hundred people attended Michael Eavis' inaugural Pilton Pop, Blues & Folk Festival, each paying £1 for a weekend of music and all the fresh milk that they could drink. The success of the festival led to Eavis restaging it the following June with a new name, Glastonbury Fayre, and an appearance from a singer who had a hit the previous summer when his single 'Space Oddity' had been rush-released to coincide with the Apollo 11 moon landing. In his first *NME* interview David Bowie was described as a 'modest, self-effacing young man' whose blond ringlets and velvet flares were an integral part of who he was. 'I refuse to have my hair cut or change my appearance for anybody,' Bowie explained patiently. 'People will have to accept me the way I am or not bother at all.'[56]

Bowie's performance at the Glastonbury Fayre took place on a stage constructed from scaffolding and metal sheeting to be a one-tenth-scale replica of the Great Pyramid of Giza and believed to lie on the Glastonbury–Stonehenge ley line, in a conflagration of music and the occult common to the time.[57] Neil Spencer was a former student journalist who had just started writing for Bob Houston's *Cream*. 'Music was understood to be the carrier for the values of the underground, and provided the slogans and the focus,' he explains. 'The music was the centrepiece of the lifestyle that it promoted. But on the fringes and within the music itself there were all kinds of other things. So they were big on drugs and all of the witchy-woo stuff. Out of the tiny little nexus of people who created the underground press a lot of other things sprang: the Notting Hill carnival, for example.'

Despite overt persecution from the police, the concerns of the underground press in the 1960s really began to gather momentum in the early 1970s. The gay rights movement held its first demonstration in Britain in Highbury in November 1970. The Green movement coalesced around the paper *The Ecologist* and the British wing of Friends of the Earth, established in 1971. The Feminist movement was led by the underground magazine *Spare Rib*, which launched in July 1972 under the editorship of Rosie Boycott and Marsha Rowe and sold 20,000 copies of its first issue thanks to its high production values and distribution network. 'We wanted to do a magazine that was largely professional,' remembers Rowe. 'We wanted to be in WH Smith. We didn't want to bring it out... the way the underground press did, when they felt like it and when they'd got enough money together'.[58]

While this all happened on the fringes, in the mainstream things were stagnating. The success of *Rolling Stone* had established that there was a market for intelligent writing about rock music, and over at *Melody Maker*, writer Chris Welch and editor Ray Coleman had been taking rock seriously, while 22-year-old Northern Irish writer Nik Cohn's very personal history of rock, *Awopbopaloobop Alopbamboom*, was a groundbreaking attempt to provide context and historical focus to the music in book form. But even following Alan Smith's summons to

Farringdon and the ensuing ultimatum, the *New Musical Express* hadn't much changed. Certainly, the *NME* Readers' Poll results for the year 1971–72 made for strange reading. In a list dominated by Elvis, Cliff, Cilla Black and Tom Jones, the sole concession to the new decade was the popularity of Marc Bolan's T-Rex, who had discarded their fey, John Peel-approved folk roots for a new sound inspired by back-to-basics rock'n'roll. It was an approach that clearly chimed with the *New Musical Express'* readers: T-Rex polled 'the biggest points total since Engelbert Humperdinck four years ago'.[59]

Yet there, buried at the back of an issue of the paper from January 1972, after the readers' letters and the classified ads promising 'the lushest gear in town – Super unisex crushed velvet loon trousers', was a shocking promise of things to come. The 'Next Week' box was usually a staid and functional preview of coming attractions, outlining the interviews and features in the following week's paper. This particular menu promised a significant change in the direction of the magazine, not least because Cilla Black and Tom Jones were nowhere to be seen. 'We're freaking out at *New Musical Express'* the ad exclaimed, boasting an issue of the paper that featured underground darling Frank Zappa talking frankly about porn and Marc Bolan proclaiming that 'I don't give a f*** as long as I can boogie'.

After Alan Smith had left Farringdon, Percy Dickins had offered him the opportunity of putting together a special separate edition of the New Musical Express, only sold in London and the South East. This special edition would be used by Dickins to test out a new direction for the paper away from the influence of Andy Gray and without fear of disturbing the *NME*'s current readership.

'I assembled a team of subversives like Nick Logan and Roy Carr,' says Smith, 'who jumped to supply me with contraband material – the real stuff that they wanted to write in the main paper but weren't allowed to.'

Smith was inspired by the success of London's listings paper Time Out, which had been started in August 1968 by Tony Elliott, a student journalist at Keele University, with a gift of £70 from an elderly aunt and featured a four-page magazine that folded out into a poster calendar of listings of cultural, musical and political events – it even had a section entitled 'Revolution'. *Time Out* had benefited from the police persecution of *IT* by stealing both their share of the listings and classified ads and by 1972 Elliott was selling 30,000 copies a week in a glossy magazine format.[60] *NME*'s response was to introduce a gig guide, edited by Nick Logan and featuring comprehensive listings of performances by groups called things like Hookfoot, Gypsy and Quiver. Previously, the only way *NME* readers would've found out where their favourite groups were touring was to comb the live adverts in the paper – now they were being compiled into one comprehensive location. Written in the irreverent style of the underground press, the editions of *NME* featuring the gig guide immediately started to sell in larger numbers and Smith was called back to Farringdon for another chat. This time he was offered the chance to edit the whole paper nationwide. Almost overnight Smith and his team changed the look and tone of *New Musical Express* completely.

'As a writer I was on £16 a week. As editor I was pushed up to £40,' he remembers. 'But apart from the increased sales in the South East, the magazine was still in real trouble. Melody Maker had become this old farts' bible. Pretentious, writing about those heavy, pompous bands. I was more at ease with the three-minute thrill of a good single and wanted to bring in passion and irreverence and jokes.'

Given IPC's sanction to completely start over, as well as a sizeable promotional budget for television and radio adverts, Smith and his team wiped the slate and remodelled the *New Musical Express* as the kind of magazine they themselves might want to read. IPC, which had been taken over by printing and packaging company Reed International in 1970, promoted Andy Gray, making him managing editor and giving him an office far away from the main *NME* writers' room, allowing Smith and the other young rebels to drag the paper into the modern era. 'I inherited Derek Johnson,' remembers Alan Smith. 'Although he didn't like what we were doing. Then there was Andy Gray's deputy, John Wells. He was a sort of RAF type. IPC sent him off to edit *Rave*.'

With the old guard out of the way Smith was able to recruit a whole new staff. One of his first appointments was a Californian hippy called Danny Holloway, just arrived in England, who had been freelancing for *Oz*, *Time Out* and the newly launched *Sounds*.

'During my job interview Smith explained that the previous regime had lost touch with the readers and he really wanted to shake things up,' remembers Holloway. 'T-Rex had recently exploded and I had spent an entire day with Marc Bolan during a period when he wasn't keen to speak to the British press.' Smith, keen to launch his new *NME* with a rare exclusive interview with Bolan, hired Holloway as a staff writer immediately.

Along with Keith Altham's Zappa interview, the T-Rex piece was one of the main features when the new-look *NME* launched on 5 February 1972. With a picture of Bolan on the cover, inside the magazine were lively, chatty pieces on West Coast rock, the experimental psychedelia of

Can and Hawkwind and an interview with Yes' Steve Howe. There was also a gossip column entitled 'Hello Sailor' written by Roy Carr and a message from the editor, setting out his stall: 'We're not going "heavy" at *NME*,' wrote Alan Smith. 'In fact, we're happy to stick pretension where it belongs. Simply, *NME* will be an intelligent weekly paper for music people who rate Beefheart, but don't necessarily slam Bolan.'

It was a shrewd piece of repositioning. By attempting to cover the serious end of rock music but at the same time retain their teenage pop readership, *NME* was placing itself in a polar position to its more serious rivals at *Melody Maker* (also owned by IPC) or *Sounds*, while using the might of the Reed publishing empire's infrastructure and distribution network to try and steal readers away from the underground press and the music 'zines.

'In the first issue I ran this funny little drawing that Roy Carr did,' says Smith. 'It was of a figure holding up a poster that said "I Will Dominate You". I don't really know why we did it at the time but in retrospect I think it was aimed at Ray Coleman, who was editor of *Melody Maker*, to let him know that this was *war*. It was as raw as that. We were up against a superior selling magazine which was for old trad jazzers and we wanted to take them down.'

With IPC's marketing muscle behind it, *NME*'s sales rose immediately. By the time that the Audit Bureau of Circulation, the publishing industry body responsible for charting and certifying magazine sales, released its mid-year figures, the *New Musical Express* was selling 175,000 copies a week. '*Women's Own* was a massive seller for IPC,' remembers Alan Smith. 'The biggest magazine in the company. In a short period of time *NME* soon took over as the most profitable magazine IPC had.'

But Smith and Logan knew that they needed to do more to make the vertiginous, dizzying spike in readership truly sustainable and safeguard the long-term future of *NME*. In an era still very conscious about the divide between the interests of the underground and 'The Man' – international conglomerates, and faceless big businesses, of the kind Reed International was – the *New Musical Express* needed to acquire some serious credibility. With a staff list that had been pared back with the departure of Gray and Wells, Smith and Logan used the opportunity to comb the underground press for the best writers and poach them with the promise of the two things that *IT* or *Oz* couldn't offer: a bigger audience to display their writing chops and a regular and dependable weekly pay packet. Everything was in place for *New Musical Express* to become an immense cultural force. All it needed was its star writers, its centre forwards, its frontmen. Nick Logan in particular proved himself to be a major league talent scout, identifying the names from *Oz* or *Cream* that deserved to be writing for a larger readership.

'I was aware of the underground press,' says Alan Smith, 'although I didn't really read it. But both Nick and I knew that our main aspiration was to get Charles Shaar Murray. He was a wonderful writer but he also represented cool. We had to have him.'

Although only 21, Charles Shaar Murray was already a veteran of the underground scene. Born into a middle-class Jewish family in Reading, Murray had progressed from reading *Fabulous* for its Beatles news, through *Melody Maker, Disc, NME* and *Record Mirror* and then on to whatever underground newspapers he could scavenge in his home town or on increasingly frequent expeditions to London. 'By the time I got to reading *Oz, IT, Rolling Stone* or *Frendz*, I was really starting to look down on the weekly music press,' he remembers. 'I found it socially conservative and not nearly as radical or fun as the underground. I liked *Oz* particularly: it was sort of halfway between *Private Eye* and the *New Statesman* until some of them started taking acid. It was more radical than *Private Eye*, which was quite conservative in the Ingrams era. They were always being very hoity-toity about homosexuals and they *certainly* didn't approve of sex, drugs or rock'n'roll.'

Escaping Reading for journalism college in Harlow in Essex, Murray spotted the advert in the back of *Oz* soliciting contributions for what was to become Issue 28, the controversial 'Schoolkids Issue' which ended in the two-month trial for obscenity at the Old Bailey at which the magazine's editors, Richard Neville, Felix Dennis and Jim Anderson were defended by the barrister John Mortimer, later to find fame as the author of the *Rumpole of the Bailey* television series and books.

'Some of us at *Oz* are feeling old and boring,' said the advert, 'so we invite any readers who are under eighteen to come and edit the newspaper. You will enjoy almost complete editorial freedom. Oz belongs to you'.

A few weeks the wrong side of his 19th birthday, Murray nevertheless responded to the *Oz* staff's promise. 'I wasn't going to turn this opportunity up so I adopted the traditional rock'n'roll practice of lying about your age – I claimed to be 18.' Rounding up a group of college friends, Murray's pitch was successful and he spent a few weekends in Richard Neville's flat in Palace Gardens Terrace off Notting Hill Gate putting together an issue of *Oz*, learning about magazine production and how to write, getting a first taste of the thrill of underground notoriety.

'It was incredibly exciting,' he remembers. 'These guys were doing the kinds of things I wanted to do – living in London, dressing funny, dropping acid, smoking lots of weed and generally bugging the fuck out of the decent folk. I just thought "I'll have some of that: it beats being a civil servant or a librarian".'

Forsaking the route of university that his family had mapped out for him, Murray decided that there was only one thing that he wanted to do: move to London and start writing for the underground press. 'My parents were absolutely aghast. They gradually relaxed when it looked like I was going to be able to be earning something vaguely approaching a living and I guess they thought that as long as I didn't overdose, get the clap or get myself arrested it was probably better than having me at home into my twenties signing on.'

Murray learnt his craft and started to find his voice alongside Neil Spencer and another future *NME* staffer, Ian MacDonald, on *Cream* magazine. '*Cream* was a vital stepping stone for lots of us. Clive James wrote for it. Bob Houston worked as a freelance sub on the sports desk on the *Observer* and edited the *Union* mag for the NUM. Bob was fundamentally a jazzer and a leftie. By going up to the NUM office to deliver copy I would find myself in smoke-filled pubs with a bunch of gravel-voiced NUM heavies which was a weird experience coming from a middle class conservative provincial background. Bob also took it upon himself to work on musical education – he'd sit me down and play me all this Coltrane and Ornette Coleman stuff.'

Developing varied tastes in music and a passionate and fannish but informed writing style with his pieces for *Oz* and *Cream*, Murray was at the top of Smith and Logan's hitlist of potential writers for *NME*. The only problem was that he was a dyed-in-the-wool, fully paid-up member of the underground, resistant to the commercialisation of rock'n'roll culture by a magazine sold in WH Smith alongside *Horse & Hound*, the *Sun* or the *Dandy*.

'Nick and I went to meet him at this pub near the office,' says Alan Smith. 'He was quite detached and cool and didn't really see why he should sully himself by joining our comic. But what I thought was my winning pitch was saying "but Charles, the moment *you* join *NME* we'll be different". And that must've swung it because he said yes.'

'Having had a pair of boots at the repairers and a pair of pants at the drycleaners for quite some time I thought "might as well do it",' remembers Murray. 'I wanted to make some money and I also wanted a bigger audience. But when I arrived at *NME* it was an odd combination of the new breed, like this ponytailed American hippy called Danny Holloway, and those people who were already there and prepared to go with the new flow, which included Nick Logan, Roy Carr, Julie Webb and Tony Stewart. Then there were a bunch of old duffers who promptly vanished. There was a guy called John Wells who looked like a seedy ex-Army type – this middle-aged guy in a blue blazer with brass buttons. He was still nominally deputy editor and then he vanished and Nick Logan moved up. When the new writers came in there was no longer any need for Derek Johnson as a writer. He was this fat old bald bloke with specs.'

Murray joined the staff of the *New Musical Express* formally in July 1972. One of his first assignments was to interview David Bowie for what became a two-part piece spread across successive issues. It was six weeks after the release of Bowie's *The Rise and Fall of Ziggy Stardust* and the *Spiders from Mars*, the record which marked his real commercial breakthrough, centred around a character inspired by Nik Cohn's novel, *I Am Still the Greatest Says Johnny Angelo*, which was itself based on the singer P.J. Proby. 'I'd seen Bowie play twice,' says Murray, 'once in 1970 at the Roundhouse, which Richard Neville took me to because he loved *Space Oddity*, and then a night or two before the interview at The Friars in Aylesbury doing the Ziggy show. I was just a hippie kid and all that glittery, genderbendery stuff was well exotic.'

Installed at a suite of the Dorchester hotel with Lou Reed and Iggy Pop lurking in the background, Bowie made an indelible impression on the young journalist. 'David was very good at making anybody feel like they're getting on really well with him,' remembers Murray. 'I was young and impressionable and I hadn't quite got used to the notion of charm as a weapon yet. It was the charm-offensive equivalent of invading Poland.' The eventual piece was to mark the real beginning of the modern *NME*: an informed, young writer, who'd grown up with rock'n'roll and was immersed in its culture-talking to the star candidly and on their own level about their approach to making music. The 'it's all happening for...' approach was finally banished forever.

With Murray on board, Smith brought Tony Tyler to the paper's staff. Tyler was a contact from Liverpool who'd been friendly with The Beatles in Hamburg and possessed a colourful background: stowing away on a merchant vessel he'd spent six months living in Germany in beatnik squalor before contracting pneumonia and being shipped home by the British consulate in 1962. Enlisting in the Royal Tank Regiment, Tyler, who was well over six feet tall, became almost certainly the only music journalist to have carried a weapon in war: shot by a sniper in the Army in Aden, Tyler's military career ended when he used some inheritance money to buy himself out of the services, becoming first a jobbing musician and then a roadie for Bob Dylan. Tyler had played poker with Lennon and been backstage at the Manchester Free Trade Hall the night Bob was called Judas by Keith Butler. Now, though, he was languishing unhappily as press officer for Emerson Lake and Palmer and snapped up the chance to become a poacher-turned-gamekeeper by being appointed *NME*'s new features editor. At the same time Keith Altham was making the reverse trajectory: leaving *NME*, he became a respected independent PR, working for many years with clients including the Rolling Stones, The Who, The Beach Boys, Marc Bolan and AC/DC.

The transition from the old guard was almost complete. But there was one more crucial part of the *New Musical Express* team still to arrive, the man who became a totem for the paper – as well as a warning to all of those who thought that rock'n'roll was anything less than a total lifestyle.

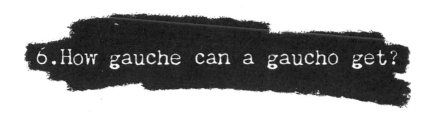

6.How gauche can a gaucho get?

'Fuck everybody else, I'm going to behave like Oscar Wilde...'

A startling physical counterpoint to the stocky Murray, Nicholas Benedict Kent was rail-thin and six feet three inches tall, a spidery, translucent figure, all sharp angles, fingers yellowed by tobacco and cheekbones accentuated by his poor diet. Born in 1951, the same year as Murray, and another child of the rock'n'roll era, Nick Kent's father was an EMI recording engineer who had worked with Beatles producer George Martin. Born in Horsham in West Sussex, Kent's family moved to Cardiff when he was eight years old. It was in Cardiff that Kent discovered rock'n'roll music. 'I saw the Rolling Stones in 1964 when I was 12, just a week before "Not Fade Away" came out,' he says, 'and they became my dark rebel princes. I saw Jimi Hendrix and Pink Floyd in 1967 in a wrestling hall. I saw Bob Dylan and The Band in a cinema where they were showing *The Sound of Music*.'

Aged 18, Kent moved to study at Bedford College at the University of London, but his academic career was swiftly curtailed when he began writing for *Frendz* and hanging out in their office on the Portobello Road, scribbling out his first pieces late at night in his university halls of residence.

'I'd done some things for *NME* and they'd liked them, so they asked me to do a piece about Iggy Pop,' says Charles Shaar Murray. 'I said "I can, but I know somebody who's really into Iggy."' Kent and Murray had met at a party and discovered a shared love of minority interest American underground bands The Stooges and The Velvet Underground. But where Murray was avuncular and clubbable, Kent's shyness made him seem aloof and cool, although his brief time writing for *Frendz* had left him well connected in the hard-rock scene centred around

'The mayor greeted us at the airport just because we were from NME...'
Roy Carr (l) and Nick Kent live the high life, 1974

West London's less salubrious neigbourhoods.

'From the underground press I knew what was happening in Notting Hill Gate or Ladbroke Grove,' says Kent. 'I knew all these people and places. I had an insight to all of these scenes which no one else on the *NME* had and I could get the news that no one else could get.'

While Murray – or CSM as he became known in print was adopted onto the *NME* staff, receiving his own desk in the office and a regular IPC wage, Kent chose to remain a freelancer, allowing him a sense of outsidership, of not being tied to the paper and its internal office hierarchy, but also meaning that he lacked the security of sick or holiday pay. 'We don't want to go into detail about how mean IPC was,' says Kent. 'I was listed as a staff member very briefly to facilitate claiming expenses, but chose to remain freelance.'

The freelance journalist lived only according to how successful they were in pitching stories or interviews to editors, supplementing their income by selling the promotional copies of albums that record companies doled out in the hope that someone might review them, surviving on free sandwiches and canapés at press receptions and creating bogus expense claims to get some extra beer money in the kind of minor-league commercial fraud that has been standard practice for journalists since the profession was invented.

'One of the first things that happened when I arrived at *NME*,' says Danny Holloway, 'was that Roy Carr schooled us on the fact that IPC owned half the magazines on the newsstand and there was one central accounts office for all their titles. With a little imagination, we could supplement our modest salaries with extravagant expenses claims and secure a few extra shekels.'

Meanwhile Carr was proving that he had a unique flair for promotion as well as fraud. 'It was Roy's idea to do things like the flexi singles which we gave away free with the paper,' says Alan Smith. 'He had the gumption and the charisma to go out and get exclusive tracks by the Stones, David Bowie, The Faces. We had Lou Reed's "Walk on the Wild Side", which the BBC wouldn't play because it was so terribly dangerous.'

The flexidisc was the perfect marketing tool for *NME*. A disposable record pressed into very thin plastic, it could be bound in to the magazine itself or glued to the front cover with a sound quality no worse than conventional LPs: following the 1973 oil crisis prompted by the Yom Kippur war, which saw the price of a barrel of oil rise from $2 in 1972 to $11 in 1974,[61] record companies were forced to start using recycled vinyl to make their records, melting down used singles and albums and recasting them. Unfortunately, sometimes the recycled records still had their labels affixed to them, so a dismayed customer rushing home to play their new T-Rex LP might find their enjoyment of the listening experience somewhat hampered by a piece of a Jim Reeves record label embedded into the grooves. The flexi remained a staple of the magazine's promotional arsenal until the 1990s, although few of the records given away with the magazine matched the exclusive Monty Python track that Roy Carr secured in 1974. Narrated by Michael Palin, it boasted that 'this tiny black round thing comes to you with the compliments of the *New Musical Express*, in the interests of promoting world peace and promoting mutual understanding between the nations of the free world. It is not in any way an attempt to boost promotion and sales of the paper in a year of increasing competition or a cheap gimmick to attract people away from *Disc* or *Melody Maker...*'

With these records mounted on the cover each week, a new design featuring the *New Musical Express* title printed in scarlet on the front cover and a young team of writers, sales of the paper began to grow exponentially, in turn attracting more advertising, until it fattened, reaching an unheard-of 96 pages every week.

'On Wednesday night the whole thing would go to the printer's in West Drayton to be pasted together,' remembers Alan Smith. 'You'd stand with the guy who was, by union agreement, the paste-up artist as he put it together. Then Nick Logan and I would stand on the bridge over the machine below and see the press turn and suddenly there was the whole week's work. It was just total magic.'

Grabbing a few hours' sleep, Smith would then round up the staff in his office on a Thursday morning, ordering in chicken sandwiches and bottles of white wine and getting to work filling the pages of the next week's issue.

In March 1973, with sales reaching record levels, the *New Musical Express*'s founder finally decided that the time was right for him to depart the paper after over 20 years, retiring to run a flower shop in Mayfair. Maurice Kinn's Alley Cat column had been renamed 'Teasers' in Alan Smith's scorched earth redesign, but the guest list at Kinn's farewell party was testament to his legacy and the range of his influence, as well as the sheer length of time he'd been working in the music business: Slade singer Noddy Holder and The Who's John Entwistle rubbed shoulders with Vera Lynn and Max Bygraves. The sexy singer from America mentioned in the first-ever Alley Cat column was also in attendance: Tony Bennett surprised Kinn by turning up to toast his future.

The 51-year-old Percy Dickins remained from the Tin Pan Alley days, combining his day job at *NME* with new innovations like the annual

NME awards for record producers and graphic designers, which recognised the importance of the album as a coherent piece of art. But as the Big Band days disappeared into the rearview mirror of history, more fresh blood arrived. Nick Kent brought in *Frendz* designer Pennie Smith as a photographer, where she joined New York snapper Joe 'Captain Snaps' Stevens to define the visual look of the paper. Tony Tyler scouted Ian MacDonald, an erudite and intelligent freelancer who wrote with great passion and authority. MacDonald, whose real surname was MacCormick, had been an acquaintance of Nick Drake while reading English at King's College Cambridge and his brother Bill had played bass in the group Matching Mole with ex-Soft Machine drummer Robert Wyatt. MacDonald had an understanding of the process of making music not uncommon at the time – *Melody Maker* had only recently abandoned the requirement that all their journalists could read musical notation – but he wore his learning lightly, bringing a madcap sense of humour to the *NME* house style, which was rapidly becoming an invigorating and frenetic polyglottal blend of Shakespeare and Damon Runyon and Goonspeak, of Fleet Street and hepcat slang, of cod-Jamaican patois and punning stoned humour and alliteration mixed up with CSM's hard-boiled Americanisms and Kent's bitchy slang.

The biggest influence on *NME*'s writing – perhaps because it was among the first journalism since Colin MacInnes' in mainstream publications to take pop culture seriously – was the New Journalism movement in America. Pioneered by Terry Southern, Tom Wolfe and Gay Talese in *Esquire* magazine and taken up by George Plimpton and Hunter S. Thompson as well as the established novelists Norman Mailer and Truman Capote, the central driving force of the form was what Wolfe described as 'the discovery that it was possible to write accurate non-fiction using techniques usually associated with novels and short stories'.[62] This meant a total revolution in the way that features writing was approached by journalists, discarding the Edwardian convention of the calm, dispassionate voice of the uninvolved observer in favour of putting the writer at the centre of the action, combining personal memoir and experience with reportage. For aspirant journalists keen to make a name for themselves in the world of rock'n'roll, the idea of a writer placing themselves in the foreground was a deeply seductive one: the writer could be just as much a part of the story as the stars that they were writing about. Of the New Journalists, it was Tom Wolfe who was most influential on the new wave of British music writers, perhaps because his work was the most readily available, having been reprinted in Britain in the *Daily Telegraph*'s colour supplement. As a result echoes of Wolfe's pacey style, with its blend of phonetic spelling and onomatopoeia, third-person narrative and experiments with punctuation and typography, were all over the *NME* of the early 1970s and beyond.

'I liked some of the guys who wrote for *Rolling Stone*, particularly Lester Bangs, John Mendelsohn and the young Greil Marcus,' remembers Charles Shaar Murray. 'I also loved Raymond Chandler, Harlan Ellison, Kurt Vonnegut, William S. Burroughs, J.G. Ballard and H.P. Lovecraft. But I was deep into the New Journalism. I learned how to describe a rock concert by reading Norman Mailer describing a riot in Miami and the Siege of Chicago. What I learned to do early on was mix high-flown theory and language with phonetic representations of dialect and street argot and try and mix it all up – high and low culture. Musicians listen to their favourite players and think 'how was that done?' and try and work it out. Ever since I was a kid I was always fascinated by my favourite writers and would try and figure out how they achieved what they were doing.'

'Truman Capote and Mailer were a big deal for us,' agrees Nick Kent. 'And I loved Hubert Selby's *Last Exit to Brooklyn*. But the big thing for me wasn't writing, it was Sam Peckinpah. When I was 17 his film *The Wild Bunch* was showing at the cinema in this little town where I lived. I went on a Monday afternoon to see it and was just hooked: I went back and ended up seeing it like 21 times. By the end of the run the fucking thing was part of my DNA to the point where it influenced my writing: *The Wild Bunch* is driven by action, but the action breeds character development: what are these people like? Are they self-destructive? Are they crazy? Or are they all totally immoral bastards?'

The same questions could perhaps have been asked of the staff of the *New Musical Express*. Where *Rolling Stone* treated stars like deities and built up the myth of the rocker as genius artist, Ian MacDonald and Tony Tyler would scour photo files for the kind of pictures any other magazine would discard: appending speech bubbles and sarcastic headlines to pictures of rock royalty snapped with their eyes closed or tripping over in an approach learned from goofy American satirical magazine *Mad*. Along with Tony Benyon's surreal and freewheeling weekly comic strip, the Lone Groover, the paper developed a unique free-form style that had no equivalent on the newsstand.

'Tony Tyler and Ian were essentially anarchists,' says Charles Shaar Murray. 'Ian was obsessed with stuff that bust the fourth wall of the paper. Everybody was into Python. That was a huge influence on the collective humour of the paper. And I loved Marvel comics, not just for the comics but for the way Stan Lee did letters pages. Basically, we wanted to establish as much of a personal relationship with our readers as we possibly could, short of going round to their houses and talking to them all individually. As well as having an underground press flavour, *NME* had a 'zine flavour. We wanted to bust down the barriers and turn each issue into this exciting, unorthodox experience.'

Part of that unorthodox experience lay in the personalities that made up the *NME* office, many of whom had never held down a proper job before, let alone one putting together a huge-selling and profitable 96-page magazine each week. It is the nature of all journalists to test the boundaries of their deadlines as much as possible. Some weeks, however, it was a miracle to all concerned that the *New Musical Express* was ever published at all. 'I remember going out to the printer's in Uxbridge on press day,' says Neil Spencer, 'and we still didn't have the front cover story. So Tony Tyler says, "I know what I'll do, I'll ring up Rick Wakeman". So he rang Rick, drove over, bought Rick Wakeman lunch in the local pub, wrote up the story and brought it straight to the printer's in time for the deadline. That was how fly by the seat of your pants it was.'

Despite the fact that he was being sent around the world on press trips to interview Led Zeppelin or David Bowie for *NME* cover stories, Nick Kent had a somewhat slapdash approach to the vagaries of journalism and publishing. Whether born of perfectionism or just a lackadaisical attitude to deadlines, he rarely delivered his pieces on time. When he did, they would be scrawled in longhand on whatever scraps of paper were to hand – cereal packets, envelopes, tissues – and had to be typed up to be edited properly. 'We all respected Nick Kent's ability,' says Danny Holloway. 'He would disappear into the small review room designed for listening to records and write his pieces out in longhand. He told me that once he had the opening paragraph, he'd be on a roll until he completed the piece. But sometimes it took him four or five hours to get the opening paragraph.'

'The way that I wrote was that I didn't even start until a deadline was two hours away,' says Kent. 'I'd write the piece in longhand with some secretary standing over me ready to take it out of my hand and type it up and hand it to the editor, so I never had time to review what I was writing. I never had a chance to reread anything until it was printed. So it was not just a case of "first thought, best thought", but "first thought, *only* thought."'

Often a replacement piece would have to be found at the last minute when Kent couldn't find that crucial opening line, to the annoyance of the paper's full-time staff, while Kent was cultivating an image as an untamable outsider.

'Alan Smith calls me into his office one week,' remembers Kent, 'and tells me that IPC have done a survey and asked a load of readers what it is about the paper that they liked, why they bought it. So I thought "I'm going to get a pat on the back here. He's going to tell me that it's all because of the new guard of writers". But what he actually said was "We found that they don't read the paper at all. They buy it to look at the photographs; the only thing they bother reading is the fucking gossip column." So this certainly knocks my ego to the ground for five minutes. But then I realised that I was writing for an audience that probably has the shortest attention span known to man. So in order to be read I did what most rock musicians do when they don't want to be ignored: I became more flamboyant in the way that I dressed, the way I wrote, behaved in public. It was like Jimi Hendrix setting fire to his guitar: to grab those 15-year-old kids' attention you just had to go to extremes and say 'look at me'. Fuck it. I didn't have a family, didn't have a wife or kids. I was only 20. I could go out and do what I wanted. I wasn't on staff so I didn't have to do the 9 to 5 routine. So fuck everybody else, I'm going to behave like Oscar Wilde.'

Kent transformed himself, becoming, in the words of Peter York, 'the only rock press boy who knows what it is like to wear make up';[63] at a time when the standard uniform for anyone working in the music business was denim flares, a moustache and a beer gut, Kent took to wearing leopardskin, feather earrings and leather trousers which were never cleaned or patched where they had ripped. Despite the effete allure of Bowie or Roxy Music's Brian Eno, it was a macho time – Lou Reed once told Kent that he was planning on writing a song called 'get back in the closet, you fucking queers'[64] – and Kent's style of dress was intended to provoke as much as get him noticed. To make things worse, he never used a notebook[65] and had a possibly apocryphal habit of leaving milk bottles full of his own urine behind him at parties.[66]

Like many of the post-Beatles generation, both Kent and Murray had frustrated musical ambitions. They didn't want to be sitting behind a desk writing about the people onstage. They thought they should be on the stage. 'Charlie is a really wonderful person,' says Roy Carr, 'who always wanted to be a rock star. Unfortunately the Gods didn't bless him with enough musical talent.' Kent had originally wanted to be a musician before he started writing. He appeared, credited as Nick Kool and the Kool Aids, playing piano on the song 'Blank Frank' on the first Brian Eno album. By 1973, *NME* was selling well over 200,000 copies a week, with IPC estimating that the average copy sold was passed on and read by three more people. Adding discounted sales and bulk retail discounts every week over a million young Britons would open *NME* and see Murray and Kent's byline, next to pictures of them – Murray in shades and sideboards under his afro, Kent wearing a single long earring and smoking. The writers became stars. 'I went to Hamburg once,' remembers Roy Carr, 'and the mayor greeted us at the airport with a big oompah band just because we were from *NME*. Ridiculous stuff.'

Inspired by the way that *Creem* mixed street-level writing about rock'n'roll with high-flown theorising about the nature and meaning of rock music, Nick Logan did a deal with *Creem*'s Detroit publishers to reprint articles by some of their star journalists, like Lester Bangs. Bangs was a dishevelled, paunchy guy who looked much older than he was: both his lank moustache and the free promotional band t-shirt he normally wore were usually splattered with mustard or bits of food. Bangs lived in the communal *Creem* house in the middle of Michigan with the rest of the paper's staff, a place where both privacy and glamour where in short supply and where Nick Kent, who idolised Bangs, once turned up one afternoon in 1973 demanding that the American teach him how to write. But Lester couldn't believe what he found when he first visited the *NME* offices, writing in *Creem* that he had 'visited our sister publication, *New Musical Express*, where the journalists are pop stars. To wit, Nick Kent, who looks just like The Stooges' Ron Asheton, and Charles Shaar Murray, who came to the office dressed as Lou Reed. Not only do they get to dud up like this, they get their pix in the mag so all the young girls in England can see them and get the hots.'[67]

'We did the autography thing,' says Murray, 'and sometimes girl attention was involved. It was stardom by proxy, really.' Naturally, this level of profile and visibility had its drawbacks. Once the fearsome manager Don Arden, famous for overseeing the careers of Gene Vincent and the Small Faces, burst into the office accompanied by two heavies to berate Tony Stewart for writing a bad review of Arden's charges ELO. 'I remember once being ringed by Steve Harley and his entire band in some godforsaken European field behind the stage at some godforsaken festival,' says Murray, 'and harangued for almost half an hour. A real "caught by the school bullies" flashback'.

The songwriters Nicky Chinn and Mike Chapman, most famous for their glam hits for the likes of Mud, the Sweet and Racey, took such exception to something CSM wrote about their production on a Suzy Quatro record that one day he arrived at the office and unwrapped a mysterious brown paper parcel to find a package of rotting pig brains.

As *Melody Maker* and *Sounds* disappeared further into the progressive rock ghetto, the writers on the *New Musical Express* were given free rein to write about the huge-selling but credible and interesting likes of Bowie, Bolan and Roxy Music. And as the rock world expanded and its stars became further removed from their fans, the weekly *New Musical Express* was a crucial link between artist and audience. It was *NME*'s job to report and inform, but also interpret, to make sense of the chaos of signs and gnomic or stoned utterances of rock stars, building significance and myth from the interview wreckage. It helped that *NME* writers, by working for the biggest paper, had the best access to the stars. 'We'd have an editorial meeting,' says Roy Carr, 'decide who we'd want to interview and just phone them up. I'd call Keith Moon or whoever and just arrange to meet him down the pub. Or if I was going to New York I'd ring Lennon and tell him I was coming.'

In a time before widespread transatlantic travel – Freddie Laker's Skytrain service, which sold flights at a third the price of his rivals, didn't launch until 1977 – *NME* journalists were being flown to America on a regular basis, holding court at the Chateau Marmont or Continental Hyatt hotels or Rodney's English Disco on the Strip, where 13-year-old groupies and, far less decadent, draught measures of Watney's Red Barrel kept the British rockstars occupied.

It was an era of unsurpassed music industry profligacy, and labels would do anything to get their act coverage in the paper. Record companies would send bottles of brandy or packages of cocaine to the *New Musical Express* office, or offer to put journalists up in five star hotels in Monte Carlo or New York for the weekend. Yet the staff of *NME* made it a point of pride to take the payola and then bite the hand that had offered it to them. They were often outwardly antagonistic – reviewing the country singer and producer Lee Hazelwood's 1974 album *Poet, Fool or Bum*, CSM simply wrote 'Bum' – while even the rock deities of the era weren't exempt from criticism. 'Oi fort your review wos bahluddy stoopid,' screamed Mick Jagger at Murray backstage after a gig in Frankfurt[68] before summoning security to chuck him out of the Stones' dressing room for not being nearly complimentary enough about the band's *Black and Blue* album.

Yet despite all of this, the staff of the *New Musical Express* took music very seriously indeed. Chris Salewicz joined the paper as a freelancer in 1974, having started out writing for the most serious of all of the early '70s music mags, *Let It Rock*, which also featured contributions from Lester Bangs. '*Let It Rock* was run by International Socialist people from Sussex University,' remembers Salewicz. 'A lot of those student socialists hated rock music, but they didn't. People had figured out with *Rolling Stone* that there was a market for intelligent writing about music.'

Salewicz's first piece for *NME* was a baptism of fire of sorts, being dispatched by Tony Tyler to review Camel playing at Wandsworth prison. Salewicz was joined at *NME* by Fred Dellar, whose encyclopedic musical knowledge was legendary. Even at its zaniest, the *New Musical Express* dealt with rock history in a way that was informed and irreverential: Kent wrote luminous retrospective features on then-forgotten artists like Brian Wilson and Pink Floyd's Syd Barrett that were among the best pieces of his whole career. Roger St. Pierre's lists of soul releases were a crucial resource for anyone into music generally dismissed as pop froth by the white rock fans. Henderson Dalrymple's 'Black and British' column covered calypso, ska and reggae. Tim Hart of folk-rockers Steeleye Span wrote a fortnightly column. As the *NME* grew in pagination, the variety of music, old and new, that was being covered expanded accordingly, from pieces on doo-wop and rockabilly to the underground German art-rock scene or heartfelt and serious-minded retrospectives by Murray on largely forgotten bluesmen or 1950s R&B artists like Bo Diddley, memorably described as playing 'a strange rectangular Gretsch guitar and produced an utterly unique sound, rubbery and shimmering, like an elastic band connected to Battersea Power Station'.[69]

'Six months after I joined the paper I was touring with Led fucking Zeppelin,' says Kent. 'The world's biggest fucking rock band. I was there backstage with them; I was watching them from the side of the stage. I had the kind of access you dream about, more than even the people at *Rolling Stone* were able to get. But I pushed myself into that role. Most rock journalists working at the time would be at the fucking bar for most of the gig. I'd be standing in the audience down the front. I was committed. I was on fire for something. It was the same thing that everybody that was seriously involved in music felt: that this music has real substance to it. That it's important.'

'I loved the music and its attendant culture and I wanted to use every tool I could find to communicate all the things I'd noticed and all the things that I'd felt,' says Murray. 'One of the things Tyler always used to say was that the *NME*'s not just about the music, it's about all of the things that the music's about. And as the music had broadened during the '60s from being about dancing and cars and girls and "aren't parents a drag" we figured we'd do the same, that it was legit. In the same way that Dylan opened up rock lyrics by importing the tradition of the topical polemic and all of his influences from literature and poetry. As a result I was getting to interview people like Michael Moorcock, Kurt Vonnegut, J.G. Ballard.'

NME became a sort of unofficial sixth form newspaper, giving readers a package of things that they wanted to read about, whether directly related to music or not. 'There were other things going on in the world beyond the experience of Tony Blackburn and Bob Harris on the *Old Grey Whistle Test*. And *NME* was the place that you found out about them,' says Neil Spencer. '*NME* and the John Peel show on Radio 1.'

While *NME* journalists were passionate and evangelical about the things that they loved, they were certainly not above pricking the egos of the more pompous rockstars. There were enough of them around, after all: the early 1970s were a time when some musicians began to take themselves very seriously indeed, either as great artists or as socialites. The staff of *NME*, mostly working-class young men from modest backgrounds, had no rapport with the likes of Rod and Britt or Mick and Bianca cavorting in St. Tropez and often treated musicians with the disrespect that they deserved, a disrespect that varied between gentle ribbing and outright venom: Nick Kent once called a new band, Queen, 'a bucket of urine' in print, while Murray referred to Elton John as 'ol' coconut bonce'.[70]

'Tony Tyler edited the gig guide,' remembers Chris Salewicz. 'One week when Elton John was going on tour he used the headline 'Hercules Unchained!'' Tyler was also responsible for the legendary headline 'How gauche can a gaucho get?' to accompany a photograph of Roxy Music's Bryan Ferry wearing South American dress to promote the band's 1974 *Country Life* tour. A furious Ferry demanded that his label, Island, withhold all adverts from *NME*, although he later defended himself in an interview with *NME*'s Max Bell by saying that the outfit was 'blowsy, romantic, swashbuckling. It fitted the songs.'[71]

Nevertheless Tyler scented blood: his response was to refer to Ferry each week by a different schoolboy nickname: Brian Ferrari, Biryani Ferret. Kent's remark about Queen cost the paper adverts from their label, EMI, and by the time Island relented and started to place adverts in the paper again, Murray was writing insulting things about a Robert Palmer album personally produced by the label's boss, Chris Blackwell. 'We weren't about to be told what to do by PRs and record companies,' says Murray. 'We were fiercely independent. We weren't going to be told what to do by our publishers and we certainly weren't going to be told what to do by the music business. Sometimes we'd take on the artists on behalf of the audience and sometimes we'd take on the audience on behalf of the music.'

Island responded to Murray's review by pulling their ads again. It wasn't a problem, particularly: *NME* was so popular that there were plenty of other people who'd take the advertising space if EMI or Island didn't want it.

The lion of the Ladbroke Grove scene reclines. Mick Farren, 1970

'I remember Alan Smith having a go at me at one editorial meeting for describing something as a bunch of crap and I had to remind him that the people who he wanted buying the paper didn't mind that kind of language,' says Murray. 'From then on we were given free rein to do whatever we wanted. Occasionally some IPC bigwig would get a complaint because the daughter of one of his golf club mates had brought the *NME* home and he'd found something in it that he didn't like, but generally speaking we kept a bit quiet for a week or two and went back to business as usual. We were a crew who were determined to be as subversive as we could be under the IPC banner. The idea was to hijack the *NME* and have an underground rock weekly being produced by a major corporation for a mass audience.'

An outraged article in the *Sunday People* decrying the kind of material that *NME* was printing appeared in 1973 following the declaration, by Cliff Richard, that he refused to have the paper in his house. The *People's* article appeared under the deathless headline 'Must we fling this filth at our pop kids?' To the staff of the *NME*, the answer was an unequivocal 'yes'.

The next logical step was for *NME* to recruit one of the underground press' most notorious and outspoken figures. Mick Farren was a sardonic rock'n'roller with immaculate underground credentials: a lion of the Ladbroke Grove scene, he'd been variously editor of *IT* and *Nasty Tales*, lead singer with biker rockers the Deviants, doorman for the UFO club and organiser of the Phun City festival in Worthing, which featured the MC5, Free, The Pretty Things, and The Edgar Broughton Band, as well as readings by William S. Burroughs and Alexander Trocchi. Farren was a professional agitant and subversive: in 1970 he'd been involved with the staging of a prankish coup along with Richard Neville, John Hopkins and various members of the underground press and revolutionary hippy group the Yippies – the Youth International Party – to gatecrash the prime-time Saturday night *David Frost Show*. Sporting a polka-dot shirt and an unruly afro, Farren joined the rest of the gang to upstage Frost in front of the camera, throwing flowers, squirting water pistols and shouting slogans after Yippie leader Jerry Rubin lit a joint and attempted to pass it to Frost. It was theatre, but it was partly motivated by a revolutionary hippy spirit that derided the passiveness of the flower power generation and wanted to overthrow the old order. Farren was perfect for the *New Musical Express'* subversive agenda.

'I knew Charlie Murray and met him at a party and he said I should go and see Ian MacDonald, who introduced me to Nick Logan,' says Farren. 'The underground press was having a hard time. By that time we'd just got to the stage where we had to make a living. Things were tough. We'd been through the *Nasty Tales* trial and the *Oz* trial and the underground press was on its last legs.'

Farren was another link with *Creem* magazine, whose staff he knew through his friendship with the MC5 and membership of the UK chapter of the White Panther party and when Lester Bangs visited Britain he'd sleep on Farren's sofa. But despite the fact that Farren had written a piece entitled 'Rock – energy for Revolution' for *Melody Maker*, he was depressed and deflated by the way that the underground press had crumbled after constant government harassment. Joining the staff of the *New Musical Express* in 1974, supplementing his income by writing pulp novels or pseudonymous pornography for men's mags, Farren just wanted to have a good time.

'Initially I just wanted to write about *Star Trek* and Bruce Lee,' he says, 'but the record companies were always offering goodies and I was basically seduced. Free trips, t-shirts, cocaine, clothes. We were never nice to them. We took everything they offered and slagged off the band. The music business had gone very corporate but we were dealing with guys like Andrew Lauder at UA – these house hippies who were working inside big corporations but hated it and were kind of depressed by what was going on.'

Sharing a love of science fiction with Murray, Farren used to frequent Derek 'Bram' Stokes' science fiction and comic shop Dark They Were and Golden Eyed on Berwick Street in Soho, where both journalists bought books on the occult and underground comics as well as the latest copies of Marvel's *Dr. Strange* or *Silver Surfer*, titles that deftly combined hippy mysticism and cosmic voyaging with underpants-over-tights superhero conventions. It all became part of the mix. Murray, Farren and Tony Tyler were dedicated to using the *NME* as a vehicle to disseminate their tastes and recommendations as widely as possible. Less than ten years before, the only way people in Britain could find out about the Beats or cult authors was through shops like Indica: now kids in Hull or Sheffield or Glasgow could pick up a copy of one of the biggest-selling magazines in the country and have it all laid out in front of them: appropriately, Mick Farren brought in his old friend Barry Miles as a freelancer.

'As far as we were concerned we were at the cutting edge of lifestyle and we were leading the way,' says Murray. 'Lots of people had never heard of William Burroughs or Jack Kerouac until they read the *NME* and then they used to go off and read their books. I decided early on that I'd rather lose a slow reader than talk down to a bright one. Talk on a total level to our readers, never condescended, ever. A lot of the other mainstream papers were talking down to their readership, treating them like they're dumb kids. We were always trying to stimulate or intrigue. Turn them on to cool stuff that they might not have been aware of otherwise.'

The staff of the *NME* were living out a newly minted version of rock'n'roll Utopia. Treated like stars, able to write about whatever they wanted with minimal interference from the company that they worked for, producing an underground newspaper while being paid regularly and free from police harassment, even getting the occasional groupies. Most of the writers were in their early twenties: even though they were working 14-hour days to get the paper out, clanging away on broken IPC typewriters, locked into an endless production cycle with no respite, churning out tens of thousands of words a week, it didn't really seem like work at all.

**Tony Tyler (l) and Charles Shaar Murray channel
Born To Run in the NME office at Long Acre, 1975**

'I'd just come down from Cambridge,' said Ian MacDonald in an interview with Paul Gorman in 2001, 'so I was used to a more elevated style of banter. When I first walked into *NME* it seemed like a loony kindergarten. Everyone was mucking around and laughing and sprawling on each other's desks like delinquent kids... being on that paper was a riot. Come lunchtime, we'd straggle off through the West End to find some lunch, preferably somewhere with a jukebox so that we could keep the soundtrack going. Early in the evening we'd reluctantly knock off and collect in the pub next door. Then it was all back to Tony's place in Highbury or Charlie's eyrie in Islington or Mickey's flat in Notting Hill or the shabby communal house Kent and I shared in Maida Vale. In the early hours we'd crash... then reassemble in the office the next morning to take up where we left off.'[72]

'I'd go round Farren's with Joe Stevens,' remembers Chris Salewicz. 'He was very fucking productive. A good journalist. I'd go to his place in Ladbroke Grove and Lemmy'd be there in the corner wearing this face mask which was in fact an incredibly elaborate hash pipe. And Farren'd be sitting there watching his rented TV, smoking a spliff, drinking brandy and writing longhand. He couldn't type. He'd be writing science fiction novels, he'd be writing his stuff for *Men Only* and he'd be writing his stuff for *NME*. Ingrid his girlfriend used to type it all up for him.'

The border between leisure time and work began to blur and then disappeared completely. When they weren't sitting around at each other's flats and digs smoking grass and arguing about music, the *NME* staff were sitting around in the office record review room, smoking grass and arguing about music.

'As well as work we were all into the idea of having big fun,' says Charlie Murray. 'During most of the '70s I didn't even own a TV. I had better things to do than sit around indoors watching the television. I'd either be at a gig or a party or we'd be hanging out at each other's houses with a stack of the latest albums, a few bottles of wine and a bag of weed arguing into the wee small hours about the greater or lesser arcana of popular culture. We were a fucking *gang*. Roy Carr wasn't much of a doper and he'd spend most of his time hanging out with his drinking buddies, but Roy hanging out with his drinking buddies, considering who his drinking buddies were, brought us a hell of a lot of good stories.'

The office haunts were the slightly faded and tatty remnants of Swinging London, like the Speakeasy, where visiting American rockers hung out with PRs and DJs and managers, or new acts performed showcase gigs to the assembled London music business: Bob Marley played his first-ever British gig at the Speak. It was also the main meeting place of the Pink Fairies All Star Rock'n'Roll Show Motorcycle Circus, a drinking club led by Farren and featuring former T-Rex member Stephen Peregrine Took, Keith Moon, Pretty Things drummer Viv Prince, Bonzo Dog Doo-Dah Band singer Viv Stanshall and various assorted Ladbroke Grove misfits, greasers, drug addicts and former Deviants. They even had a uniform of matching pink velvet jackets made up to give them more of a Hells Angels feel – although the well-connected Farren was naturally an honorary member of the bona fide Angels anyway.

'You'd be out five nights a week with whoever was around,' remembers Roy Carr. 'We were all silly little boys running around town. Keith Moon was usually the one instigating things. One night we all went down to the army surplus shop at Laurence Corner and got these tropical summer outfits for sailors – white suits with shorts, although they'd obviously been in the shop a while, as they weren't so much white as green and yellow. We all got dressed up: beards, long hair, cowboy boots and these sailor outfits, and went out on the town in the West End. We ended up in the Speakeasy at two in the morning. The guy Nino who ran the place wouldn't let us in until he recognised Keith, who managed to convince him that he'd left The Who, joined the Navy and was out on shore leave.'

Most of the staff were winging it and getting by gloriously. 'Charlie Murray had actually been to journalism school, he'd learned to type and put a story together,' says Nick Kent. 'Before I started on *NME* I'd written essays for school and a couple for university, plus three or four articles for the underground press. The only way I knew how to put a story together was by reading *Rolling Stone* and the only advice I ever had was from Roy Carr who said "Don't ever write anything bad about Elvis or you'll get your legs broken".'

'At the *NME* no one gave a fuck about what you did as long as you did your job,' says Charles Shaar Murray. 'If you maintained your professional standards no one was going to get censorious about your lifestyle. It was rock'n'roll, not children's television.'

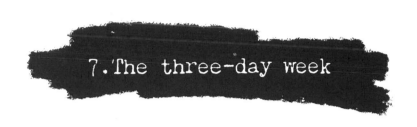

7. The three-day week

'It was basically weed from mid-morning on, pint or two at lunchtime and all bets are off after about six o'clock...'

During the latter years of his tenure at *NME*, Alan Smith and his wife had been running a sideline buying run-down houses in fashionable parts of London, doing them up and selling them on at a profit. Embittered at the fact that he'd saved *NME* but barely been offered a pay rise by IPC, Smith left the magazine at the end of 1973 to move to Spain with the cash he'd made from the property market. He was replaced as editor by his right-hand man, Nick Logan, and Ian MacDonald was promoted directly from a freelancer to being deputy editor.

'Nick had gone the conventional mod route,' remembers Mick Farren, 'got some girl pregnant, dusted off his Lambretta and moved to the suburbs. He had an inferiority complex that he'd never been to college – metaphorically speaking he'd worked his way up from the mail room and was trying his damnedest to make something out of his situation to make himself happy.'

Nick Logan's first major challenge as editor was a printer's strike organised by the National Graphical Association, the union which represented 7,000 printers in London and Manchester. Logan and his staff were placed in the dispiriting position of having to produce a magazine every week for over two months, without ever knowing whether it would come out or not. The strike lasted well into 1974, during which time the Conservative government had introduced the three-day week in an attempt to conserve electricity during a period of work-to-rule by the National Union of Mineworkers.

At *NME*, though, some of the staff were already living their own version of the three-day week. 'I went through a period of well over a year of only sleeping three nights a week,' says Charles Shaar Murray. 'Basically I would start going up on speed on a Thursday and stay awake and working until we'd go to the printer's on Tuesday, at which point I would crash, stumble through Wednesday and most of Thursday daytime. Then mid-afternoon on Thursday I'd start doing speed again. I kept this up for about a year and a half.'

The combination of their intense work rate combined with the unrelenting weekly pressure of putting the paper out, as well as the heavy-duty socialising began to take its toll on the health of the journalists. Drugs were also beginning to be more prevalent courtesy of a celebrity dealer. 'In Covent Garden, Lemmy would wander in, give out a line of speed to anyone who wanted it, see if anyone wanted a pint, or pick up some back numbers of the paper with pictures of him in,' says Farren.

'Generally Tyler would roll the first spliff at half past eleven in the morning,' says Murray. 'We'd be smoking weed at editorial meetings. Other stuff you had to be a bit more subtle about. I don't know if anyone ever actually shot up in the review room but there were certainly a lot of powders about. I don't think anyone took acid in the office – even an office as groovy as the *NME* is not conducive to happy tripping. But it was basically weed from mid-morning on, pint or two at lunchtime and all bets are off after about six o'clock. Most everybody smoked like chimneys. It was a very smoky office. I don't think that there was anyone there that didn't smoke. If there was they were probably really uncomfortable.'

Generally speaking, the music business attracts misfits and hucksters, people who can't really fit in anywhere else. The *New Musical Express* was no exception. 'There was a general lack of life experience,' says Chris Salewicz. 'I'd driven vans for Barclays Bank before I worked at *NME* and I was amazed that no one else could drive. They didn't seem to have life-skills. It was a home for dysfunctional people. A lot of rock'n'roll's like that.'

The natural oddness of some of the staff, mixed with drugs and stress, was not a healthy combination. 'Tony Tyler was a very funny guy,' remembers Salewicz, 'although probably quite psychologically damaged. But then everyone back then was in one way or another. Ian MacDonald was very troubled. I always remember this story about how when he'd been at Cambridge he'd taken acid and got a swan from the river and killed it and eaten it. A very traumatic experience.'[73]

It perhaps didn't help ers that it was a fiercely competitive atmosphere, with the star writers jockeying for position and approval from Logan, at the same time as attempting to curry favour with bands and get exclusives. This, combined with drugs, comedowns, hangovers and testosterone led to the kind of occasionally fractious atmosphere that occurs whenever a group of young men are cloistered together for hours on end, whether on a tour bus or a midget sub. Like the rest of the mid-'70s music business, it was an overwhelmingly heterosexual male atmosphere – Fiona Foulgar and Julie Webb apart, the only other women in the office were secretaries and receptionists. At a time when even the TUC conference would end with rounds of beer and strippers, record companies would occasionally send up semi-naked women to the office armed with balloons and copies of whatever new album the company were plugging that week. But the tension was exacerbated by a series of unspoken resentments, about class, status, position.

'A lot of people had dropped out and not gone to university and sometimes it showed a bit,' says Chris Salewicz. 'Kent dropped out. Nick Logan left school at 15 or 16 and did the trainee journalism thing, a classic old school journalist. But he'd also had to grow up fast – he had a young family and was holding it all down among the chaos. Nick was from a different world and we were able to sort of rampage around him. There was a 'spliffs in the review room' coterie and also a harder drugs coterie as well. I think it was a bit baffling for him.'

The problems were exacerbated once harder drugs started to creep in. At the end of 1973, Nick Kent was sent to interview Can at their studio in Cologne. It was there that he was introduced to heroin by the band's keyboard player Irmin Schmidt.[74] Perhaps unsurprisingly for a man whose twin idols were Iggy Pop and Keith Richards, it wasn't long before Kent started to become in his own words, one of the 'championship-level London-based substance-abusers of the late twentieth century'.[75] Kent himself admits that one of his first experiences taking heroin ended with him vomiting on Keith Richards' welcome mat. The good times were vanishing fast.

'1973–4 was a cultural black hole into which many strange and terrible things were drawn,' writes the journalist Robert Elms[76] and, against a backdrop of IRA bombings in Birmingham and London, of strikes and blackouts, a sense of extreme disaffection began to manifest itself on the fringes of popular culture.

In November 1971 there had been serious conversations within Whitehall about the need to activate regional government centres in case of a nuclear war. This dystopian feeling was reflected in a string of grim books and films portraying an immediate future that was violent and impoverished, where people were dehumanised by their environment. Science fiction is rarely actually about the future and the prophecies of

NME office favourite J.G. Ballard's *Concrete Island* of 1974 or *High Rise* from the following year, coupled with Stanley Kubrick's screen version of *A Clockwork Orange* or Peter Watkins' 1971 film *Punishment Park* – which portrays members of the counter-culture being chased across the Californian desert in a scenario that is part game, part social experiment – worsened the speed paranoia already at large in the *NME* office. The portrayal of the future in books and cinema made the present seem a very grim place indeed.

A new comedy show which started on BBC2 in September 1975 starring former Monty Python member John Cleese wasn't much better: *Fawlty Towers* portrayed a hotelier who stood for the worst of Britain – uptight, sycophantic, class-obsessed, xenophobic, Basil Fawlty was a nightmare portrayal of the kind of man rock'n'roll – a libertarian *lingua franca* that broke down class barriers and united young people everywhere in a shared set of values – was supposed to rail against.

But somewhere along the line rock'n'roll had failed. *NME* was still putting out 96-page editions and its features were getting longer, but the music it was supposed to be covering had become remote, bloated, self-satisfied or ineffectual. There was also a sense of rootlessness at large as pop culture began to move away from its unifying '60s one-world vision, opening up and fragmenting into more select sub-cultural shards. Hippy mixed with glam and people's dress got stranger and more magpie-like, as detailed by the novelist Malcolm Bradbury's description of the scene at a student party:

'People in old suits that look new and new jeans that look old... students and youths in Afghan yak, loon-pants, combat wear, wet-look plastic; bearded Jesuses, long-haired androgynes, girls with pouting plum-coloured mouths.'[77]

By 1975, Dylan was in the process of converting to Christianity. Elvis' June tour that year was a farrago. Led Zeppelin's double album, *Physical Graffiti*, consisted mostly of songs recorded for earlier albums. Lennon was in exile in New York, complaining of being persecuted by the Nixon administration, of having his phone tapped, getting increasingly paranoid about the power rockstars have and how that power threatens the status quo. 'If you get Bowie on TV and somebody switches on in Ohio or Bradford,' he told *NME*'s Andrew Tyler, 'and they see this person looking out at them, it's going to affect their whole way of life. He doesn't have to say Power To The People Right On. He is the message in himself. It's like holding a mirror up to society.'[78]

The high points of the *NME* critics' 1975 albums of the year list were few and far between. In an issue which contained a piece by Lester Bangs on Kraftwerk under the bad taste headline 'Kraftwerk – the final solution to music's problem?' and picturing the band juxtaposed against a backdrop taken from a Leni Riefenstahl film, the prestigious list of the *New Musical Express* star writers' favourite music of 1975 contained Dylan's *Blood on the Tracks*, Patti Smith's *Horses*, a Neil Young album, *Tonight's the Night*, actually recorded in 1973 and a compilation of Elvis' Sun singles put together by Roy Carr. Over in the readers' poll, the best female singer was Kiki Dee, best male singer Paul Rodgers from Free, best disc jockey Noel Edmonds and the best new groups list included Ace, Pilot, Hunter, Splinter. The *NME* journalists interviewed within were disconsolate.

'1975 was the year that half the people I know ritually stayed home every Saturday night to debate whether rock was dead or not,' wrote Charles Shaar Murray. 'Bob Marley aside, nothing happened this year,' complained Neil Spencer. 'Rock in general seems to have plodded on in an increasingly predictable course.'

The lives of the writers were in no better state. Ian MacDonald left the paper to freelance for classical music magazines, moving into a Sufi commune in Maida Vale with the folk singers Richard and Linda Thompson. Charles Shaar Murray had a complete and total speed-induced breakdown. 'I absolutely crashed and burned and had to take six weeks off work to recover,' he says. 'Basically I went to my doctor and confessed everything. He prescribed some pills and I really liked them, which immediately set off an alarm bell. I gave a few of them to a friend and he came back to me a week later saying "Those were really good, got any more?" so I thought "this is probably not what I should be taking to get off speed". I basically stayed indoors, slept a lot, ate a lot, drank a lot of wine and avoided bright lights and loud noises. It was rough. Physically and psychologically immensely debilitating. I would not recommend it as a lifestyle. If I'd attempted to keep it up much longer I'd've probably killed myself.'

Most troubled of all was Nick Kent, who had been temporarily sacked from the paper as punishment for constantly missing his deadlines, becoming a homeless couch surfer. When Logan relented and started to employ him again, Kent would commandeer the *NME* record reviewing room as his own personal study, leaving behind a fetid collection of empty Heinz tomato soup cans and mouldy yoghurt pots, the extent of his diet. Apart, that is, from heroin.

Following his first introduction to the drug, Kent had developed a full-blown habit. For one article on Keith Richards in 1974, Kent spent 40 sleepless hours in the company of the Stones guitarist, fortified by what Richards called 'the breakfast of champions', a mix of heroin and cocaine. In February 1975, Kent was sent to Los Angeles to write a piece on Jethro Tull, simultaneously researching his article on Brian Wilson. Tull were in the middle of a sold-out six-night stand at the 18,000-capacity LA Forum, for which they were accompanied by an orchestra. Kent contented himself with holing up at the Continental Hyatt House hotel on Sunset Boulevard with his hero Iggy Pop. Penniless, the pair paid for their heroin by allowing drug dealers to take luxury items from the hotel lobby shop downstairs, paid for by the unsuspecting Tull. Soon afterwards Kent OD'd for the first time and was resuscitated in a hotel room bathroom by a panicked Iggy.

'From 1972 on I lived a charmed life,' Kent says. 'I felt very strongly that nothing bad could happen to me. I was like the gambler at the roulette wheel that feels as though nothing bad can happen, that I could do anything. I was on a lucky streak. Time and time again I found myself in these dangerous situations and walked out of them. So I got to thinking that I was invulnerable, that I was fucking *Superman*. And for a long time that was the case. '72, '73, '74: three years of good luck. That all came to an end when I got involved with heroin. It really fell apart in the middle of '75. My lucky streak was over and a bad streak was coming.'

Writing his personal reminiscences of the year alongside Spencer and Murray, Nick Kent was just as candid. '1975 has been a bloody miserable year as far as I'm concerned… for the past few months I've not even had a record player to call my own.'

If the idea of a music journalist without a means of actually listening to music seems odd, it could be taken as proof that rock'n'roll was in a dire state. Co-opted by the establishment to a point where the old symbols had lost all of their resonance and power, it flailed along in a self-satisfied haze of private jets and backstage parties.

Ever prescient, David Bowie summed up the mood in August 1975 in a particularly strange interview with *NME* writer Anthony O'Grady. Under the headline 'Watch Out Mate! Hitler's On His Way Back',[79] Bowie, fresh from the *Young Americans* tour and sacking manager Tony Defries, started out by condemning what he described as the decadence abroad in the world, before suggesting that the answer to this global problem was in all probability an 'extreme right' dictatorship. 'The original aim of rock and roll when it first came out was to establish an alternative media,' said Bowie, 'to speak for people who had neither the power nor advantage to infiltrate any other media or carry any weight. But [rock'n'roll] has just become one more whirling deity… going round that never-decreasing circle… rock and roll is dead. It's a toothless old woman. It's really embarrassing.'

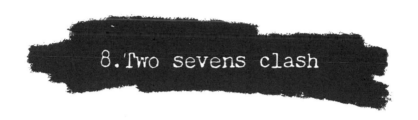

8. Two sevens clash

'Glam Rock, Heavy Metal Panzers, Techno-flash and dry ice machines...'

In January 1959, the first-ever Notting Hill Carnival was held. An attempt by Trinidadian civil rights activist Claudia Jones to showcase African-Caribbean arts and culture following the Notting Hill riots of 1958 – depicted in Colin MacInnes' 1959 novel *Absolute Beginners* – the carnival took place indoors in front of a few hundred people at St. Pancras Town Hall and was later televised nationwide by the BBC.[80]

The origins of the modern carnival parade, however, lay in the London Free School, a temporary adult education project organised by Ladbroke Grove community activist Rhaune Laslett in collaboration with future *IT* publisher Hoppy Hopkins. Uniting local residents, former beatniks like Jeff Nuttall and Grove-based musicians like Pink Floyd, the short-lived LFS put on a weeklong series of events, which culminated in a street party for West London children. The party turned into an impromptu parade when jazz musician Russell Henderson's steel band decided to go on a spontaneous walkabout around Ladbroke Grove and Notting Hill, establishing one of London's best-loved cultural events.

Only ten years after this first parade the 1976 carnival was ending in a pitched battle between almost 3,000 policemen and a large crowd of mostly working-class black teenagers resentful of constant police harassment under the so-called 'sus' law. The law, which allowed police to stop and search suspected persons without reason, was used as a form of racial profiling by the mostly white Metropolitan Police to harass and oppress young black Britons with impunity. At the 1976 carnival, against an aural backdrop of soundsystems playing the latest reggae tunes imported from Kingston, rioting began in late afternoon and carried on until the small hours of the morning. Almost 100 policemen were hospitalised and 66 carnival-goers arrested.

For some of the middle-class white liberals at *NME*, a love of reggae music was the perfect way to display a bit of underclass cred and show solidarity with oppressed black youth. John Peel played the occasional reggae record on his radio show, alongside new tracks by the freakier, hairier end of the British progressive rock movement like Caravan, Gentle Giant or Henry Cow, while in December 1973 a new magazine, *Black Music*, was launched, covering the reggae and roots scene in detail. But the music reached the radar of the mainstream white rock fan with the release of the 1972 Jamaican crime film *The Harder They Come*, starring reggae singer Jimmy Cliff.

'Reggae was a sort of underground music,' says Chris Salewicz. 'Most white rock fans fucking hated it because it was indelibly associated with skinheads. But then after *The Harder They Come* came out you'd go to dinner parties and people would suddenly be playing the soundtrack album and smoking grass.'

'I remember being in the office once,' remembers Neil Spencer, 'and Pete Erskine had been sent this Bob Marley album, *Soul Revolution*, on Trojan records. He made a ridiculing comment and threw it in the bin.'

Not all of the *NME* staffers were so opposed to reggae. At a time when the paper's pages were enlivened only by the increasingly ridiculous behaviour of Bryan Ferry, the lunkhead pop thrills of glam or a campaign to get readers interested in Iggy Pop's back catalogue which smacked of a valiant but fruitless personal crusade, reggae music was adopted as an alternative to the increasingly decrepit spectacle provided by mainstream rock music. 'Reggae became big,' says Neil Spencer, 'simply because it was the most interesting noise being made.'

Spencer and Salewicz wrote about reggae consistently throughout their time on the magazine. 'I went to Jamaica for *NME*,' says Salewicz. 'I woke up early in the morning because I was jetlagged and went up to 56 Hope Road which was Bob Marley's headquarters and Bob turns up and I introduce myself and show him the articles I'd written. Within about 15 minutes I'd been given a spliff by him and we were in a minivan on the way to the court at the governor's office to plead for someone's life. But you could do that back then. He encouraged it because he knew that he needed good stuff written about him in the British press.'

There was also an apocalyptic strain to reggae that chimed with the mood among certain sections of the British public. At the end of 1976, the Jamaican reggae trio Culture recorded their debut album, *Two Sevens Clash*, the title track of which predicted apocalypse on 7 July 1977. It came after a national heatwave which began in late spring and lasted until late August, producing the hottest summer since records began, as well as conditions of pestilence: ladybird swarms and a drought which meant that lawns and parks were burned to a drab, dull brown.[81] The *NME* responded by producing a cover dedicated to the history of sunglasses in rock,[82] but this drabness was only another manifestation of the disrepair and decline being suffered in the inner cities. The national birth rate had peaked in 1964 and the population of Britain fell in the period between 1974 and 1977 as emigration increased.[83] London began to empty and atrophy[84] as people fled the unrepaired Second World War bombsites, broken-down docks and empty warehouses remaining from a Victorian industrial and seafaring past that now seemed impossibly remote.

The middle of 1976 also found Mick Farren on the verge of a nervous breakdown only worsened by the unrelenting heatwave. At 33, a battle-scarred hero of the underground, he had settled reluctantly into a cosy life on the IPC payroll, augmented by the more ludicrous examples of record industry profligacy. Farren's workload and alcohol intake increased in tandem, but he was bored and itchy: for all of his adult life he'd been a *provocateur*: now he needed a new battle to fight. He looked around him at the pathetic state of the rock'n'roll music that he'd grown up on and decided that someone needed to take a stand against the mediocrity that was engulfing the music that he loved.

As rock music had grown up and become more socially acceptable, so it followed that it needed a new home, away from the dingy pubs and smoky clubs where it had been born. Instead the rock aristocracy, the major league earners, realised that by playing conference halls or sports stadiums they could make more money in one night than in a month of playing mid-sized venues or even the larger clubs. So while Led Zeppelin were breaking attendance records set by The Beatles all over America, their peers were playing huge gigs at Earl's Court or Wembley Pool or Charlton Athletic Stadium. These stadium gigs demanded a means of communicating that suited the architecture of the venues: grand gestures were needed to make an impact when playing to audiences of tens of thousands of people. Subtlety was jettisoned in favour of the kind of pyrotechnics that had moved on since The Who's smoke bombs to the point where a band like Kiss would put on a show that included exploding guitars, a drum riser that shot off sparks and a bassist, Gene Simmons, who spewed fake blood – actually made from yoghurt and red food dye – over the audience. 'Mainstream rock had… escalated into a spectator sport,' wrote Roy Carr in a retrospective piece on the '70s rock scene at the end of 1977, 'with Glam Rock, Heavy Metal Panzers, Techno-flash and dry ice machines dominating the international arena to the exclusion of almost everything else.'[85]

The scars of the Second World War had left a deeper mark on those bands old enough to have been born during the Blitz: both The Who's 1969 album *Tommy* (filmed by Ken Russell in 1975) and Pink Floyd's later album *The Wall* featured main characters recovering from the emotional scars of losing fathers to war. But while they worked out their problems onstage at Earl's Court, Mick Farren decided that he had had quite enough. In June 1976, he closed himself off in one of the *NME*'s meeting rooms and hammered out a page-long editorial piece for the magazine railing wildly against the state of the world. Entitled 'The Titanic Sails at Dawn',[86] in his screed Farren predicted that the iceberg of public dissatisfaction with the state of rock would threaten to rip open the hull of the 'dazzlingly lit, wonderfully appointed Titanic that is big-time, rock-pop, tax exile, jet-set show business'. He knew that audiences were sick of queuing to stand in huge stadiums to see their idols, of rock'n'roll's promise and danger being neutered by commerce following 'a determined effort on the part of some artists, promoters and sections of the media to turn rock into a safe, establishment form of entertainment. Has rock and roll become another mindless consumer product?' he asked, 'one that plays footsie with the jet-set and royalty while the kids who make up its roots and energy queue up in the rain to watch it from two hundred yards away?'

'Things were ready for a change,' argues Neil Spencer. 'Things had become stagnant and dreary. We were lost in a sea of fucking triple albums and epic works and prog rock and a popocracy who'd pulled up the ladder behind them. There was this phrase going around; "you've got to pay your dues", which meant that if you had a dreary band and if they went on the road long enough they deserved their success. Well *fuck* that.'

Farren's answer to the problem of rock's stagnation was a simple one. He advocated a total cleaning of the slate, a regeneration, a revolution, a process of 'taking rock back to street level and starting all over again'. Even someone as prescient as he was wouldn't know just how soon he would get his wish.

In June 1975, the *New Musical Express*' American stringer, Lisa Robinson, delivered a piece for the paper about a new set of bands that were emerging in New York. Gathering around a Manhattan dive bar called CBGB's previously favoured by winos and where the owner, Hilly Kristal, allowed his Saluki dog to wander through the bar freely, fouling the floor or sitting on the stage while the bands played, Robinson profiled some of the main players – Television, the Dictators, Debbie Harry and the Heartbreakers – of the scene. The piece made the squalor of CBGB's sound so exciting that Charles Shaar Murray followed Robinson to New York in July 1975, finding Kristal's bar looking as though 'the proprietors kick holes in the walls and piss in the corners before they let the customers in'.[87] Clearly this was a world away from the speaker stacks and exploding guitars of the mainstream rock milieu. In the piece that he filed for *NME*, the enthusiastic but sceptical Murray wrote that the bands he saw at CBGB's embodied 'both the traditional and the revolutionary... that a band like Television are currently happening and that people are listening to them,' he suggested, 'is indisputable proof that rock is a hardier beast than much of the more depressing evidence would suggest... they represent an escape from the roller-coaster to oblivion into which rock is currently straitjacketed – i.e., an imaginative return to basics.'[88]

The return to basics was already in full-swing back in London, where some of the larger and more run-down Victorian gin palaces were using their empty function rooms to host nightly gigs. A hangover from the same R&B scene that birthed The Who and the Rolling Stones, pub rock gave ordinary jobbing musicians an opportunity to earn some cash well away from the stadia and the mainstream music industry. On any night of the week the *NME* gig listings would be advertising cheap entry three-band bills in the back room of The Nashville in West Kensington or the basement of The Hope and Anchor in Islington,[89] where audiences sustained by warm bitter and cold chips could go to hear bills encompassing country rock, hard-edged R&B revivalists, proto-metal boogie and beer-soaked funk. But the pub circuit existed below the radar: so much so that the staff of the *New Musical Express*, while desperate for new thrills, didn't really pay much attention to it.

'One of the problems with the *NME* was that no one went out,' says Neil Spencer. 'If you look at the people on the staff they all went home to the suburbs every night. So nobody was actually out there checking out what was going on at a grass roots level. Tony Tyler lived across from The Lord Nelson on Holloway Road and one morning he came in and said "I've seen this group, you've got to come down, they're there every Tuesday." So I dutifully go down with Tony and see this band Dr. Feelgood, who were just fantastic. I'd never seen anything like it, they were just the total opposite of everything else that was going on at the time. Pub rock was cheap, local and accessible, while rock music had marched on and become arena music. It was inflated to the point where they'd lost touch with what had originally made the music exciting. With bands like Dr. Feelgood you didn't get long guitar solos.'

"FUCKIN' ell somebody CAll AN

Back row, l-r: Nick Kent, Mick Farren, unknown, Dr. Feelgood singer Lee Brilleaux.

bulance, ya know what I mean!^{pi}

Front: Pete Erskine, Deviants manager Jamie Mandelkou

While most of the pub scene consisted of journeymen musicians playing cover versions, Dr. Feelgood stripped R&B back to the point where it became almost avant-garde. The band's guitarist was the bug-eyed, bowl-cutted Wilko Johnson, an ex-hippy former schoolteacher whose style of playing was sinewy and redacted. Singer Lee Brilleaux was well read and cultured but a menacing presence who stalked about the stage in a grimy white suit. The Feelgoods' reductive, minimalist R&B resonated with the staff of the *New Musical Express*, many of whom had grown up with the harder, Dexamyl-fuelled end of the beat boom or idolised the tough, streetwise music being written about by *Creem* magazine and longed for an indigenous British equivalent. 'The music sounded like they'd strip you from ear to ear as soon as look at you,' wrote Mick Farren of the Feelgoods.[90] So while *Creem* had the Dictators and the Ramones, *NME* championed Dr. Feelgood, prompted in small part by frequent office visits from the band's tour manager, Jake Riviera. 'Jake used to come by Long Acre and give Tony Tyler big parcels of speed or hash,' says Chris Salewicz. 'Total payola. The Feelgoods would always come in as well. They became the *NME* house band.'

The staff of *NME* rapidly awarded Dr. Feelgood the highest accolade possible for a new band: they put them straight on the front cover of the paper without waiting for them even to sign a record deal or release an album. In January 1975, just before the release of Dr. Feelgood's debut LP, *Down by the Jetty*, Neil Spencer went to interview the band at their rehearsal room on Canvey Island in Essex, but he wasn't expecting the reaction that he'd get when the magazine with the group on the cover appeared in shops. 'One public relations person rang me up, outraged: "You've put a band on the cover that haven't even got a record out!" To which I could only say "Yeah, great, isn't it?"'

Fired up by pub rock, the staff of the paper began getting back to grass roots – still covering their bankers like Led Zeppelin or the Stones in order to keep the readers happy, but slipping in coverage of new bands wherever possible. In the wake of Dr. Feelgood came another band from Essex, Eddie and the Hot Rods, who played a weekly residency at the Nashville, alternating the headline slot with a group called the 101'ers. Sent to review the Hot Rods at a headline gig at the Marquee Club – site of The Who's famous Tuesday night residencies in the mid-'60s – in February 1976, Neil Spencer happened to catch a performance by the support act. When the piece was printed the following week, there was absolutely no mention of the headliners at all.

'Don't look over your shoulder,' warned the headline on Spencer's review, 'but the Sex Pistols are coming'. In the piece, Spencer described 'a quartet of teenage misfits from the wrong end of various London roads' who had played less than a handful of gigs, threw chairs at the audience, chatted to their mates in the crowd in between songs and played '60s-styled white punk rock'. Rushing backstage to interview them after the shambolic gig, Spencer grabbed a member of the band to find out more about them. 'Actually, we're not into music,' one of the Pistols confided, sharply. 'We're into chaos.'[91]

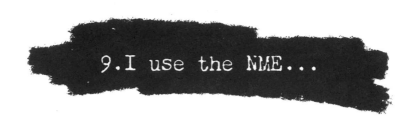

9. I use the NME...

'Let's really get on their nerves, flood the market with punk writing!'

Despite Neil Spencer's excitement, for one member of the *New Musical Express* team at least, neither the Sex Pistols nor punk rock were particularly news at all: Nick Kent had actually *been in the band*.

In his first piece for the *NME* back in July 1972, Kent wrote an article reappraising Iggy and The Stooges' first album from three years before in particularly enthusiastic terms. The record, which had sold poorly and been badly reviewed on its first release, was, Kent believed, 'perhaps the finest example of pure punk-rock ever recorded'. The Stooges, another Detroit group beloved of the *Creem* staff in general and Lester Bangs in particular, were exactly the kind of act that the more discerning *NME* writers loved: edgy, tough, heavy, blue collar and American. They were also fairly obscure, a fact which routinely appeals to music critics because it gives them an opportunity to demonstrate in print how much more discerning and attuned they are by picking up on a band that their peers have overlooked or dismissed.

'Iggy and The Stooges had only sold 500 records when I was writing about them,' says Kent. 'CBS were going to delete *Raw Power* – just before punk happened – but I went into their offices in 1975 and said "You are not going to delete this record".' I had the best taste of anyone at the *NME*. More than anyone else in music journalism, certainly in Great Britain. I knew the best music that was happening at that time and the best subjects to write about. My instincts were 100 per cent.'

As well as having punk rock in his vocabulary, Kent made a Sex Pistols connection in April 1974 when he interviewed the band's future manager, a shopkeeper called Malcolm McLaren, for a piece discussing his boutique, Too Fast to Live, Too Young to Die, which was situated at the wrong end of the King's Road at World's End, Chelsea, just around the corner from where Gandalf's Garden had their hippy head shop.

In 1975 McLaren had returned from a disastrous spell living in America managing The New York Dolls and reopened his shop as Sex, stocking rubber and leather clothes bought wholesale from suppliers that included AtomAge, John Sutcliffe's fetishwear company. Undeterred by his experience with the Dolls, McLaren decided that he wanted to assemble a new band around a teenager from Shepherd's Bush that he'd seen in his shop called Steve Jones. Kent, who still harboured dreams of actually being a rock star instead of just reporting on their activities, joined Jones and the rest of his fledgling band, Kutie Jones and his Sex Pistols, for three months of rehearsals as guitarist. 'I wasn't in the Sex Pistols in the same way that Pete Best wasn't in The Beatles,' Kent says. 'I was in a work in progress that was called the Sex Pistols. My biggest contribution was saying to them "Forget all this Small Faces and Who stuff you're doing", because back then they were a retro band. It was a tribute to that mid-'60s mod thing. It had no currency in the '70s. I turned them on to The Stooges. I had a tape of the early Modern Lovers demos, which I played to them again and again, telling them to use these things to write their own songs. Without that they would've been just a rockabilly group, which was what McLaren wanted.'

Despite its reputation, later cultivated by McLaren, as a 'year zero' movement, the early punk scene had a distinct sense of its place in rock music history. Although McLaren's assistant at Sex, Jordan, claimed that the only music that she and her friends danced to was reggae,[92] her boss had started off his career selling drape coats and brothel creepers to aging Teddy Boys, and was fixated on Larry Parnes, explaining in an *NME* interview that punk possessed 'the same attitude… that Eddie Cochran probably had, that any real rock and roller had'.[93]

Prescient coverage of the CBGB's scene had given *NME*'s sales a boost in early 1976, and even the jaded Murray was inspired to follow Kent into the punk frontlines, forming his R&B band Blast Furnace and the Heatwaves at the start of the year. He was partly inspired by the success of the Patti Smith Group, whose singer and guitarist Lenny Kaye had been a music writer. 'We all like him because he's a rock critic,' wrote Barry Miles in a review of Patti Smith's first London gig. 'Patti's one as well. They wrote for *Creem* and *Crawdaddy!*.'[94] Meanwhile a former *NME* freelancer from Dún Laoghaire in Ireland called Bob Geldof was abandoning his dream of starting a weekly music paper in his native country and, inspired by Dr. Feelgood, formed a band, The Boomtown Rats, signed to Phonogram in 1976.

'There were punk precursors,' says Murray, 'depending on how far back you want to trace the bloodline. But it really reached crucial mass with the emergence of the CBGB's guys in New York. The tipping point in the UK came around the time when I was recovering from speed and I didn't go out for a few months. By the time I'd emerged blinking back into the world it was in full swing.'

Despite Spencer's enthusiasm for the Sex Pistols, the *New Musical Express* was slow to totally commit to covering the British punk movement : the next time the band was mentioned by the paper was in a round-up of the London pub rock scene which included half-hearted reviews of deeply unpromising-sounding bands called Giggles, Bearded Lady and Dog Watch.[95] While Logan was making his mind up, the competition took up the advantage. Inspired by *NME*'s review of the Pistols at the Marquee, *Sounds* journalist Jonh Ingham sought the band out for an interview: his piece, the first on the young group in the rock press, appeared at the end of April 1976. Meanwhile *Melody Maker*'s Caroline Coon had attended early Pistols gigs after being tipped off by the band when shopping at Sex. Coon had strong ties to the hippy underground; in 1967, while studying at Central St Martins College of Art, she founded Release, a 24-hour 'underground welfare service' which arranged legal representation for people charged with drugs offences. George Harrison and John Lennon were two high-profile recipients of Release's assistance, while Coon also testified for the defence during the *Oz* obscenity trial.[96]

But despite *NME*'s enthusiastic coverage of pub rock, many of the staffers didn't engage with the fledgling punk movement, deriding it either as amateurish and lacking in musical and artistic credibility or simply unaware of what was happening. 'All this stuff was going on under people's noses,' says Neil Spencer, 'and there weren't many people on the *NME* who were paying attention. Nick or Tony or the rest of them were driving back to the suburbs to be with their families.'

Jon Savage was a trainee solicitor who committed to punk early on with his fanzine *London's Outrage*, starting to write for *Sounds* in April 1977. 'By 1976 all of the stars of the *NME* were failing,' he says. 'Ian Macdonald had left the paper and Charles Shaar Murray was burned out. There was aggravation between Nick Kent and the Pistols. Mick Farren had the sympathies and the right background but at that point he was far too old. Which meant that the other papers were able to write about this new music first. At Sounds the original editors had fucked off in about '74 so the paper was able to reinvent itself totally. We broke bands and wrote about new bands first while *NME* hung back and waited to bestow its imprimatur on anything because it had a reputation to think of. The *NME* brand was a blessing and also a curse. Being the market leader meant that it was very slow to react.'

While *Melody Maker*'s financial reliance on classified adverts for musicians meant that it was tied to a notion of 'musicality' and musicianship in the bands that it covered and *Record Mirror* was more pop-orientated, *Sounds* rapidly became the punk paper of choice. '*Sounds* jumped in with punk because we were the fourth-selling weekly music paper so we had nothing to lose,' says the magazine's then-editor, Alan Lewis. 'Our reputation wasn't on the line but *NME* were seen as the tastemakers and the gatekeepers of the whole music culture so they were very slow to make up their minds about punk. Some of the very senior people were very reluctant.'

However, the gap in sales between *NME* and its rivals remained so great that there was never any sense of commercial peril. 'We never paid attention to them,' says Mick Farren, 'because we were trashing them. Roy Carr used to socialise with the *Melody Maker* guys but as far as we were concerned they were just keeping the boring shit in business, going around after ELO and whatever the fuck else.'

'I remember meeting Allan Jones when he'd first started writing for *Melody Maker*,' says Murray, 'and he said 'I decided to go to *Melody Maker* because if I'd gone to *NME* I'd have a harder time finding what I might do that several other writers aren't already doing'. He was brought in to be their Nick Kent or Charlie Murray, to try and give them a bit of the *NME* flavour. As it was he really annoyed Ray Coleman by turning up to the interview with a copy of the *NME* sticking out of his pocket.'

In July 1976, the same week that *NME* boasted The Who's Roger Daltrey on its front cover, alongside mentions of Jethro Tull ('Ian Anderson just wants to be loved') and the Doobie Brothers ('beating the boogie backlash'), a teenage bank clerk from Deptford called Mark Perry was putting the finishing touches to his first fanzine, inspired by the Ramones' debut London performance at the Roundhouse. Things had changed since the days of the mimeograph machine, and *Sniffin' Glue and Other Rock'n'Roll Habits* added headlines that were hand-written in felt tip pen and biro to typewritten text and then photocopied. While Malcolm McLaren's art school friend Jamie Reid defined the visual look of punk – ripped and patched, collaged and repurposed – with his artwork for the Sex Pistols, *Sniffin' Glue* set the tone for its verbal style with its vernacular and slightly earnest writing. Soon it was selling 15,000 copies every issue, a not insignificant amount when it lacked the kind of established distribution network enjoyed by the mainstream papers. Instead, like the early underground press, Perry had to build his own network of vendors willing to take *Sniffin' Glue* on a sale or return basis, or through Better Badges, who occupied the former offices of *IT* on Portobello Road and became a pioneering punk and indie marketing company.[97]

Soon the shelves of Rough Trade records in Ladbroke Grove were full of photocopied punk fanzines inspired by Perry's success: *Moron*, edited by teenage schoolkids; *Chainsaw*, which featured a cartoon strip by future BBC Political Editor Andrew Marr and hand-lettered 'n''s because the key was missing from the editor's typewriter. *Peroxide*, edited by Norman Cook, who later found chart success as Fatboy Slim. *Jamming!*, *Vague*, *Burnt Offering*, *Sideburns*,[98] *Censored* in Birmingham, *Kingdom Come* in Edinburgh: all short-lived and homemade efforts which established a fanzine culture that would last for 30 years, providing an alternative voice and a feeder pool of new talent to the mainstream rock weeklies. 'All you kids out there who read SG, don't be satisfied with what we write,' wrote Perry in issue 5. 'Go and start your own fanzines or send reviews to the established papers. Let's really get on their nerves, flood the market with punk writing!'

Mark Perry left *Sniffin' Glue* after issue 10 to form his own punk group, Alternative TV, leaving the magazine in the hands of co-editor Danny Baker. Baker, also from Deptford, had left school at the age of 15 to work in One Stop records near Bond Street. Unlike his punk 'zine peers, however, Baker was happy to satirise the groups that others fawned over. Worse still: he had long hair and liked Philly Soul.

It didn't bother the readers of *Sniffin' Glue*, but at *NME* Nick Logan was starting to panic, not that the mild and guarded editor would've ever let it show. At an early Sex Pistols gig John Lydon, fortified by a quantity of speed and LSD, had confronted Nick Kent with the words 'Nothing's happening at the *NME*, is it?'[99] Further mortification came for the ultra-hip staff of the *NME* when the Sex Pistols released their first single, 'Anarchy in the UK' in November 1976. Reviewed by Cliff White, the paper's soul correspondent, as a 'third-rate Who imitation', there in the third verse was a reference to the nation's best-selling rock weekly: 'I use the *NME*,' howled John Lydon, with no little disdain, 'I use anarchy…'

In the spring of 1977, that old *NME* standby, Marc Bolan, released what was to be his final album, *Dandy in the Underworld*. Only 29, in pop terms Bolan was a Methuselah whose career stretched back to the distant past of Tin Pan Alley and the 2i's coffee bar. After a period spent living as a tax exile in America and Monaco, Bolan and manager Tony

Secunda were nervous that some of his fans would've forgotten about him, or worse, see him as old news. Bolan's response was to pick a punk act to support him on tour, pulling in the floating voters and gaining a bit of cutting-edge cred. 'I remember going to Portsmouth or somewhere to review this tour Bolan did with The Damned,' says Mick Farren, 'and suddenly before your eyes you see all these Bolan fans morphing into Siouxsie and the Banshees fans, into punks. You didn't have to be smart to release that hey! here comes a new youth movement.'

More than that, punk was newsworthy in a way that music hadn't been since the *Rock Around the Clock* riots of the 1950s. Ever since the Sex Pistols had appeared on the Bill Grundy show in December 1976, punk had been a constant fixture in tabloid headlines, while within six months, the image of the safety pin, chains and flying phlegm was embedded enough in the culture to be sent up by *The Goodies*. Logan had known that something needed to be done to properly get to grips with the most exciting British youth movement since rock'n'roll began, that it needed its own house punks to regain its credibility or face looking old like Bolan. Luckily, though, he had his secret weapons.

10.Hip young gunslingers

'Not just taking heroin but taking heroin with Keith Richards. Not just
smoking dope but smoking dope with Bob Marley...'

For two weeks in July 1976 among the small ads offering records for sale
or selling 'washed indigo scoop pocket' flared trousers and cannabis leaf
silver pendants, a small advertisement ran in the pages of the *New Musical
Express*. Written by Charles Shaar Murray in a partial echo of the Oz
Schoolkids ad he had replied to six years previously, it was immediately
eye-catching:

'Attention hip young gunslingers. The *NME* has a vacancy for a
STAFF WRITER. Previous experience in either journalism or the music
business is not essential, but a good knowledge of rock and enthusiasm
are, together with the ability to write lively and incisive prose. All
applications must be accompanied by a sample 5–600 word review of
any album of the applicant's choice.'

Quite apart from Nick Kent's obsession with *The Wild Bunch*, there
was much gunslinging imagery at large on Long Acre in 1976. From Roy
Carr's cowboy boots and fringed Buffalo Bill jacket to the Zapata-style
bullet belts that both Mick Farren and Lemmy would wear on their visits
to the office, the house style was part outlaw cowboy and part army
surplus leftovers. The logo of the magazine that appeared on the masthead
was even written in a pastiche of a Western wanted poster.

The punks didn't approve of this kind of macho posturing. One of
Malcolm McLaren's best-selling items of clothing at Sex – after the cap-
sleeved unisex t-shirts featuring a black and white photo of a pair of bare
breasts and the shirts depicting the homemade leather hood worn by
Peter Cook, the recently convicted Cambridge rapist – was a t-shirt
featuring an illustration by the American artist Jim French.[100] The shirt

depicted two gunslingers, both smoking cigarettes and wearing Stetsons, one adjusting his colleague's bandana. They were both naked from the waist down, and their penises were almost touching,[101] in the style of Tom of Finland.[102]

One of the people who read the *NME* advert was a 17-year-old schoolgirl from Bristol whose father was a Communist union activist and shop steward who worked in a distillery. Having recently completed her O-Levels and being unusually well read, Julie Burchill was half-heartedly contemplating a future as a schoolteacher until the advert caught her eye. 'I thought – eww, macho cowboy imagery, they must be really sexually inadequate up there,' she says,[103] although she nevertheless applied, sending in a review of Patti Smith's *Horses* written in biro on a scrap of paper. 'I was just really keen to get out of school and get to London. I was 17 and doing my A-Levels and it didn't suit me. I never thought about it in an intellectual way – it was more like letting the greyhound see the mechanical rabbit. Leave school, move to London, be paid for writing.'

Burchill wasn't alone: it seemed that a whole generation of bright, creative, frustrated people from around the country had found inspiration or comfort in the weekly connection to the rock mainframe *NME* provided. Over the course of the next month, Logan and Tyler received over 1,200 applications for the job on offer. From London, an editor at Marvel comics, bored with his job anglicising American slang for British editions and desperate to break into pop journalism. Neil Tennant didn't get the job, although he ended up being Assistant Editor of *Smash Hits* before leaving to form The Pet Shop Boys. From Bromsgrove in Worcestershire a prog obsessed schoolboy called Jonathan Coe, later to draw on his fixation with the '70s music press in his novels. From Camden, a schoolteacher with dreams of being a novelist called Sebastian Faulks. From Liverpool and Manchester and Sheffield and Glasgow, a generation united in one ambition: to see their photo next to a byline in the *NME*.

A Liverpudlian who had settled in London after studying at the LSE, Paul DuNoyer was one of the applicants. 'The idea at the time was that to be an *NME* writer was to aspire to a kind of stardom yourself,' he remembers. DuNoyer had grown up reading *Merseybeat*, the paper founded in 1962 by Bill Harry, a former art school colleague of John Lennon,[104] the fortunes of which were tied irrecoverably to that of the local music scene. 'The *NME* became for me the idealised older brother which I didn't have in real life. I worshipped those guys and regarded them as the fount of all wisdom on ers musical and cultural.'

DuNoyer submitted a review of Ian Dury's pub rock band Kilburn and the High Roads, receiving a telegram inviting him to an interview. He was unsuccessful, but by this stage Tyler and Logan had narrowed their shortlist down to four: Burchill, a PhD student from Edinburgh called Ian Cranna, a fanzine writer and bookshop assistant from Stockport called Paul Morley and a wiry 23-year-old gin distillery worker from Billericay in Essex called Tony Parsons.

'I loved the *NME*,' remembers Parsons. 'I used to travel in to Central London because you could buy it a day earlier than everywhere else from a stand at Tottenham Court Road tube station. I thought I was the only person who did that, but it turns out later that Jonathan Ross did that, Neil Tennant did that: an entire generation that just couldn't wait to read the *NME* every week and had to get it a day early. I didn't read the underground papers because I wasn't a hippy at all, I was a little suedehead, but when my feelings about music were changing in the early '70s *NME* seemed to articulate that. I was a David Bowie fan and I took my first girlfriend to see him at Earl's Court on the *Aladdin Sane* tour and it was a horrible experience – there were people everywhere being drunk and vomiting and the bouncers were very rough and Bowie was disengaged and probably coked out of his mind and it was not that intimate inclusive experience that the music was to me. Nick Kent wrote a very vicious, bitchy review in the *NME* and I just thought "that's exactly how I feel. Maybe it's over. Maybe music is over".'

Of the chosen four, Parsons was the oldest and the only one with any experience of actually having writing published: while working as a shipping clerk he'd written a novel, *The Kids*, which was put out by pulp publishers the New English Library early in 1976. Specialising mostly in cheap science fiction and horror paperbacks, the NEL also published a strain of garish novels written by the Canadian author James Moffat under the pen name Richard Allen, concerning the various misdeeds of different British youth sub-cults: *Skinhead, Suedehead, Mod Rule, Glam, Punk Rock, Smoothies.*[105]

Parsons' book earned him £700, but the money wasn't enough to establish him full-time as a professional novelist. Instead he worked on the night shift in the Gordon's Gin Distillery on Moreland Street in Islington. It was there that he first discovered punk. 'We'd fuck around with the machinery,' he says, 'which meant that the engineer wouldn't be able to come out until 5 o'clock in the morning and we'd just slip away into the night.

'The only places that were open in London at that time were Dunkin' Donuts or punk gigs. The pub rock thing had opened up a lot of venues and pubs or jazz clubs like the 100 Club had realised that you could put on a rock band and make good money over the bar. I hadn't been to a gig for a few years. I'd given up going to see live music. I'd followed The Faces or The Who around but I just kind of got put off because it was too big. I hadn't read about any of these punk bands but I'd literally be looking for somewhere to go at night and end up in the 100 Club watching The Damned or whoever.

'So I'd had a novel out and I'd actually seen a few of these punk bands. I was published, I was 22 and I had a leather jacket: I was practically a shoo-in for the job.'

Burchill was less of a sure thing: bonding with Nick Logan in her job interview over a shared love of American soul music, she was sceptical about music made by young angry men with guitars, but nevertheless judged sufficiently pale, youthful and working class to be able to cover the punk beat. 'Julie was a strange girl,' says Neil Spencer. 'Very young and very naïve. Just out of school. She was a good writer, but she couldn't talk to anyone or go anywhere.'

Cranna, Morley and DuNoyer were taken on as freelance writers. Tony Parsons and Julie Burchill were both made staff writers, becoming the hip young gunslingers upon whom instant stardom and the hopes of the *NME* in credibly covering punk were bestowed. First they needed to make a grand gesture, a break with the past, an irreverent show of punk fearlessness and contempt for the music business. Burchill obliged when she was dispatched to her first interview for the paper, with hippy veteran Country Joe MacDonald, then plugging a greatest hits album. Burchill slipped amphetamine sulphate into MacDonald's drink, leading to a fulsome interview but also complaints from the singer and his record company. Logan responded by banning her from more interviews, instead assigning her to help Mick Farren compile the magazine's gossip section, *Teasers*. 'We had a very lively, gossipy magazine,' says Farren. 'Pennie Smith or Joe Stevens would come by with these paparazzi-type shots of Mick Jagger or whoever backstage which we'd run alongside strange stories from other magazines. So I'd send Julie up to Old Compton Street to buy all the magazines that she could carry – everything from *Esquire* or *Paris Match* to *Guns & Ammo* – then come back to the office and scour them for interesting stories or photographs.'

While Burchill was being kept occupied by Farren and taken in as a lodger by Charles Shaar Murray, the rest of the office circled Parsons nervously, conscious that he was the new star set to put them all out to pasture. 'He looked like he could be handy in a fistfight, something that couldn't be said about any other male in the office,' says Nick Kent.[106]

But more than that, the arrival of Tony Parsons made some of the staffers feel something they never had done before: old and uncool.

'Parsons thought he knew it all,' says Mick Farren. 'He was a real asshole. Julie was 17 and liked to be the centre of attention, but she was actually a very good writer. Mad as a hatter, but I don't think Dorothy Parker was a day at the beach either really.'

'The job interview was more like an audition,' says Parsons. 'They were picking people who looked the part more than anything. It was about the image, about the *NME* as a brand, about it being cutting edge and dangerous.'

With Logan feting his new protégés in print and around the music business in a high-profile attempt to reposition *NME* as the punk paper of choice, some of the *NME*'s former stars gradually began to feel uncomfortable. 'I don't think I was a good writer,' says Burchill, 'although obviously I had something. But Tony and I had a very high profile right from the start.' It was a very territorial world, one that only two or three years previously they had ruled totally. But while Kent's heroin addiction worsened and Murray was still recovering from his breakdown, a whole generation divide had opened up. At its inception, punk was tied in completely with the hippy underground – as well as Caroline Coon's links to the underground press, Malcolm McLaren was a keen student of the rhetoric of 1968's student unrest, having been involved, along with Jamie Reid, in a sit-in while a student at Croydon Art School. Few people involved with punk at the beginning didn't have a past. But as the music spread out away from the cities, the bands and audiences involved grew younger and less connected with the '60s. At 22, Tony Parsons was only three years younger than either Kent or Murray. But their distant association with the hippy underground marked them out as antediluvian in the light of the new punk scene.

'At my interview Tony Tyler said that there had been "a shift in the tectonic plates",' says Paul DuNoyer. 'I didn't understand what he meant at the time, but I've since realised he was talking about a kind of generational watershed. Charlie wasn't much older than the punks, but he was Charlie of the afro hair and loon pants and his problem was he'd started so young on *Oz* magazine that he was permanently associated with the hippy underground.

'Mick and Charlie understood punk as well as anybody, being the great prophets of punk. They knew what was going to happen but were forever associated with the old guard. People like Tony didn't carry any of this baggage.'

'Joining the *NME* was like joining bohemia,' says Parsons. 'I was 22 years old, probably a *young* 22 years old, and suddenly I was surrounded by people who spent the weekend not just taking heroin but taking heroin with Keith Richards. Not just smoking dope but smoking dope with Bob Marley. People were impressed by the fact that I had a book out, even if it was through an act of will rather than any great literary ability, and they were all fantastically friendly to me. Nick, Charlie, they were all friendly to me. But they were rivals. They were the top dogs. My writing wasn't as good as theirs, but I had access that they didn't. I remember going down the Speakeasy with Mick Jones and Paul Simonon from The Clash and not being allowed in because we weren't cool enough. Those kind of experiences produced a bond between us.'

Even though Derek Johnson was still on the staff, suddenly an *NME* star writer's career came with something that it never had done previously: a lifespan, determined by how young and hip you were. 'The writers, when they're twenty-nine they retire,' wrote Peter York in a piece on Tony Parsons and Julie Burchill[107] published in his book *Style Wars*. 'They leave to become PRs at record companies or… disappear entirely.'

'I was only about a year older than Joe Strummer turned out to be,' says Charlie Murray. 'In 1976 I was 25 and Tony was 22. Basically it had got to the point where a rock generation had shrunk to something like three years. Up until punk I only knew three or four professional musicians younger than I was. I'd spent my entire working life talking to people who were older than me. Most of the Ramones were actually older than I was. Blondie, Talking Heads, all those people. I'm younger than Patti Smith.'

Murray trimmed his afro and bought some straight-legged jeans in an attempt to shed some of the remnants of his hippy past. Mick Farren, who had been the other side of 30 when he joined the paper, refused. 'Mickey's attitude was "I've been listening to fucking wankers telling me to get my hair cut since I was 15 and I'm not going to tolerate it now",' says Murray. 'But by the time I'd come back to work following dire warnings from my doctor about the consequences of long-term amphetamine abuse, Parsons and Burchill had arrived and I was getting a lot of "don't take it out on us because you can't handle your drugs, granddad".'

An air of fundamentalism bred about which members of the old guard were acceptable in the light of punk's brave new dawn: Bowie and Roxy were allowed. The Faces had the right kind of terrace credibility. Reggae was de rigueur. Pretty much everything else was old and boring and the punks united in their novelty.

'The great thing about punk was its egalitarianism,' says Chris

Salewicz. 'Everyone was in it together. If The Clash liked you, you could have endless access. All of those punk people gave you their phone numbers. Jimmy Page wouldn't have done that. Ozzy Osbourne wouldn't have done that. It was very good fun and very intelligent. I met Rat Scabies or The Clash and they were all really bright blokes – and then you realise that this was actually an art movement. You could have good conversations with people, talk about books. Most people on *NME* hated punk. I remember Nick Kent saying to me "You're writing a lot about this punk stuff aren't you?"'

Despite the nervousness of some of his staff, Nick Logan had committed to punk totally. At the end of 1976, he fixed the traditional annual readers' poll, replacing the readers' choice as the brightest hope for 1977 – Brand X, a jazz-fusion side project of Genesis drummer Phil Collins – with the Sex Pistols.[108]

'Prior to punk rock *NME* had a serious debate over Mick Farren's Titanic piece,' remembers Neil Spencer. 'Which was about questioning where it had all gone wrong. Mick was basically an unreconstructed rock'n'roll fan who liked Gene Vincent and the MC5. So on the one hand there was an appetite out there for something new and different, but on the other hand once they got what was going on they didn't all like it. Punk was aggressively young, so you had people who were 19 or 20 years old confronting people who were 29 or 30 years old. It seems ridiculous now but there was a frisson because of it. And of course it wasn't easy for everybody to get their hair cut and lose their flares. It wasn't easy for people to abandon Led Zeppelin or Genesis or whoever they liked.'

'Robert Plant and Jimmy Page came down the Roxy one night,' says Parsons, 'and John Lydon was sneering at them. I liked them. Ultimately Robert Plant's just a bloke from Wolverhampton and punk reminded him of when he was first in bands, of when people had more enthusiasm than technical ability. And they were just interested. They wanted to know what was going on. Bowie was the same. And I got into a lot of great music, like John Martyn or Bert Jansch from Jimmy Page recommending me stuff.'

Not everyone was so comfortable with the new wave. 'You had reactionary old hippies, successful musicians who had made a lot of money and sold millions of records, getting on their high horses and railing against a bunch of 20-year-old spiky-topped kids because they dared to do something different,' says Spencer. 'You saw it with journalists too: "it's not real music", all that rubbish.'

As the schism developed between pro- and anti-punk factions on the *NME* staff, the circumstances that they were all forced into only made things worse. In February 1977 IPC magazines published the first issue of a new weekly science-fiction comics anthology called *2000AD*. *2000AD*'s early copies featured both a revamped version of the old Radio Luxembourg favourite Dan Dare and a green extraterrestrial as editor: with his silver ponytail and motorcycle boots, Tharg the Mighty looked not unlike one of Mick Farren's Ladbroke Grove drinking buddies. Tharg edited 2000AD from his 'Nerve Centre', a futuristic tower block that bore a distinct physical resemblance to IPC magazines' new headquarters at King's Reach Tower, overlooking Blackfriars Bridge on the River Thames.

Completed in 1972, King's Reach Tower was a 31-storey tower designed by the architect Sir Richard Seifert. Seifert had been responsible for the Central London office block Centre Point, which now towered, unfilled, over Tin Pan Alley. The rest of IPC magazines moved in to their new homes at the tower in 1975. *NME* followed in February 1976.

On a clear day from the *NME*'s new office on the 25th floor, one could see across the whole of London, from Hampstead Heath and Parliament Hill to the north down to Crystal Palace in the south. From the outside looking up at the building, however, the impression was a different one: not just an anonymous tower block, King's Reach Tower was actually actively *ugly*. Among the concrete of the redeveloped riverbank, the tower was, in Jonathan Coe's memorable phrase, 'a monstrous symphony of variegated browns, jutting over the others like a sculpted turd'.[109]

Whatever the sense of entitlement provided by the view, inside the new *NME* eyrie the tower's large open plan floors were separated into a dingy warren by felt-covered wooden partitions. According to IPC fable King's Reach was built on the site of a 17th-century plague pit and strange smells and the sound of the wind whistling in the lift shafts lent the place a suitably eerie air. Worse still, the staff were now surrounded on all sides by IPC's other titles, so that they could no longer kid themselves that they were an underground paper operating independently within the machine. Suddenly there was no way of escaping the fact that *NME* was just one of many titles in a large portfolio of magazines that included sports titles, women's mags, children's magazines and hobbyist mags of all kinds. Every Monday morning, the staff of the *NME* arrived at work, passed through a check-in desk and shared a cramped lift upwards with the staff of *Horse & Hound* or *TV Times* or *Angler's Mail* or *Women's Own* (or *Woman's Weekly*) or *Yachting World* or *Shooting Times*. At Long Acre, the accepted office culture was that a large communal joint would be passed around in weekly morning editorial meetings while the contents of the following week's magazine was formulated and commissioned. At King's Reach this tradition was swiftly curtailed following complaints from the other occupants of the building about the behaviour and appearance of the *NME* staff emerging from the cloud of fragrant blue smoke.

'There was friction with other magazines because of the noise and our physical appearance,' says Parsons. 'People would regularly complain about Nick Kent's bollocks hanging out of his torn leather trousers.'

By 1977, Nick Kent had developed from a glammed-up peacock into something wholly cadaverous: he's there in Julien Temple's Sex Pistols documentary *The Filth and the Fury*, hollow-cheeked and swaying gently, looking grubbier and more otherworldly than any punk could ever hope to. 'Kent was the thinnest man on Wardour Street,' wrote Peter York. 'His leathers were peerless, the leather trousers on pipe-stem legs, meatless thighs, bone shanks, lapping tightly over painted black boots with the little spur strap around the instep... the most exquisitely grimy, neo-decadent get-up in London.'[110]

'The presence of Kent at King's Reach would cause a total furore,' says Salewicz. 'You'd be in the lift and these Harris-tweeded guys with moustaches from *Country Life* would get in, smoking Senior Service in the lift. Then you'd go up a few floors, the doors would open and there would be Nick, with his bollocks on show to everybody, not caring.'

'One time Julie had been chucking roaches in the wastepaper bin,' says Parsons, 'and one of the cleaners emptied out the bin and found the remains of all of these joints.' Logan punished her and Parsons with the ultimate punk penance – being sent to review Queen at Earl's Court Arena.

'One of the many reasons that we hated being moved to King's Reach Tower was that it made it harder for Lemmy to come round and sell us our speed,' says Murray. 'Previously he'd been able to come straight up the stairs. Now he had to sign in and out via an IPC Commissionaire. At 128 Long Acre we had an enormous degree of autonomy. We had an entire floor to ourselves, we could play music very loudly, behave extremely badly and we could pretend to ourselves that we were an independent underground publication because the IPC bureaucracy was somewhere else. Moving to King's Reach meant that we were suddenly squashed into these horrible identikit offices, the IPC bureaucracy was above us, below us, next to us and we felt that our independence and privacy had been totally compromised. It was made damn clear to us who we were working for and under what conditions. It drove us nuts, in some cases literally.'

'We'd stay up for three nights, crash for a night and then stay up for another three nights...' Julie Burchill and Tony Parsons, Dingwall's, Camden, 1978

The staff did their best to decorate the office by installing plastic tat salvaged from kitsch shops around the corner in Waterloo – and in Julie and Tony's case, a noose – decorating with plastic garden gnomes and cheap lava lamps and consoling themselves that they didn't work for *Melody Maker*, whose offices were in a pre-fab Second World War Nissen hut in a forlorn street behind Waterloo station.

'Everyone got stressed out about the move,' says Salewicz, 'partly because it was badly planned. I remember going in and there was one of the writers, Steve Clarke, sitting in Nick's office with headphones on because there was no record review room. King's Reach was difficult to fucking get to and it always seemed cold. There was a restaurant on the ground floor. Farren and I'd smoke spliffs on the roof and go down to this restaurant and eat whitebait or whatever, absolutely off our heads, not speaking because we were so stoned.'

The combination of noxious IPC whitebait, marijuana and stress was a potent one. People began to complain of headaches and vertigo, of poor ventilation causing sore throats and eye irritation.[111] Tempers that had already been exacerbated by hangovers and speed comedowns began to fray further. Nick Logan became trapped between the demands of the paper's writers and those of the publishers, who began to pressure him to control the behaviour of his staff, who had taken to daubing graffiti on the office walls and removing ceiling tiles.[112] One day features writer Monty Smith lectured Burchill about the mess she'd left behind in the office; Parsons grabbed him by the throat. It was a minor infraction by the standards of what was to happen later on, but it widened the gap between the punk gunslingers and the rest of the office.

'The offices were partitioned,' claims Burchill, 'so to heighten and glamorise our outsiderness we decorated our corner with nooses, broken glass, KILL THE HIPPIES spray paint and so on. Their worst fears that the working classes were wild animals were confirmed.'

'Everybody was young and out of their mind on drugs and very afraid that this was all going to suddenly disappear and you'd be sent back to wherever you came from,' says Parsons.

The answer was to drink more and take more drugs. The office's alternative home became Dingwall's, a bar and gig venue in an old Victorian warehouse in Camden. 'At King's Reach we drank an awful lot,' says Farren. 'We were practically on strike at the time because we hated it so much and spent most of the time in the pub over the road. Then most nights we'd go to Dingwall's and run into Lemmy and Wilko Johnson and all kinds of people. I managed to short-circuit Paul Weller from hitting me one night at Dingwall's. I'd written a review of The Jam's third album, saying that they hadn't moved on, and he went to punch me but I shook his hand very quickly instead.'

While Parsons and Burchill derided Murray and Farren as superannuated old flower children, the older pair were enjoying themselves. 'Punk was interesting to write about,' says Farren. 'They'd mouth off about boring old hippies but that didn't apply to me and Charlie. The hippy thing was something that happened out in the suburbs. We were meaner and tougher, more like old gangsters. We were quite capable of dealing with any punks because we'd been through the mill. The Deviants played the same music except our songs lasted twenty minutes instead of three. Plus I knew all the punk bands from Ladbroke Grove. I knew The Clash from when they were the 101'ers or the London SS and drank in The Elgin Arms.'

Nevertheless, the pressure grew. Lemmy stopped popping in to the office. Kent disappeared. Logan grew paler and more stressed. Burchill and Parsons began to wind up the rest of the staff more and more. 'There was genuine friction,' says Parsons. 'Very few people in that office were not taking drugs. With a few exceptions everyone was either taking a lot of drugs or recovering from taking a lot of drugs. It was unbelievable. People were staying up all night.'

Charles Shaar Murray bridges a generation gap with John Lydon in Neil Spencer's office at King's Reach Tower, 1977

Unlike opiates, which work by stimulating the part of the brain which produces pleasure, amphetamines take effect by short-circuiting the receptors which tell the body to *stop* producing pleasure. The result is a surge of dopamine and adrenaline that produces an empathogenic effect while the user is high. However, long-term use affects the limbic system, the part of the brain associated with emotions and memory. In this respect speed was the perfect drug for punks to sharpen their sense of alienation: providing an energy rush while simultaneously fostering feelings of isolation and abandonment by attacking the part of the brain that breeds empathy with other people.

In April 1977, Barry Miles was sent to review The Clash at London's Institute of Contemporary Arts, just down the Mall from Buckingham Palace. The veteran of the counter-culture reacted with cynicism about the possibilities offered by the punk scene, but even Miles, who perhaps had every right to feel jaded, was shocked by an incident in the crowd.

'A young couple, somewhat out of it,' he wrote, 'had been nibbling and fondling each other amid the broken glass when she suddenly lunged forward and bit his ear lobe off. As the blood spurted she reached out to paw it with a hand tastefully clad in a rubber glove, and after smashing a Guinness bottle on the front of the stage she was about to add to the gore by slashing her wrists when the security men finally reached her, pushing through the trance-like crowd who watched with cold, calculated hiptitude.'[113]

With the appointment of his new journalists, Logan had rebranded the paper entirely, a process that Tony Parsons and Julie Burchill were happily complicit in: a few weeks before Miles' ICA review, Tony Parsons wrote a piece on The Clash which set the intellectual and aesthetic tone for the rest of punk, steering it away from its roots in the bohemian intellectual fashion milieu of Malcolm McLaren, repositioning it as the authentic expression of working-class street life. 'Thinking men's yobs,' ran the headline on a piece[114] which omitted the fact that all three current members of The Clash had been to art school and instead played up the fact that guitarist Mick Jones lived in a tower block overlooking the Westway and bassist Paul Jones had once been a football hooligan who enlivened Saturday afternoons by fighting on the terraces.

London in 1977 had the capacity to be a violent place. Shortly after the Jubilee bank holiday in early June, the *Sunday Mirror* ran an editorial prompted by the release of the Sex Pistols' 'God Save the Queen' single. 'PUNISH THE PUNKS' screamed the headline[115] and some readers happily obliged. Jamie Reid had his nose and leg broken by strangers in the street. Sex Pistols singer John Lydon was attacked with a machete in a pub carpark. A gang of Teddy Boys armed with metal bars assaulted the band's drummer, Paul Cook.

'It was quite dangerous to walk round dressed as a punk,' says Parsons, 'a violent time. The Roxy was in Covent Garden, which was in the process of changing from the old *My Fair Lady* Covent Garden to the new kind of tourist palazzo Covent Garden. You came out of the Roxy onto Neal Street and it was just rubble everywhere. There was nothing else there, just this bomb site.'

With this background it was inevitable that violence would spill over into the *NME* office in a way that was a lot more raw and less stylised than punk observers might've expected. One Monday lunchtime Charlie Murray was writing a review when his phone rang. It was Farren, calling on an internal line from the conference room next door where editorial meetings were normally held. 'I had gone into my usual writing trance and was pretty much oblivious to everything,' remembers Murray. 'The internal phone rings and it's Mickey saying "ere Charlie, come in here and roll me a joint, I just had the fucking shit beat out of me".'

Tony Parsons had punched Farren in the face after finding out that Burchill, who'd developed a crush on the older man, had slept with him. 'It was all a bit sordid to be honest,' says Burchill. 'I was a punk. Mick was an old hippy. I was only 17 and conceived a rotten crush on him, had my way with him, Tony found out, beat him up. We weren't even going out together then, the nutter.'

'Julie was just discovering her sexual power and all the chaos that it could exert,' claims Murray. 'She pestered Mickey to initiate her into S&M. Mickey later said to me "I felt a bit funny about it, so I just decided to take her far enough in for her not to want to go any further." Of course the next thing Julie did was to tell Tony that Mickey had done unmentionable things to her.'

'Julie was a 17-year-old girl,' says Salewicz, 'so I was a bit surprised that some people took advantage of her. I mean, she seemed quite damaged. She seemed troubled. I walked in to King's Reach to find that Tony had knocked out Mick Farren's teeth. There was a deathly silence about the place.'

Parsons downplays the incident. 'I came from Essex and it was natural to be around bands like The Jam where you'd go to some gig and Bruce Foxton would have a black eye because he'd had an argument with Paul Weller. They'd have a fight and it would be over but that was how they resolved their differences. The *NME* was a middle-class environment and they weren't used to that kind of thing. So the violence that there was got overstated because they were so shocked by it. To me it was working-class rough and tumble.'

While the punk wars raged, things were getting worse for Nick Logan. With the staff engaged in internecine arguments and IPC pressuring him to push sales even higher, he had a kind of nervous breakdown.

'I was not easy to deal with,' says Nick Kent. 'Murray wasn't easy to deal with. Lester Bangs, who Nick had to phone and talk to, was hard to deal with. Tony Parsons and Julie Burchill were *very* hard to deal with. Nick had a hard time at the *NME*. He was the architect of everything. He could instinctively see that although some writers might have problems and be hard to work with they could really deliver.'

Logan had been on the staff of *NME* for ten years, but the stress of the move to King's Reach Tower, compounded by his workload, having to deal with the demands of both his staff and IPC and the process of buying a new house, finally got to him. In early 1977 he was sent to America for six weeks by IPC to recuperate, during which time Neil Spencer stood in as editor. When Logan returned he announced that he was leaving the company. Spencer expected to be promoted to editor, as he was already doing the job, but IPC decided to bring in a friend of Mick Farren's called Richard Williams instead. Spencer was aghast and preparing his resignation letter when news came through that Williams had been busted by police for possession of cocaine. 'IPC decided that he would make a better editor than me, perhaps because he was an outsider,' says Spencer. 'But then he was busted in Camden Lock with six wraps of coke in his pocket and IPC had to say to him "Look, are you a journalist or are you a dope dealer?" They were left in the lurch so I was called in to do the job.'

Thankfully for Spencer, IPC had realised that the *NME* could not thrive on the 25th floor of King's Reach Tower and, under considerable pressure from the magazines with whom the *NME* staff were lodging, decided to move the paper out after eight months' residency. It was Tony Tyler who eventually engineered a change of heart on the part of senior management, following a week where the staff went on strike and the magazine wasn't published. 'Tony was Nick's number two so he did a lot of the dirty work,' says Spencer. 'First he sent me home complaining of vertigo. Then he went to IPC and said "Nick's in America, Neil's gone home, it's impossible for us to put the paper out." Tony had started going out with Kate Phillips, whose father Ron was the MD of IPC so Tony confronted Ron face to face. IPC caved in and they pretty quickly found us somewhere to go to.'

To the obvious relief of all concerned, *New Musical Express* was extracted from its place within the IPC corporate hub and moved to a new office on the third floor of a building at numbers 5 to 7 Carnaby Street. Downstairs were the offices of *Billboard* magazine, The Who's management company, Track, and Lew Grade's television company ITC, then just branching out into film production. It was also the exact address where a young Glaswegian tailor called John Stephen had opened his first shop in 1957, transforming the street and making it a world centre for fashion. By 1978, however, Carnaby Street was long past its 1960s prime, but the staff of *NME* didn't mind: it was a return to the Long Acre days, when Joe Strummer or Elvis Costello or Paul Weller or Lemmy could walk up from the street without being bothered by an IPC security guard. 'IPC obviously thought Carnaby Street was rock'n'roll and hip, when of course by 1978 it was the complete antithesis of rock'n'roll and hip,' says Salewicz, 'the absolute nadir of fashionability.'

'You'd go to the toilet and see Bob Hoskins on his way to ITC,' remembers Roy Carr, 'and outside you'd have all the bloody boutiques playing The Bee Gees at full blast.'

It didn't er. *NME* was out again. The staff were free to smoke joints in editorial meetings, or decamp to a Swiss restaurant in nearby Leicester Square for lunches that lasted all afternoon. Tony Parsons and Julie Burchill reached a new level of notoriety with a Sunday Times interview and photoshoot. Even Mick Farren seemed happier and was getting his musical career going again, releasing an EP on Jake Riviera's Stiff label.

'We weren't paid very much, but all of our needs were catered for,' says

Parsons. 'If you were going to do an interview with Bruce Springsteen in New York or go on the road with Thin Lizzy you didn't really need anything. I was sent on the road with Lynyrd Skynyrd and I had a big stack of amphetamine sulphate with me and was really generous with the lines, chopping them out for everyone. Then when I was leaving the tour in Glasgow the tour manager came up to me and said "We really appreciate your hospitality," and gave me this big wad of greenbacks. And I didn't know what to do with this huge wad of dollars. I'd just been happy to share what I had. You didn't imagine that you could live in a good flat or have a car. No one we knew had cars or television sets. We were doing the job we loved and it was exciting and that was enough.'

Again freed from the stultifying commercial demands of the IPC management, the staff of the *NME* carried on their dedication to Logan's pro-punk vision with renewed vigour. 'Punk rock was like somebody chucking a brick through the shop window,' says Neil Spencer. 'It was fun and of course young people thought it was great. It was very empowering and it was very easy to become a punk – cut up your old man's shirt, scrunch up your school tie. Put a safety pin through your school blazer, tighten your jeans. It was very DIY.'

'There was a lot of whining and moaning at the record companies because we were doing too much about punk and not writing nice things about ELO or not really being terribly interested in Yes,' says Farren. 'But that's what the kids wanted to read about. Nick made a decision that *NME* was going punk and the sales figures proved his point. A lot of kids were wanting to find out what was going on in London. When the first punk tours started, like the Pistols and The Clash, they'd go and play in Birmingham or Manchester or wherever and there was a whole audience of kids there ready for them, they knew what was happening because they'd all read the *NME*.'

But while *NME* promoted The Clash, employing cartoonist Ray Lowry to send regular visual reports back from tours with the band, as well as giving away a free EP, *Capital Radio* (which featured a recording of an interview between Tony Parsons and the band recorded on a Circle Line tube train), to coincide with the band's second album, they were free again to cock a snook at any of the stadium rockers unwise enough to stick their heads above the parapet ('I like the bits between the tracks best' wrote Max Bell in a review of Aerosmith's *Rocks* album[116]) or take cheap shots at passing pop stars. A bewildered Mick Farren was dispatched to Sweden to meet Abba, the record-breaking chart sensations who counted Sid Vicious of the Sex Pistols among their many fans. He was astonished to find that the history of Abba and the *NME* were intertwined when one of the band's songwriters, Benny Andersson, confessed to a love of the accordion.[117] 'An accordion!' wrote Farren. 'As far as I've ever been concerned, the only good accordion is a dead accordion. I think we have maybe defined the culture gap, if not bridged it.'

For most of the staff of the *NME*, life was good. For their most famous freelancer, however, things were rushing downhill without brakes.

11.An obituary of rock'n'roll

'We'd stay up for three nights, crash for a night and then stay up for another three nights. People I knew were killing themselves with smack...'

Unlike in America or parts of Europe, until the late 1970s the use of heroin in Britain was not epidemical. Instead it was a select pastime, confined mostly to London's bohemian fringes[118] and only available to those with the money or the connections to actually procure the stuff. As the hippy trail to India opened up, travellers would return bearing Afghan coats, joss sticks and the occasional illicit parcel of brown. Smack was an exclusive, mostly middle-class drug favoured by a minority and denoting a taste for the exotic that marked the user out from the square, straight world. A habit was a badge of disregard for society. 'We are not old men, we are not worried about petty morals,' proclaimed noted user Keith Richards at the trial resulting from the Redlands bust.[119]

Towards the end of the decade, however, all of this began to change as cheap Pakistani brown heroin began to arrive in Britain, taking the drug far beyond the coterie of London users to the housing estates of Glasgow, Manchester and Liverpool, finding young working-class men and women who faced an uncertain future as unemployment figures spiralled from a million out of work in 1972 towards three million in the early 1980s. The punk scene, which had spread from the King's Road and Chelsea out to the inner-city housing estates across the country, rapidly became awash with heroin.

'It was *soaked* in smack,' says Tony Parsons. 'It was pre-Aids and the last great hurrah of chemical promiscuity. People would find that they no longer got the buzz from speed that they were used to so they'd shoot up heroin instead.'

In January 1978, the Sex Pistols had split up after a disastrous US tour. Shortly afterwards, the band's bassist Sid Vicious slipped into a methadone-induced coma during a transcontinental flight from San Francisco to New York. When Vicious arrived back in the UK, Chris Salewicz received a phone call at the *NME* office, demanding an interview. Salewicz, who was working as a consultant on what was to become the punk documentary *DOA*,[120] took a camera crew with him for the arraignment. Arriving at the West London mews cottage Vicious shared with his American girlfriend Nancy Spungen, Salewicz found him strung out on smack, jetlag and Valium,[121] nodding off in mid-sentence and being slapped awake by Spungen whenever he dropped lit cigarettes or boiled sweets on the bed where the interview took place. Almost exactly a year later Spungen and Vicious were both dead.

'What's really remarkable is how much death there was,' says Parsons. 'In a time of peace and prosperity a lot of people died.'

As far as heroin went, Nick Kent's habit extended back to the first half of the 1970s. Needless to say, as the drug became more common in the London music scene, his predilection for heroin began to worsen. By 1976 his work rate had gradually slowed to a trickle and then dried up to nothing. He'd occasionally float in to the *NME* office, pick up some promotional copies of LPs and then float out again to sell the records for drugs. At one point Nick Logan had even offered Kent more money if it meant he'd get his pieces in on time. Needless to say, it didn't make any difference.

'By 1975 the actual skills that I had were being diminished, partly by the drug use and partly by the fact that I was just *jaded,*' says Kent. 'I had a lot of great times but at the same time it was a very cold world. The people that I really admired and looked up to were just rotting on the vine. It was depressing. Listen to the great records of the period, like David Bowie's *Low* or Neil Young's *On The Beach* or Iggy Pop's *The Idiot* and you get a sense that the person who's singing on those records is literally in hell. I think that feeling was about more than just the drugs. But the drugs certainly spearheaded that sense of isolation. That's what drug addiction is about. It starts out splendid and gets less and less splendid. That was certainly my experience, but I wasn't alone in feeling like that. It was a shared phenomenon.'

Homeless and penniless, Kent was reduced to camping out in the *NME* offices overnight as he ran out of sofas to crash on. But as well as feeling jaded by the music business and the weekly grind of producing copy he was also recovering from the emotional fallout of a brief but intense fling with another *NME* freelancer, an American called Chrissie Hynde.

Doomed love: Chrissie Hynde and Nick Kent, 1975

'I used to get the *NME* at my local mall in Ohio, where it was always a couple of weeks late,' Hynde says. 'It was the only English paper I'd see and I didn't know much about the English rock scene but there was one piece which I cut out and sellotaped to my wall, an Iggy Pop review. That review was one of my inspirations to leave America and move to London: "at least they get Iggy Pop there".'

Born into a middle-class family in the small city of Akron, Ohio, Hynde attended Kent State University's Art School, and was on campus during the May 1970 shootings, during which National Guardsmen opened fire on unarmed college students, killing four and inspiring the Crosby, Stills, Nash and Young single 'Ohio'. Obsessed with rock'n'roll and its peripheral concerns, in October 1973, aged 22, Hynde moved to London. She didn't know anyone in the city, or indeed the country.

'A few months after I arrived I went to some student party in Acton and I walked in and I was in a bad mood because some guy had nicked my records. So I was grumbling about how someone had stolen my copy of *Raw Power* and this voice from the back of the room says "I know Iggy Pop". I was pleased because I'd been in London for months and no one I'd met had even *heard* of Iggy. Anyway, weeks later I realised that this was the guy who had written the article that I had stuck to my wall.'

Nick Kent rapidly moved himself and his few possessions into Hynde's shared flat in Clapham. In return, he introduced her to Ian MacDonald, who offered her some freelance writing work when her job answering the phone in an architect's office fell through.

'I didn't have a work permit and was doing all this hand-to-mouth illegal stuff so I thought I had no choice but to take the work,' says Hynde. 'I never thought of myself as a writer but they kept bigging me up – they'd print pictures of me in the paper and I didn't want to be known as a writer because I didn't feel like I was very good at it. Then one day they asked me to write a piece looking back at The Velvet Underground and I thought well, "I don't want to be doing looking back pieces", so I quit.'

Taking up a job at McLaren's Too Fast to Live, Too Young to Die, by now renamed Sex, Hynde also split up with Kent after he gave her gonorrhea. He repaid her by turning up at the shop one day, removing his leather belt and whipping her with it, drawing blood while the rest of the shop's staff cowered behind the counter.

It didn't end there. One night in July 1976, the day before Mick Farren's Titanic piece was published in *NME*, Kent was watching the Sex Pistols and The Damned play at the 100 Club when he was approached by Sid Vicious and a friend from his pre-Vicious days. As John Beverley, Vicious had attended Holborn's Kingsway College of Further Education with a kid from Stepney called John Wardle. Now renamed Jah Wobble, Wardle was one of a motley gang of Johns, including John Lydon, who frequented McLaren's shop and who Kent knew vaguely on a social level from the tight-knit and small London punk scene. As the band took to the stage, Vicious took his place in the audience immediately in front of

Kent, his gangly six foot two frame entirely blocking the writer's view of the stage. Kent asked him to move aside, but when Vicious turned around, he realised that he'd made a mistake. 'Sid… looked positively scary, as if he'd partaken in a gargantuan quantity of amphetamines just prior to his arrival… and I soon became uncomfortably aware that he had picked me as the intended victim on which to vent his spleen, so to speak.'[122]

As Wobble brandished a flicknife, Vicious produced a cycle chain from his inside pocket and whipped Kent with it, spotting the walls of the 100 Club with the writer's blood before being wrestled to the ground by bouncers as Kent stumbled up the stairs of the club to street level, blood gushing from the cut on his forehead.

McLaren, who'd failed to recruit Kent into the Sex Pistols, had instead decided to use the journalist as a vehicle for achieving some more press notoriety for his band, a literal whipping boy who served as a handy totem for the decadent music business, strung out on smack and self-importance, that the new wave would wipe out.

Kent lost half of one of his front teeth in the attack, which pleased him terribly. 'I always thought Nick was secretly very pleased with losing that tooth,' says Hynde, 'because it happened right at the peak of his obsession with Keith Richards, and he was always very impressed with Keith's dreadful dental state.'[123]

'Chrissie Hynde actually bought the bike chain that was used on me,' claims Kent, 'although that event was more about my relationship with the Sex Pistols than Chrissie. McLaren was poisoning everybody.'

McLaren, displaying his customary genius for promotion, put together a press release disassociating the Pistols from the attack and sent it out to all of the music papers, from where the name of Sid Vicious was picked up by the national press as one more example of punk rock degeneracy. Within a fortnight, Sid was a household name. By the end of the month, Glen Matlock had been fired from the Sex Pistols and replaced by Sid. Meanwhile Kent became a walking target for random acts of copycat punk violence: one night he was attacked and stabbed by a group of Vicious clones in King's Cross. It was no real surprise that his career was unravelling at the same rate as his personal life.

'Kent got fired a couple of times,' says Murray, 'because he was becoming a liability because of his quote/unquote "lifestyle" and he wasn't delivering. If he'd continued to perform to the standard at which he'd performed in his first two years there'd have been no way in hell they'd even have considered getting rid of him. By the time he'd got serious with junk his writing was deteriorating. He'd become a rather embarrassing parody of himself. He also developed a massive persecution mania.'

'A number of people looked at me like a fucking leper,' says Kent. 'Those weekend pot smokers couldn't even bear to be in the same room with me. The usual '70s drug snobbery. The guy in the corner with the alcohol problem wouldn't look at me because I had a heroin problem. I was homeless, but no one offered me a spare room because I was a drug addict and therefore untrustworthy – which was actually probably true.'

As Nick Kent turned into a parody of himself, another *NME* writer was rapidly turning into a parody of a parody. Pete Erskine had joined the paper from *Sounds* and *Let It Rock*, where he was a colleague of Chris Salewicz. 'Pete was a good guy: a very sweet, innocent kid,' Salewicz says. 'But he became very quickly enamoured of what he thought was the *NME* lifestyle. There was one problem with the *NME*, which was it pushed people as star writers when it wasn't necessarily very good for them. Pete wanted desperately to be one of those star writers. He suddenly became very fey. Then Nick introduced Pete to Keith Richards who introduced Pete to heroin.'

Pete Erskine succumbed to heroin with the same speed that Kent had and rapidly developed a debilitating habit. His marriage fell apart and Charlie Murray installed him in his spare room temporarily. One night Murray came home to find that both Erskine and a large part of his record collection had vanished.

'One day I go in the toilets in Long Acre and find a spoon and all the paraphernalia,' says Roy Carr. 'Then things started to disappear from your desk. Pete had this bike and he would ride around the record companies and get free records to sell for drugs. Some of them banned him from their buildings.'

Sacked by *NME* and unable to pick up work elsewhere, Erskine ended up in prison. One day in 1984, he had an asthma attack and died, barely out of his twenties, leaving behind a young son. 'Pete tried too hard to be Kent by proxy in the same way that Kent tried to be Iggy or Keith by proxy,' says Murray. 'Pete was a nice bloke,' says Roy Carr. 'Nick got Pete onto smack and one day he had a fit and died. A lot of people held it against Nick Kent. Nick didn't give a shit, but then he didn't know what day it was half the time. Nick was so smacked up that he didn't realise everyone was taking the piss out of him all the time.'

'A lot of people were completely enamoured of Keith Richards at that time,' says Chris Salewicz. 'And guess what? They're all dead.'

'Peter York wrote this piece about *NME*,' says Tony Parsons, 'and he said "You wouldn't believe the stuff that's in this paper: politics, sex, drugs".

And this was true. We were in this tower block with security guards and yet there were people working there who had just fallen out of a drug den with Keith Richards.'

York was right. Under the auspices of IPC, *NME* carried on the ethos, style and content of the underground press well past punk, up to the end of the decade and beyond. In 1976, John May, an old friend of Kent's from *Frendz* began to contribute to the paper, both under his own name and a pseudonym, Dick Tracy. May's forte was serious investigative journalism, and *NME* readers soon found lengthy and well-researched pieces on human cloning, the recently founded militant Animal Liberation Front, record piracy or the environment running alongside the usual interviews with Graham Parker, Thin Lizzy or Pink Floyd.

Elsewhere the magazine ran a regular drugs news and information column called, perhaps inevitably, 'The Inside Dope', and providing in-depth coverage of Operation Julie, in which undercover officers disguised as hippies provided surveillance evidence leading to the closure of industrial-scale LSD laboratories across Britain.[124] John May also worked with Ian MacDonald to produce a special four-page *NME Guide to the Nuclear Age*, a serious and chilling examination of the effects of a disaster at one of Britain's nuclear power stations which made the front of the magazine in June 1977. It was a bold and even foolhardy choice of cover, followed swiftly by a return to business as usual in the form of a Stranglers interview on the front of the following week's issue.

But May and MacDonald's investigation reflected the broad range of interests held by the people who produced this paper each week and the high regard with which they viewed their readers. In 1980, Andrew Tyler left *NME* to set up the charity Animal Aid, while the paper played a large part in the formation and promotion of the renewed anti-Nazi and anti-Racism movement in Britain.

In June 1976, as membership of the racist National Front reached 17,500, the first reported racially motivated attacks on the Bengali community in Brick Lane in London occurred. That August Eric Clapton made a drunken speech from the stage at a concert in Birmingham in which he endorsed Conservative MP Enoch Powell's anti-immigration 'Rivers of Blood' speech, made in the city at a meeting of the Conservative Political Centre in 1968. Clapton then repeatedly shouted the National Front's slogan 'Keep Britain White' and called for action to be taken to 'get the foreigners out, get the wogs out, get the coons out'.[125] In September 1976, a letter appeared in the *NME* expressing disgust with Clapton's comments, pointing out that one of his biggest hits had been a cover version of Bob Marley's 'I Shot the Sheriff' and that Clapton had spent most of his career since his days in The Yardbirds playing the blues. The letter signed off by announcing the launch of a new movement called Rock Against Racism (RAR) and provided a PO Box in East London for interested *NME* readers to contact. The response was overwhelming. 'We got so many letters,' says Roger Huddle, one of the founders of Rock Against Racism, '200 or 300, in the first week, mainly from soul fans or mixed-race couples, that we felt confident.'[126]

In April 1978, RAR was so sure of the level of popular support for their cause that they organised a march from Trafalgar Square to Victoria Park in East London in association with the Anti-Nazi League, which was followed by a free concert headlined by The Clash. Eighty thousand people attended.

Pro-Labour, anti-corporate, egalitarian: NME editor Neil Spencer, King's Reach Tower, 1978

'Part of the vision for *NME* under my editorship was inspired by the spirit that was on that Rock Against Racism march down to Victoria Park,' says Neil Spencer, 'that there was another Britain coming into being, one that wasn't populated entirely by people who were white or male. People like Linton Johnson and Benjamin Zephaniah were first written about in *NME*.'

Reggae was still big news at *NME*. In 1978 Chris Salewicz was sent to accompany John Lydon on a trip to Jamaica, where the former Sex Pistols singer had been sent by his label boss, Richard Branson, on a recuperative holiday, partly in an A&R capacity to sign new reggae acts to Branson's Virgin Records, and partly to keep him out of the way during the acrimonious legal battle between Branson and McLaren. Lydon, accompanied by his friends the DJ Don Letts and photographer Dennis Morris, spent his time smoking weed, checking out the local music scene and licking his wounds after the grim fallout of punk.

'Lydon was probably a bit vulnerable but very good fun,' Salewicz says. 'There was a spirit of adventure about the whole trip: going downtown with Tapper Zukie to Trench Town where everyone would be zonked off our heads on this weed that was so strong you'd be tripping and all this weird stuff going on – people with machetes and guns wandering around.'

Lydon wasn't the only one feeling disillusioned with the way the promise of punk had fizzled out. After the incident with Farren, Tony Parsons and Julie Burchill had commenced a relationship.[127] After mocking their predecessors about their inability to stand the pace of life at *NME*, the strain was starting to show in both of them.

'It just burned you out,' says Parsons. 'I did three years at *NME* and it was enough. We'd stay up for three nights, crash for a night and then stay up for another three nights and it got too much. People I knew were killing themselves with smack. I had just had enough.'

Parsons and Burchill collaborated on a book, *The Boy Looked at Johnny*, which expressed their dissatisfaction with the punk movement that had made their names. Subtitled 'An obituary of rock'n'roll', it was a funny and dogmatic attempt at a personal history of punk, which dismissed most of the main players as no-tune, no-talent poseurs. Shortly afterwards, the couple left it all behind and moved to suburban Essex to start a family.

Lydon was one of the few people to be spared in Parsons and Burchill's book. After his three weeks in Jamaica, he'd immediately started rehearsing a new group, Public Image Limited, inspired partly by reggae but also by the kind of experimental rock music that punks were supposed to show disdain for.

In the meantime Danny Baker had been recruited from *Sniffin' Glue* to work as a receptionist at *NME*'s new Carnaby Street offices. 'On Wednesdays or Thursdays when *NME* came out I would just gobble it up,' he remembers. 'People like Tony Tyler and Charles Shaar Murray were as big as rock stars to me. I remember reading something that Charlie wrote where he mentioned he'd popped out to get some milk and I was just astonished – I didn't think that the rarified life of an *NME* journalist would involve having to buy your own milk.

'The culture which it invented is now the culture. At the time it was the underground and now it's the culture – the way it dealt with celebrity, the way it wrote in this breathless prose, the way it understood that the writers and the readers were more important than the celebrities. Those *NMEs* from '72 or '73 tore a new culture right out of the air.'

'I was doing *Sniffin' Glue* and that came to an end and Tony Parsons told me that they were looking for a receptionist, so I had a terrific time earning £15.58 a week on the phones. Nick Kent's mum always used to ring up and say "Could I speak to Nicholas Benedict please?" and he'd sit there waving his arms saying "no, no", but I'd always make a point of putting her through.'

Baker joined the *NME* at the same time as Mark Ellen, a former university friend of Tony Blair from Oxford, who had played with the future Prime Minister in a Stones-style band called Ugly Rumours. 'I'd look around the office,' says Ellen, 'and there was Julie Burchill and Tony Parsons and Nick Kent and Danny Baker on the front desk at reception – Danny used to answer the phone by saying "City Morgue – you stab 'em, we slab 'em" – and it was a very exciting place to be. These people were big stars.'

Before long Baker worked up the confidence to write for the paper, becoming one of *NME*'s funniest and sharpest journalists, giving up his job on the phones and becoming staff writer. In June 1979, he was dispatched to interview Public Image Limited at their favourite pub in Notting Hill Gate. Baker found them to be in a sullen and combative mood following the lukewarm critical reception afforded to their recently released debut album.

Baker: Were you disappointed at the reaction to the LP?
Lydon: Not really. It takes time and people are stupid.
B: What do you mean, 'people are stupid'?
L: I mean journalists are stupid.
B: Is that what all journalists are?
L: I think they're creepy, spineless parasites.

B: What are you talking about?

L: Name me one that has got integrity?

B: (calmly) I have.

L: Well, show me your work and I'll tell you.

B: Yeah, but I don't need to.

L: So prove me wrong.[128]

The tense mood was lightened by the arrival of the band's bassist, Jah Wobble, but even he was in an edgy mood. 'I tell ya,' he said, downing another pint, 'all that punk achieved was a load of crap.'

'I had a terrific time earning £15.58 a week on the phones...' Danny Baker in the office at Carnaby Street, February 1979

12. The ghost of Roland Barthes

'It was a psychedelic pirate ship. A free-floating raft of misfits...'

As 1978 turned inevitably but not without warning into 1979, the 26-year-old *NME* found itself with a smart new set of clothes. Under his pen name Barney Bubbles, the graphic designer Colin Fulcher was one of the pre-eminent rock artists of the 20th century.[129] He'd started out producing lightshows for Pink Floyd and designing for *Oz* and *Frendz* while working as a design assistant at an ad agency; work which led, through the usual Ladbroke Grove connections, to commissions for sleeves for the likes of Hawkwind and West London squat legends Quintessence. In 1977 Bubbles joined Stiff Records as art director, establishing a sparse visual style that had much to do with the label's success: at a time when dedicated indie record fans were likely to buy anything on their favourite labels, the Stiff logo was a mark of, if not quality, then certainly a kind of shared aesthetic.

At the same time as he worked at Stiff, Bubbles also undertook freelance commissions to help pay the rent on his Old Street studio. 'My first job when I took over as editor,' says Neil Spencer, 'was to straighten out the staff situation and get Tony and Julie off the staff. They were getting paid but I hadn't seen them for months and I wanted to get some new blood in.

'My second job was hiring Barney Bubbles to redesign the *NME* because he'd designed all those Stiff covers. And he absolutely delivered. He redesigned the paper, redesigned the logo, and *NME* stopped being *New Musical Express* and became *NME*.'

Inspired by a sign on a warehouse near his Old Street studio, Bubbles junked the old-fashioned Western-style logo on the paper's masthead and replaced it with clean, stencilled military-style lettering[130] of the kind found on army surplus wear. Inside the magazine, Bubbles cleared out the accumulated mayhem of the last six years and developed a unifyingly sleek, forward-looking style as much influenced by 1920s Russian poster art as it was by Pop collage. Bubbles wasn't the only artist looking to the past to define the *NME*'s visual style: around the same time Alan Moore, later recognised as comfortably one of the 20th century's greatest visionaries, was paying his rent with ornate illustrations for the singles and albums pages, including one accompanying a piece about Malcolm McLaren's Sex Pistols film, *The Great Rock'n'Roll Swindle*, which depicted the band's manager holding John Lydon's severed head in homage to Aubrey Beardsley's 1893 illustration 'The Climax'.[131]

'Lydon was a bit vulnerable but very good fun...' John Lydon and Chris Salewicz at Public Image Limited's headquarters in Gunter Grove, Fulham, 1978

With its new style in place, the paper was ready for a new decade. Freed from the IPC machine, meanwhile, the *NME* offices at Carnaby Street rapidly descended into mild, student bedsit-level squalor.

Ian Penman joined the paper as a freelance writer in 1977, moving to London from Norfolk to write full-time in 1978. 'Paul Morley and I started at about the same time,' he says, 'and I remember going to the *NME* offices for the first time, expecting this glamorous, Algonquin Round Table-type of environment and instead it was a fucking dump full of people who were past their best and in some cases in very deep personal trouble hacking away on these metal typewriters which weighed a tonne and had half the keys missing.'

'It was a psychedelic pirate ship,' says Danny Baker. 'A free-floating raft of misfits. We used to push the desks back and play football in the office. Charlie Murray used to be furious whenever the ball came near him because he always hated sport.'

Karen Walter was hired by Neil Spencer as his PA in 1983. Her memory of the office at Carnaby Street is one of similar disarray, worsened by the fact that, as an outpost of IPC based in central London, the staff of the paper were left to fend for themselves when it came to resources. 'We never got any new furniture,' she says. 'The carpet tiles were coming up and people would be tripping over them. Or the backs of chairs would fall off and it would take seven months to get a new one from IPC. I had an electric typewriter at home but I'd come to work and have to use this old manual typewriter.'

'The kitchen at Carnaby Street was an absolute tip, absolutely filthy,' says Baker. 'Half-eaten ready meals with joints stuck in them everywhere. My wife Wendy was the editor's assistant and used to go and clean it up when it got too bad. She always says that the only person who'd help her was Paul Weller.'

His excellent manners obviously endearing him to the more fastidious members of staff, The Jam's frontman was a frequent visitor to the office. Indeed, in the absence of the King's Reach IPC registration desk, pretty much anyone could walk in off the street, dodging the stalls selling plastic policeman's helmets or the punks posing for tourist cameras, braving the rickety lift and finding themselves in the editorial hub of the country's most cutting-edge publication almost immediately. The young Boy George used to hang around perching on the edges of desks offering to run errands or nip out for sandwiches at lunch. Elvis Costello and Sham 69's Jimmy Pursey were regulars. Joe Strummer would sit on reception and chat to Baker or his successor, Gary Crowley. Promoting his 1979 album, *Do It Yourself*, Ian Dury arrived unannounced one day and started to wallpaper the office. 'All of these people would just materialise there at your desk,' says Paul DuNoyer. 'I very much regret that modern magazines retreat behind corporate reception desks with plastic identity tags and entryphones, as it was a tremendously exciting atmosphere for a newspaper to exist in. People would just turn up at reception ranting, whether it was musicians or fans, and that gave you a feeling of intense connection with the world you were covering.'

'People stayed the night and slept in the record review room, which was a sort of windowless room with bits of paper and LPs strewn everywhere,' says Karen Walter. 'Often I'd be the first to arrive at work in the mornings and all of these bedraggled people would emerge from inside the review room.'

By 1979 the music business had slipped its Denmark Street moorings and floated across Tottenham Court Road into Soho on the start of a slow journey that would eventually take it a few miles out to West London. But in the late 1970s, booking agents and managers and PR companies were all based around the corner from Carnaby Street. Interviews for the magazine would invariably take place in one of the pubs nearby – The Cumberland Stores[132] or The Sun and 13 Cantons or The King of Corsica – and drag on way past their allotted time span, until whole days and nights were lost in a blur of cheap lager, given slight focus by amphetamines.

'It was a big drinking culture,' says DuNoyer. 'The big schism was between the dope smokers and the beer drinkers. Neil and his friends were not big drinkers. But Monty Smith, Ian Penman, Danny Baker and I went to the pub most lunchtimes.'

'We'd collect our post,' says Baker, 'then be waiting outside The Cumberland Stores as they slid the bolts off the doors in the morning. We'd open our mail and go straight round to Cheapo Cheapo records to sell the albums we'd been sent to buy more beer.'

'It was all so *ad hoc* and amateurish,' says Ian Penman. 'We'd go for very long lunches most days and sometimes go to a film screening in the afternoon. At King's Reach there was a sense of 9 to 5, of going in to "A Job". At Carnaby Street you didn't have that. I used to go to the pub to sit and write all of my articles.'

But the rowdy, laddy culture was not endemic of the *NME* as a whole. In May 1979, Margaret Thatcher's Conservative Party won the General Election, performing especially well among younger voters.[133] Under the editorship of Neil Spencer, a committed Labour Party member, the *NME* set itself up as a voice of dissent, discarding the fashionable nihilism of punk or the blank-eyed decadence of its early '70s incarnation to become increasingly politicised. 'Tony Tyler was older,' says Danny Baker, 'and marginally less to the left than everyone else. We responded by calling him "Hang the Irish Tyler", just because he wasn't swallowing whatever Socialist Worker's Party rubbish the rest of us were that day.'

However, Spencer's position as editor left him divorced from his political beliefs. During the mass strikes of the 1978–79 winter of discontent, the *NME* had appeared in shops every week without fail. But in April 1980, a strike by the National Union of Journalists, of which many employees of IPC were members, ended in a deadlock when negotiations failed. IPC responded by locking 1,500 staff out of their offices for five weeks, meaning that no issues of *NME* appeared on newsstands. The lockout was only called off when *Melody Maker's* Allan Jones, drunk and frustrated at the state of affairs, threw a typewriter and a couple of chairs out of the window of the *Melody Maker's* office hut. News trickled back to the IPC negotiating team that a riot was breaking out and they quickly caved in, but not before IPC had lost an estimated 35 million magazine sales due to the strike[134] and former *Melody Maker* and I*T* journalist Mark Williams had launched a short-lived rival weekly, *New Music News*, published by ex-*Oz* man Felix Dennis' Dennis Publishing.[135]

Spencer was forced to mediate between his staff and IPC. 'That was always a problem for *NME* editors,' says Charlie Murray. 'They had to represent the staff to the corporation, or so we thought, and the corporation thought that the editor was there to represent the corporation to the staff. When crunch times emerged this was always a problem for the editors. This was a particular problem for Neil Spencer was spiritually and intellectually on our side, but in terms of his contract and his pay grade and his job description he was suddenly the local representative of the bad guys.'

The writers of *NME* responded by entrenching. In the 1970s, rock was controlled by a small group of multi-nationals with non-music interests: EMI, CBS, Warner Communications, RCA, Phillips-Siemens: all were international operations with British offices based in London. Then, in the immediate pre- and post-punk period a sudden rash of independent record labels sprung up, arising partly from the remains of the hippy underground but galvanised by punk's DIY impetus. *NME* soon started receiving new music from labels like Stiff, Rough Trade, run initially out of the shop in Ladbroke Grove, Cherry Red and their tiny studio in Notting Hill or Beggar's Banquet and 4AD.

From Sun Records through Northern Soul or the hundreds of 1960s garage imprints, the local independent label had long been a staple of the music business, feeding new bands through to the majors. But by the time that the trade paper *Record Business* introduced their indie chart in 1979, a new infrastructure had developed around the indies which allowed them to compete for sales and chart positions properly for the first time. Independent distribution companies like Pinnacle, Spartan and the regional Cartel, which included Rough Trade, Backs and Red Rhino, took on the records released by the smaller labels and got them into shops nationwide. *NME* was key to the survival and success of this new movement: the paper's influence meant that a positive review made the difference between selling a few hundred and thousands worldwide.

After punk the production and distribution of music also began gradually to devolve from London to the regions and local labels, like Postcard in Glasgow, Fast Product in Edinburgh or Factory in Manchester. Many of these operations relied on willing volunteers, ready to hand-fold record sleeves and box them up to be sent out. But they also formed a focus for self-contained local scenes to grow and be sustainable, rather than just developing bands who would eventually move to London in an attempt to sign a record deal. *NME*'s coverage of gigs and scenes outside of London began to mushroom, as some of the influx of applicants for the gunslingers jobs began to file reports from their home towns. 'When I became editor I made much more use of stringers from out of London,' says Spencer. 'One of the things that punk had engineered that nobody foresaw was that the DIY ethic meant that the music business would devolve to the regions in a way that it had never done before. Prior to that you'd always had to come to London to make it. After punk you had scenes which were self-contained in cities, notably Manchester. So I made much use of Andy Gill, Paul Morley. Tried to make it much more national so we had people reporting back from the regions.'

From the early 1970s onwards, *NME* had always had its strongest readership outside of London. Now those readers were able to find out what was happening on their doorsteps, as well as in the capital. 'The archetypal *NME* reader was someone who lived out of London,' says Spencer, 'someone who lived in Sheffield or Glasgow or Bristol who was either in the sixth form and hoping to go to university or someone at university or someone who had not gone to university but was clever.'

Lucy O'Brien was one of those readers. Growing up in Southampton she idolised Charles Shaar Murray's writing in *NME* before forming teenage punk band The Catholic Girls and moving to Leeds for a period of undergraduate study. 'At that time in the early '80s it was the paper's policy to have correspondents in all the major cities in the country,' she says. 'Post-punk was about distinctive regional identities – so that what was happening in Manchester was different to Birmingham or Leeds. Writers living in those cities were encouraged to write regular reports on what was happening in their home town to increase the regional news element of *NME*. I remember that being a policy – of nurturing the talent of these regional stringers – writers were encouraged to be a champion of what was going on in their local scene. And of course in those pre-internet days the weekly music papers had an A&R function – finding new bands outside of London that hadn't yet been co-opted into the music business there.'

So while O'Brien was writing about Leeds' Gang of Four and Delta 5, Andy Gill in Sheffield was hanging out with Cabaret Voltaire and the Human League, Paul DuNoyer had the Liverpool connection, former fanzine writer Gavin Martin was drafted in to cover his local scene in Belfast and Paul Morley was managing Manchester punks The Drones. Morley's confederate in Manchester was the photographer Kevin Cummins, who'd graduated from blagging his way into gigs for free by turning up with an empty camera case borrowed from the college where he studied photography to obsessively documenting the city's music scene, inspired by the photojournalism of Bill Brandt. 'Paul and I did a piece in May '77 about the Manchester scene for *NME* but it didn't run,' says Cummins. 'So we phoned Tony Stewart who was features editor and said "Look, Giovanni Dadamo from *Sounds* is coming up at the weekend to do a big piece on Manchester" and Tony panicked and agreed to run our piece. Obviously we'd just made up the thing about Giovanni but it was the only way to get *NME* to take notice of what was happening in our city.'

The piece became a two-page round-up of the current Manchester scene, comprising bands formed in the wake of the Sex Pistols famous second show at Manchester's Lesser Free Trade Hall and including the Buzzcocks, Magazine and a new group called Warsaw in homage to the David Bowie album track 'Warszawa'. In January 1979, Morley and Cummins were encouraged to revisit their home town for another round-up. Picking three new local bands – Spherical Objects, The Passage and the band formerly known as Warsaw, now renamed Joy Division. Joy Division were to be accorded the least amount of space in the piece, but, tramping around Manchester's brutalist housing estates of Hulme in the snow one Saturday morning, Cummins took a photo of the group's singer, Ian Curtis. Clad in an ex-army greatcoat, red-eyed, smoking a Marlboro,[136] the shot of Curtis was stark and startling and chosen by Neil Spencer for the front cover at the expense of the other groups. 'Spherical Objects were going to be the main thrust of the piece because their singer Steve Solomar used to DJ at the Electric Circus,' says Cummins. 'Joy Division weren't really part of our social scene. They were outsiders who didn't really mix with anybody. But they were serious about what they were doing, very intense about it.' Joy Division released their debut album, *Unknown Pleasures*, in the summer of 1979, winning support from John Peel and a small national fanbase. 'Joy Division had a support slot on this Buzzcocks university tour in '79,' says Cummins, 'and the buzz about the support band was bigger than the main band. There was a real comedown when they came offstage.'

'Seeing Joy Division,' wrote Paul Morley of the band's last-ever

London appearance, at the 700-capacity University of London Union in February 1980,[137] 'is a jarring experience... the introversion and singularity of the four musicians is fitfully held under control, and private music is forced out into the open. The tension is startling... the presentation is as grey and bland as the noise is volatile and deeply black – singer Ian Curtis' comical trapped butterfly flapping the only real stage movement, a visual representation of the struggle inherent in Division's music.'

On 18 May 1980, Ian Curtis hanged himself in the kitchen of his home in Macclesfield after listening to Iggy Pop's *The Idiot*. Curtis' death came during the NUJ strike, but the first issue to be published once IPC called the lockout off, billed as the 'Back On The Streets Special', contained his obituary. It sold 270,000 copies, but *NME* would never again achieve the same kind of sales.

Following the relative stylistic homogeny of punk, the late 1970s were distinguished by a total musical free-for-all. The 1960s one-world view, where debs and scroungers were as united in their love of *Rubber Soul* had finally evaporated, replaced by an excitingly polyglottal mix of styles and tones, assembled almost like collage: the underground became a lab in which funk and dub and R&B and punk and primitive electronica grew in the same musical Petri dish. In January 1981, *NME* responded to the indie boom with a co-promotion with Rough Trade records. The C81 cassette was the '80s version of the flexidisc: cheap to manufacture, *NME* readers could collect two tokens from the paper and send £1.50 to receive a cassette that reflected the disarray of the current indie scene. From scratchy almost-funk (Essential Logic), jazz (James Blood Ulmer), long-serving avant-garde heroes (Red Crayola), spoken word poetry (John Cooper Clarke), ska (The Beat, The Specials) and sundry lo-fi legends, the cassette was an immediate success. 'Walkmans were the big thing then,' says Roy Carr, who compiled the tape, 'we sold about 15,000 copies, which for mail order was a phenomenal figure.'

Despite the diverse array of musical styles, many of the artists on the tape did share a few things in common: extreme poverty, a disregard for the mainstream rock beast and a belief that ideas and innovation were more valuable commodities than musical proficiency. Barney Hoskyns was one of the *NME*'s post-punk intake, joining the paper after freelancing briefly for *Melody Maker*. 'Punk overthrew that idea of rock giants in limousines,' he says. 'It took a long time before the dinosaurs weren't regarded as dinosaurs any more but were regarded as the guardians of Rock Greatness. So for a good decade rock wasn't cool. It was anathema. There was a collective sense that rock had become a tired cliché and that it was important to identify anything that wasn't about power chords and leather trousers and heroin. So you end up with post-punk, where what was celebrated was anti-virtuosity and lo-fi production. Post-punk was very much about "we've just recorded in the back room". Proficiency wasn't cool.'

"His leathers were peerless... lapping tightly over painted black boots with the little spur strap around the instep..." John Cooper Clarke and Nick Kent, Manchester, August 1978

'There were a lot of people who came through during punk rock who'd been excluded by the music business,' says Spencer. 'Look at Ian Dury: Ian was just too leftfield for people, too weird before punk.' In April 1978 Dury, 35-year-old former frontman of Kilburn and the High Roads, who had been making music in relative obscurity for seven years, had his first top ten hit.

This post-punk mood of pro-Labour, anti-corporate, egalitarian righteousness was a reaction against the standard rock modes of behaviour common five or ten years before, ones that *NME*, for all its posturing, had occasionally subscribed to. 'In the '70s there would be pictures of topless girls in the magazine,' says Hoskyns. 'Just gratuitous objectification and sexism. But it was part of the culture. By the early '80s that had started to change. This was post-Slits, post-Au Pairs. Neil Spencer was very right on and politically correct before the term existed. It was a little bit po-faced and earnest and Neil was mocked for it. But he also brought in women writers: Lynn Hanna, Cynthia Rose, Julie Burchill, Kath Carroll, Lucy O'Brien.'

'There was such hypocrisy and sexism in that hippy world,' says Ian Penman. 'The women were supposed to be in the back cooking the brown rice while the men sat around smoking dope and discussing how heavy Dylan's lyrics were or whatever. Danny Baker was going through the *NME* photo archive one day and he found this photograph of Charlie Murray in the mid-'70s. Charlie was holding this inflatable plastic Led Zeppelin PR thing, this plastic zeppelin, between his legs. Danny ran off 40 copies on the Xerox machine. Charlie was really not amused.'

'Before punk rock there were no women in bands,' says Neil Spencer. 'There was a group called Fanny and that was about it. Then after punk you get The Slits. A big difference. I recruited a lot of female writers and tried to create an inclusive atmosphere. But a lot of the writers that I brought in were either ignored or propositioned or people called them names. You also had a cadre of homophobes. Almost obsessively anti-gay. Then on the other hand you had people like Phil McNeill who'd worked for *Gay Times*.'

As Spencer tried to drag the paper into the 1980s, there were still remnants of the old rock culture around. The *NME* office was not a welcoming atmosphere for women writers – it still had one foot in the world of dinosaur rock music, rather than modern consumer journalism. 'It was a very intimidating place,' says Lucy O'Brien. 'The aura of a sixth-form boys' common room. I felt isolated as a female. Certain editors weren't very encouraging – they thought that because I was a woman I wouldn't know as much or take things as seriously as the men.'

'I remember thinking "What's the currency here?' And I decided that it was knowledge. So I really made sure that I knew my stuff – went to as many gigs as I could every week. I even had a little box file where I'd write the names of bands I'd seen and a little description. It was quite trainspottery really. When I amassed this knowledge I began to feel really accepted. But I had to be twice as good as the men to get anywhere.'

As well as tension between staff and publishers, the *NME*'s new editor had to deal with new tensions between the staff and the IPC advertising executives, based back at King's Reach Tower. As the '70s had progressed and the *New Musical Express*' sales and influence increased, more and more non-musical advertisers were vying for spots on the paper's pages. Now Spencer had to explain to his staff why *NME* was starting to run more adverts from very uncool and corporate non-music brands at the point where he was trying to reposition *NME* as a left-leaning inclusive environment.

'We couldn't believe the adverts that they were still accepting,' says Ian Penman. 'It was old school. You'd have these articles on The Fire Engines or Kid Creole and then on the facing page there'd be an advert for David Coverdale with a photograph of a big dragon coming out of his crotch and two writhing women at his feet. It was bizarre.'

Any kind of residual façade of counter-cultural cred that the paper's journalists might've tried to maintain in their writing was undermined when it was juxtaposed with, say, recruitment adverts for the British Army or ads for Woolworth's. '*NME* occupied a central position within British youth culture,' explains Andy McDuff, then the paper's advertising sales executive, 'and suddenly we started to attract advertising not just from record companies, but anyone keen to sell their product to 15 to 24-year-old men. Coffee companies, car companies, banks; they were all falling over themselves to give us money. We had adverts for Jaguar XJS and for Red Mountain coffee which were particularly unpopular with the writers.'

The staff of the *NME* responded by burrowing deeper back into the underground. The decline of rock'n'roll in the mid-'70s and the failure of the first-wave punk bands to notably reverse the decline led to a generation of bands who attempted to strip music back to its atomic level and reassemble it in new forms. So it was with writing about rock music: in an almost self-flagellating way, some of the writers on the *NME* attempted to invent an entirely new way of reviewing records, believing that their predecessors had failed.

'I didn't really like punk,' says Ian Penman. 'It promised all of this change but soon we were just going back to the same old rock'n'roll thing, which I had no emotional investment in. I knew next to nothing about rock music history. If you'd quizzed me about The Byrds or Iggy or The Velvet Underground, I'd be lost. I knew nothing. I'd never read Lester Bangs.'

Penman and Paul Morley responded by attempting to write in a way that was alternately brave and baffling, employing punctuation like a weapon, conjuring images that were abstract and evocative and occasionally downright meaningless. It was gloriously provocative but at times very long-winded and egocentric writing, inspired by French philosophers Michel Foucault, Roland Barthes and Jacques Derrida and the work of the Frankfurt School of dissident Marxist social theoreticians. Whether this approach had any place in a weekly music paper is a moot point, but suddenly the pages of *NME* assumed something of the atmosphere of the staff common room of the philosophy department of a small provincial university.

'Compendium Books in Camden had a great section of French philosophy,' says Penman, 'and I just started getting into all of these great writers. I didn't understand half of it at the time, but I remember opening a book of Jacques Derrida and it just *looked* amazing: all this playfulness with the layout and white space. Roland Barthes was the same. It was wonderful writing but it was laid out and played games with the reader. It was immensely pleasurable and refreshing when everyone else was trying to write like Martin Amis, which was just stale and airless and like something from 1964.'

'A tear-stained pillow turned inside out,' wrote Paul Morley of a Human League album, 'not really a best-seller lethargically bandaged up! We've talked for long enough time about the tart appeal of the beggars and their maids. It was easy. Entertainment is always JUST entertainment.'[138]

'Ian Penman's stuff was at times very dense and elusive and metatextual,' says Barney Hoskyns. 'Pretty hard to grapple with. When he reined in his more esoteric tendencies he was very good. Paul had a pretty innovative and radical approach to pop culture in retrospect.'

'The cliché that grew up at the time around me and Paul was that we were pretentious, which I'm not ashamed of,' says Penman. 'Pretentious is just another word for aspiring to something, for trying something out. There was this idea that we were these grey long-coated Echo and the Bunnymen fans sitting in darkened rooms reading French philosophy. It wasn't like that at all. We were having *fun*. Because I didn't know about rock'n'roll history and rock'n'roll writing I didn't realise that you had to write in a certain way about things. In the middle of a singles column once I started writing about Marks and Spencer's mayonnaise, recommending this mayo instead of some single. It was supposed to be funny.'

Not everyone saw the joke. To accompany Ian Penman's review of Blondie's single 'Rapture' ('is it at all possible – the reciprocity of sensations between mythical Debbie Harry and your solitary wallpaper self?'[139]) an aggrieved sub-editor appended the headline 'The Ghost of Roland Barthes is Suitably Perplexed'.

'He had an innovative and radical approach to pop culture...'
Paul Morley, 1980

'Paul Morley always delivered great interviews,' says Neil Spencer, 'and Ian was very bright. But their egos went absolutely out of control. They were writing pretentious bullshit.'

'Ever since the underground press people had been imported wholesale into the *NME*, there had been a culture of writing in your own voice, or writing whatever you felt like,' explains Paul DuNoyer. 'It was an ethos which had replaced the old '60s mode of writing, which was a sub-Fleet Street policy of writing in a certain style for the biggest possible readership in a way that was unlikely to rock the boat for the music industry. The class of '72 brought in a new policy of writing the way that they wanted. Luckily for them – Charlie Murray, Nick Kent, Ian MacDonald – the way that they wanted to write happened to be the sort of thing that lots of people wanted to read. Their successors wrote in an individual way that didn't seem to be so broadly appealing and seemed to strike a lot of readers as self-indulgent. I was struck by the number of letters we'd get from people complaining about it.'

The bands that were being reviewed in this way weren't necessarily too amused either. Following a damning review of their debut album ('willowy songs wallow in the marsh of tawdry images, inane realisations, dull epigrams'[140]), a new act from Crawley in Sussex called The Cure debuted a half-hearted riposte during a session for the John Peel show. Entitled 'Desperate Journalist In Ongoing Meaningful Review Situation', it was an attempt to parody the dense prose style of Morley and Penman that suggested that the band's singer, Robert Smith, had recently taken ownership of a new thesaurus. 'The lads go rampant on insignificant symbolism,' he sang, 'and compound this with rude soulless obliqueness.... Ian Penman... uses long words, like semiotics and semolina... sometimes they sound like an avant-garde John Otway.'

'Neil Spencer would give people their due,' says Roy Carr, 'and he hired Paul Morley and Ian Penman and their writing was just impenetrable. Overnight there was a revolt amongst the readers. They just left in their droves and never came back. And *NME* never recovered.'

13.Scum

'My colleagues were like the Red Guard of the
Chinese Cultural Revolution. Just fanatical...'

Since he'd left *NME* in 1978, Nick Logan had been getting more and more restless. Freed from the pressures of dealing with IPC management, but still recovering from the experience, he nevertheless had a magazine-shaped itch to scratch. One thing was certain, though: Logan wanted to start a new magazine on his own terms, without the interference of the big corporations. Bouncing ideas off some of his former *NME* colleagues, Logan mocked up dummy copies and worked on plans for specialist country and western and reggae mags, as well as a monthly British equivalent to *Rolling Stone*. Nothing really seemed to click until a conversation with *NME*'s printers in Kettering lead him to EMAP publishing's new magazine division. The owners of the Kettering press, East Midlands Allied Press, were a small family-run local newspaper group based in Peterborough who had successfully branched out into magazines in the 1950s with their successful weekly titles *Angling Times* and *Motorcycle News*.

Initial conversations between Logan and EMAP were slightly strained: he wanted backers but didn't want to go back on another publishing company's payroll and EMAP weren't convinced by the handful of magazine ideas that Logan had presented to them. Only one took hold: inspired both by the pop magazines that he'd read in his youth and the high-end glossy production values of *Tatler*, Logan had mocked up a version of a magazine prospectively called either The Hit or The Pop, featuring printed song lyrics of current hit singles in a poster pullout. Resisting pressure from EMAP Magazines' CEO David Arculus to turn the mag into a John Travolta and Bee Gees-themed publication called

Disco Fever, Logan instead compromised by naming his new magazine *Smash Hits*.

The timing was perfect. When *Smash Hits* launched as a fortnightly in November 1978, singles sales were at an all time high. Crucially, though, the charts were full of the kind of credible New Wave artists who'd broken through to the top ten with punk: in its first issue, *Smash Hits* carried the lyrics for songs by The Jacksons, Abba and Leo Sayer, but also the Buzzcocks' 'Ever Fallen in Love', The Rezillos' 'Top of the Pops' and Siouxsie and the Banshees' 'Hong Kong Garden'. While it was written in a way that echoed the days of *Fabulous* magazine, there was a definite punk flavour to the publication: printed on glossy A4 paper, the early issues of the magazine made use of the kinds of lurid pinks and greens favoured by Jamie Reid for his Sex Pistols posters.

Dispensing with the sense for meaning and authenticity that was the staple of N*ME*, *Smash Hits* celebrated pop music's surface culture without recourse to Roland Barthes, ably catering for both younger music fans and those readers of weekly music titles who had grown disaffected with the way that they were taking themselves a little too seriously. Produced around Logan's kitchen table in Wanstead by a team of three people, he was so nervous about *Smash Hits*' success that he edited the first three issues under a pseudonym. He needn't have worried. By reviving a neglected market for younger pop fans and bolstering their number with older readers sucked in by coverage of the post-punk mainstream plus a crossword provided by *NME*'s Fred Dellar, Smash Hits was an immediate success. By June 1979, it was regularly selling 150,000 copies a fortnight, enough for Logan to pass the editorship onto Ian Cranna, simultaneously managing a new band called Orange Juice, and become editorial director. Within three years of launching, *Smash Hits* was selling half a million copies of each issue, prompting IPC to react by launching their own carbon copy, Number One, edited by *NME*'s Phil McNeill, in 1983.

Within a very short period of time, *NME* went from being comfortably the biggest-selling music magazine in the country to third place bronze medal holders. To make ers worse, *Smash Hits* took the lease on an office practically next door to *NME* on Carnaby Street. '*NME* was pretty tedious at that stage,' says *NME* freelancer Mark Ellen, who joined *Smash Hits* as features editor in 1981. 'Neil Spencer was a rather serious and academic type and that didn't quite make for a very interesting paper, but the music wasn't very interesting either. New Wave had a tremendous energy: if you put someone like Cabaret Voltaire on the cover of *NME*, they were a band with a powerful identity as rock musicians in full control of their artistic destiny, and probably taking a lot of drugs and sleeping with a lot of girls at the same time. *NME* readers loved that. But the early '80s was a dismal time. *NME* desperately tried to attach themselves to the pop thing that we were doing at Smash Hits but they just didn't have the apparatus to do it. *NME* was printed on broadsheet old bog paper and *Smash Hits* was a shiny full-colour pop concept. The *NME* office was directly opposite – I could look out of the window and see Charlie Murray or Adrian Thrills and whoever else writing up their interview with Devo or their Crispy Ambulance review, but they didn't have the necessary filter to deal with pop music and instead they tried to take it all too seriously.'

There was another important factor underpinning *Smash Hits'* rapid success. At midnight on 1 August 1981, an obscure new 24-hour cable television channel launched itself to a million subscribers in a limited number of American cities with the words 'Ladies and gentlemen, rock and roll'. With a promotional budget of $25 million, the backing of Warner Amex Satellite entertainment and a rapacious approach to growth, within two years MTV was a global phenomenon.

With the exception of the odd small local afternoon pop show and closed-circuit university television stations, until MTV America had no real outlet for promotional videos. The pioneering music video directors like former Monkees guitarist Michael Nesmith were working mostly for the European market, where shows like Germany's *Beat Club*, *Top of The Pops* or *The Old Grey Whistle Test* would regularly fill airtime by playing clips of bands produced by record companies. Lacking a bank of videos by American artists to fill their 24-hour schedules, MTV's programmers and VJ's were forced to look to the UK to find stars who understood the importance of video as a promotional tool, no er how famous they were.[141] The first clip that the station broadcast was of an obscure song called 'Video Killed the Radio Star' by British synth-pop band The Buggles. Before long, a new MTV-sponsored British Invasion was underway. The clip for Duran Duran's third single, 1981's 'Girls on Film', was banned at home by the BBC, but picked up for heavy rotation on MTV along with songs by Adam and the Ants, Flock of Seagulls and Culture Club, all of whom went on to sell huge amounts of records worldwide after breaking America through MTV. Until MTV, radio and press had been the most important way for record companies to break new bands. Now that it was shifting to television, a generation of new British bands appeared without the sanction of *NME*'s writers. The paper was left at a loss as to how to deal with them, but *Smash Hits* thrived.

'*Smash Hits* became sort of an MTV in magazine form,' says Barney Hoskyns. 'The primary focus was on pop groups that looked good and were colourful and the treatment of them was quite superficial. It was very much a reaction to this legacy of pseudo-intellectual deconstruction of pop culture that you got at the *NME*.'

Following the success of *Smash Hits* and MTV, *NME* was no longer the sole source of information about rock music. Noticing the success of the *NME*'s content in attracting advertisers keen to sell to young people, Fleet Street started to cover pop music in more detail in the 1980s, attracted by the advertising revenue opportunities that new readerships presented. *NME* writers found themselves with career options outside of the rock press world, once they'd left the indies, although in some cases it was a culture shock. 'One of the first grown-up jobs I did was to interview Harrison Ford,' says Tony Parsons, 'and I was told by the PR that I'd only have 55 minutes with him and I couldn't believe this – that we wouldn't stay up all night taking drugs and fuck each other's girlfriends at the end of it was a total shock, because that was what I was used to from writing for the *NME*.'

In November 1982, Channel 4 launched with a remit of public service obligations attached to its charter that included creating programmes that appealed to the tastes and interests of a culturally diverse society, including young people and teenagers. The station's flagship music show, *The Tube*, had a specific editorial policy of showcasing new acts, meaning that national TV was no longer a closed shop only accessible to bands who'd had chart success. Meanwhile on the channel's new soap opera, *Brookside*, one of the teenage characters, Karen Grant, was heard remarking to her aghast parents that she wanted 'to be like Julie Burchill and write for the *NME*'.

Over at the BBC, producer Janet Street-Porter, then married to *Time Out* founder Tony Elliott, launched a series of youth-orientated programming called 20th Century Box, presented by *NME*'s Danny Baker. *NME*'s monopoly on information and power to influence, always out of proportion to its actual sales, was under attack. 'The *NME* sold about five times as much as the bands it covered,' says Mark Ellen. 'The Clash would be on the cover of the magazine and you'd go and see them the following week and the gig would be half empty.'

There was another problem. One of MTV's most-requested videos in its first year was for David Bowie's single 'Ashes to Ashes', at that point the most expensive music video ever made, costing a quarter of a million pounds. For extras in the video, Bowie had raided the clientele of a fashionable new nightclub just round the corner from the Roxy in Covent Garden. Called Blitz, the club was run by two minor faces on the London punk scene: Steve Strange, who'd worked designing Sex Pistols artwork for Malcolm McLaren, and DJ Rusty Egan, who'd played drums in Pistols' bassist Glen Matlock's short-lived New Wave act The Rich Kids. Blitz had one foot in the early art school roots of punk, but its main influences were austere and Germanic: David Bowie's Berlin period, Kraftwerk and the more sleek disco of Italian producer Giorgio Moroder. While the music might've been slightly sombre, there was nothing restrained about the Blitz clubbers' sense of dress: a riot of glitter, make-up, militaria from Laurence's Corner, Harem pants and Ali Baba-style curly-toed slippers, shoulder pads and gaucho jackets, sequins and cutaway dinner jackets with tails or Second World War GI uniforms, it was a fun and flamboyant scene. Crucially, although Spandau Ballet played their first-ever gig at the Blitz Club, the currency of this milieu was not the same as the staple of the *NME*, four men with guitars. 'With the downturn in punk there was a cultural shift beginning to happen which the *NME* could not accommodate without becoming a different publication,' says Charles Shaar Murray. 'People OD'd on the gritty social realism of punk and they wanted fun pop and bright colours and *NME* couldn't do that. Poor Neil had the misfortune to preside over *NME*'s identity crisis and a larger one in the rock community.'

As the bands and people who had frequented Blitz went on to become more famous, *NME* struggled to deal with so much frivolity and face paint. 'The concept of Spandau has grown so distended that it has slipped its guy ropes and overtaxed,' wrote *NME*'s Richard Cook in 1982.[142] The *Smash Hits* approach was more straightforward: 'Spandau Ballet – another band with weird clothes and strange haircuts,'[143] they raved.

Smash Hits was not the only paper thriving. Following its assiduous punk coverage, the circulation of *Sounds* was rising thanks to their reporting on both the New Wave of British Heavy Metal and the nascent West Coast American glam metal scene. Metal and heavy rock had undergone its own identity crisis in the mid-'70s and a pub-based underground scene of new young hard rock bands like Londoners Iron Maiden, The Tygers of Pan Tang from Whitley Bay or Yorkshiremen Def Leppard and Saxon were applying punk energy and pace to heavy rock. Under the editorship of Alan Lewis, *Sounds* launched a special one-off heavy metal supplement called *Kerrang!* in 1981, while elsewhere the paper covered the politically dubious *Oi!* and streetpunk genres, linked to the emergent racist skinhead movement which culminated in a riot in July 1981 when Sikh youth from the predominantly Asian London district of Southall attacked a pub hosting a gig by skinhead bands.[144]

Somewhat ironically, given the way that *Smash Hits* had undermined the *NME*'s cultural and commercial importance, the magazine that really understood the importance of the Blitz scene and club culture was also created by *NME*'s former editor Nick Logan. As a former mod, Logan understood the importance of dancefloor style to British youth culture and his next project, *The Face*, placed music as only one aspect of a metropolitan lifestyle. Launched with a budget of £4,000 that Logan had saved up from royalties editing the book the Illustrated *NME Encyclopedia of Rock*, *The Face* was aimed at London club kids, or people who wanted to one day be London club kids. It catered to an urbane, fashion-conscious audience with a measured prose provided by ex-*NME* staffers like Parsons, Burchill and Adrian Thrills and was published monthly on glossy paper in magazine format. 'I'm looking for the kids who participate in the music scene,' said Logan on *The Face*'s launch in 1980. 'The ones who have a good time rather than just sit at home listening to the hi-fi. What *The Face* does is combine racy copy with a lot of photography – people do underestimate the power of good pictures.'[145] The Face took the expensive and unattainable world of the high-end fashion magazine and recreated it in a street-level manner. With *Smash Hits* undermining its commercial potential and *The Face* undermining its position as the arbiter of youth cool, *NME*'s sales began to flounder.

'The explicit way in which [*Smash Hits* and *The Face*] celebrate the glossy dance of image and identity makes the old time pop papers like *New Musical Express* and *Melody Maker* seem positively analytical, even a little crusty,' wrote sociologist Laurie Taylor in July 1984.[146]

'We had to labour with the problem that the 1970s was increasingly seen as *NME*'s golden age,' says Paul DuNoyer. 'I presume that Neil Spencer must've felt this quite keenly because he was somewhat in the shadow of his predecessor Nick Logan. Our sales peaked in 1980 with the Joy Division edition which came out after the long strike and thereafter they seemed to decline pretty relentlessly.[147]

'The '80s was a time of circulation decline and a certain decline in esteem. For the first time the *NME* was no longer seen as the hippest kid because it had lost ground to *The Face* and then literally a few yards across the street was *Smash Hits*, which was a different kind of magazine but nevertheless stole a lot of *NME*'s thunder. So it was a challenging time to be on the *NME* and one could never take its continued existence for granted. There was a constant anxiety about the future of the *NME*.'

One of the main currencies of the journalist on the weekly music press is the esteem of peers in the profession. Unable to engage with the new pop movement, made to look old-fashioned by *The Face* and with sales in terminal decline, the staff of the *NME* fell to reactionary in-fighting.

'After punk my feeling was that now the excitement had died down and there was no single movement to sustain the paper the *NME* needed to broaden its view again and not just be a corporate fanzine,' says DuNoyer. 'But my colleagues were like the Red Guard of the Chinese Cultural Revolution. Just fanatical. We'd be in this smoke-filled room in Carnaby Street and Neil would point out that the sales figures were going south and people would say quite defiantly "Well, we're better off without those people because they don't understand what we're doing'. That was the mentality – that if the *NME* pursued its vision with enough intensity it would shed the riff-raff and arrive at a hard core of readers who truly understood what we were doing. That was how it went on for most of the 1980s; a very stimulating place but very beset by its internal politics.'

Somewhat seduced by the success of *The Face*, Neil Spencer tried to ape some of the things that had made it successful: lacking full-colour reproduction, the *NME* had to rely on broadening its non-music coverage. At the close of the 1970s, punk's manic recycling and juxtaposing of past styles, pioneered by King's Road shop Acme Attractions – '50s quiffs and drape jackets with mod-style pork pie hats and three-button suit jackets – gradually calmed into more distinct and purist looks. A full-scale mod revival was prompted by the success of The Jam and the film version of The Who's rock opera *Quadrophrenia* in 1979. On Easter bank holiday weekend 1980, there were even reruns of the seaside riots of 16 years earlier, as mods, punks, Teddy Boys and skinheads clashed. In London, the three branches of the shop Flip imported 1950s vintage Americana, selling bowling shirts, puffball skirts and baseball jackets to the burgeoning rockabilly revival scene, which featured on the cover of *NME* in February 1980.

NME's music coverage fragmented: as well as new wave and rock and the mod and rockabilly revivalists, it still prided itself on its coverage of black music. In 1977, one of Nik Cohn's short stories, 'Another Saturday Night' had become the basis for the third biggest-grossing film of the year, behind *Star Wars* and *Close Encounters of the Third Kind. Saturday Night Fever* brought disco to small town nightclubs across the world, to the dismay of white rock fans: in the summer of 1979, Chicago DJ Steve Dahl led an anti-disco rally at the White Sox baseball team's Comiskey Park stadium. Encouraging fans to bring disco records to burn, the rally ended in a riot. In August 1979, Baker awarded Chic's single 'Risque' the coveted single of the week, passionately defending disco music against its bigoted dismissal by white rock fans, igniting a debate which would continue on the pages of *NME* for the next 15 years.

'I remember being in Neil Spencer's office for meetings and sometimes it got heated,' says Barney Hoskyns. 'It seemed like this unifying idea of pop counter-culture was diffusing and that there wasn't a centre to any of this. There was a sense of there not being a strong clear identity any more that had been there during the punk era. There was a consensus of what was cool and what wasn't and by 1981 that consensus wasn't there any more. You had different factions lobbying for different things: I remember being in a meeting where we were seriously debating whether to put Paul Young on the cover or Tom Waits. It really didn't seem clear which was the right choice. We didn't like Paul Young but he was number one and it felt like he should be on the cover. But then Tom Waits was much more interesting and the kind of artist that *NME* should be celebrating. It was an identity crisis.'

Paolo Hewitt had been brought onto the staff of *Melody Maker* in the fallout from the 1980 strike, joining the *NME* in 1983. 'One of my first jobs for *Melody Maker* was going to the Electric Ballroom to review Madness and being surrounded by 2,000 skinheads *seig heiling*. But *Melody Maker* was a real laugh. There was the person that liked heavy metal and the person that liked jazz and the person that liked Fairport Convention but we all got on really well. At *NME* there was so much backbiting and factions and politics. It was a bad time for *NME*. In the '70s it had ruled. Everyone at my school read *NME*. But when they brought Paul Morley and Ian Penman on it turned a lot of people off. The readers didn't know who Roland Barthes was and they didn't care. You had *Smash Hits* taking off and we didn't know what to do with people like Boy George and Simon Le Bon and Duran Duran. There were no rock acts and the *NME* was just flummoxed. Meanwhile *The Face* was covering drugs, fashion: I used to read *The Face* rather than *NME*, although I never told anyone that at the time, but it knew what it was doing. One week we'd have Boy George on the cover, the next week Yoko Ono. It was just mad.'

The *NME* of the early 1980s did have its bankers, however. At the 1980s Readers' Poll, The Jam had won top position in almost every category including best group but also best sleeve and best bassist in what the paper called 'an across the board triumph that even eclipses the kind of silliness that used to go on when berserked-out Led Zeppelin fans would slap the relevant members of the band down in every section'.[148] It was a situation that would be perpetuated until the band split up in December 1982. Paolo Hewitt, who was brought up in Woking in Surrey, had known Weller as a teenager. 'When I got to *NME* I didn't want to write about The Jam,' says Hewitt. 'Neil badgered me into interviewing them but I tried to keep my friendship with Paul separate from work.'

'Paul Weller was a very big deal in *NME* for about ten years solid,' says

Mat Snow, a schoolfriend of Barney Hoskyns who joined the *NME* as a freelancer in 1980 while working for Texaco. 'You put Paul Weller on the cover of the *NME* and it would sell. Paolo was brought over from *Melody Maker* because he was Weller's pal.'

'The Jam, The Clash and Madness were central to the magazine,' says Paul DuNoyer. 'My view was we should just hammer away at these bands and put them on the cover every week. We shouldn't wait a year for them to put out another album. We don't even need an excuse, we just keep hammering away at them. You don't apologise and you don't put challenging techno-pagan experimentalist from Belgium on the cover. That's brave but it's stupid. But then the *NME* was often brave but stupid.'

Two generations of mod: Paolo Hewitt interviews Paul Weller and Pete Townshend for a Melody Maker feature, Soho, October 1980

Instead, *NME* followed *The Face*'s lead and expanded its non-music reporting. The paper had already built up a good reputation for its film coverage – director Francis Ford Coppola proclaimed that Angus McKinnon's review of his 1979 film *Apocalypse Now* was the only one really to understand the film – while a series of print advertisements placed in other IPC titles played up the broad range of material sceptical buyers could expect alongside the live reviews of Alien Sex Fiend, 23 Skidoo or the Comsat Angels.

'We here at *New Musical Express* believe there's more to this rock'n'roll lark than music. It might come as a surprise that in the last year *NME* has interviewed not only Johnny Rotten and Jimmy Page – as you'd expect – but also such noted non-guitarists as Mel Brooks, Woody Allen, Steven Spielberg, Laurie Cunningham, Keith Waterhouse, John Cleese, RD Laing, Robert Jung and more. Besides a film page to rank with anything other weeklies offer, *NME* also carries a regular books column, TV and radio reviews, and informed commentary on a host of topics that relate to rock and young people from Nuclear News to Animal Liberation.'

It was a smart piece of positioning on Spencer's part, designed to put water between the paper and *Smash Hits*. In August 1984, the cover of the paper featured a long and erudite essay by Ian Penman, which quoted Baudrillard but attempted to dissect the appeal of pop music. It was the kind of ambitious project that *NME* was still the only magazine on the newsstand able to tackle.

In 1985 Neil Spencer appointed Stuart Cosgrove as *NME*'s media editor, a role created to reflect the burgeoning coverage of non-music material. A garrulous soul-loving Scot who arrived at the paper from the unlikely background of the cultural studies department of Reading University, Cosgrove set the agenda for much of the decade.

'While I was studying for my PhD I was writing for this fanzine, Collusion, as well as *Black Echoes* magazine,' he says. 'I was writing about Northern Soul using things I'd learnt from cultural studies, coming out of being a practitioner as well as a theoretician. I'd been lecturing in film and cultural studies at Reading University, but I wasn't an academic in that dusty sense – academia at that time was just beginning to explore the idea of popular culture.

'But when I arrived on the *NME* the idea of the media as a phenomenon was growing. And of course I had a PhD in media studies and could write about it authoritatively and had an understanding of film and television. And through this writing I started to get noticed by people at the *NME*, of whom Neil Spencer was the main one. Neil did a deal with *Black Echoes* to get me to come and write for them. I think I was the first ever journalist in the history of pop journalism to have a transfer fee like a Premiership footballer.'

Following 1979's Militant Entertainment tour, which featured 40 groups at 23 different venues, Rock Against Racism collapsed in 1981 after being unable to repay its debts. Instead *NME*'s cause célèbre became Red Wedge, the left-leaning political activism group founded by Billy Bragg, Jimmy Somerville and Paul Weller in November 1985. Taking its name from a Bolshevik-era Soviet propaganda poster[149] and with a logo designed by *The Face*'s designer Neville Brody, Red Wedge was a general attempt to engage young people with the democratic process that had the specific aim of electing Neil Kinnock's Labour Party and toppling the Thatcher government when the country went to the polls at the 1987 General Election.

'The *NME* in the '80s was a continuation of that radical press of the 1960s,' says Billy Bragg. 'People like Neil Spencer were children of 1968 and believed that music should say something, that at its best it provided a commentary about what was going on in society. Both Neil and Paolo Hewitt were involved heavily with Red Wedge and attended early meetings. A lot of the energy of punk had dissipated and turned into nihilism and after the 1983 election and the miners' strikes our aim was to start up a debate about what the Labour Party could do behind a coalition of artists determined to bring down the Thatcher government.'

Because of its roots in both punk and the hippy underground, the indie music circuit, and its in-house paper, *NME*, were the sole section of the media who took the Labour Party seriously. '[I remember] going into places like WH Smith and seeing the narrow range of literature that they would have on sale,' Rough Trade boss Geoff Travis told the author John Harris in 2004. 'Things like *Spare Rib* and *New Left Review* wouldn't be in those shops ... It was all slanted towards the middle of the road: the left wing wasn't represented. We felt the music business was analogous to that.'

The idealism of *NME*'s involvement with Red Wedge was a continuation of a process that had been underway since the late '70s. As a result of the paper's virulent pro-RAR and anti-Nazi stance in the post-punk period, Spencer claims that he was worried that the National Front would send a letter bomb to the office. This never happened, but in late 1978, Spencer had enlisted Clash frontman Joe Strummer to write a personal election manifesto ahead of the General Election in May 1979. Strummer advocated the reunification of Ireland. Soon afterwards, a handwritten letter appeared in the post. It was a death threat from the loyalist paramilitary group the Red Hand Commando, directed at Joe Strummer.

Worse was yet to come. During Operation Julie, the police had borrowed secret telephone monitoring equipment from Whitehall[150] in a continuation of the campaign to vilify the latent underground movement. 'We had a switchboard with about five or six lines but we also had two direct lines,' says Karen Walter. 'I had one and Derek Johnson had the other. I was told never to say anything personal on the direct lines because they were bugged.

'I took this with a pinch of salt and then one day Cynthia Rose was writing a piece on Karen Silkwood,[151] because there was a film about her coming out. Cynthia finished her call and I picked up the phone to call someone and her last conversation was being played back at the end of the line. Presumably by some government department.'

Whether a bona fide case of bugging or simply some kind of mechanical malfunction, nerves in the *NME* office began to jangle. Red Wedge's Billy Bragg was a constant presence in the office and played the office Christmas party in December 1983. He saw the *NME* as a viable way of communicating left-wing politics to the mainstream. 'The *NME* really helped to promote and create an atmosphere in which to talk about politics,' he wrote in his autobiography.[152] In April 1985, the paper put Neil Kinnock on the front cover and enlisted Chris Dean, singer with the socialist band The Redskins, as a writer under the pseudonym X Moore. It was a provocative move, especially as the paper's journalists had only recently emerged from a long and protracted further period of strike.

Prompted partly by an NUJ show of solidarity with the striking coal miners[153] and partly over demands to bring pay more in line with Fleet Street,[154] the strike of the summer of 1984 was far more painful and drawn-out than previously. For June and July no copies of *NME* were produced.

'A lot of the staff kidded themselves that they worked for *NME*,' says Neil Spencer. 'They didn't. They worked for IPC. I tried to shield them from that reality. But when the strikes started I couldn't do that any more. The strikes were half to do with the intransigence of the management and half to do with the intransigence of members of the NUJ. You can't scab and you have to be on the side of the union but it broke my heart. All that fucking work getting the editorial standards up and improving readership was wasted. It's very hard to make a paper good and very easy to lose readers. It really damaged us and I don't think *NME* ever really recovered. I wasn't in the NUJ so I could go into the office, where there'd be a couple of guys standing outside picketing, but I'd get there and there'd be absolutely fuck all to do.'

'We lived in a bubble of ignorance about what was going on with IPC,' says Snow. 'We were just of the opinion that out of sight was out of mind. Nobody even knew the name of the publisher. Then a big shock came with the strike of 1984. Suddenly people had to take notice of IPC because we were striking for pay and conditions, as well as to show solidarity with the miners. At that time, which was a very inflationary period, the pay rise we were offered was less than the rate of inflation, so it was in effect a pay cut. We all knew that *NME* was making money and were furious that we weren't seeing any of it.'

'The main problem with IPC and the *NME* was that they could never see what they'd got,' says Spencer. 'All they did was milk the paper for all they could. They didn't reinvest the money in decent offices or infrastructure or in colour reproduction or improving the product. They just took the fucking money. My beef with IPC was always financial. They wouldn't give us more pages – *Sounds* had more pages of editorial, which is one of the reasons why they gave *NME* a good run for a while. I wanted better paper, ink that didn't come off on your hands, staples. But they wouldn't spend money on improving the paper.'

ers were made worse by the fact that the *NME*'s IPC rivals, *Melody Maker*, ended their strike early and went back to work. 'The *Melody Maker* staff were better paid than us because they were in a different section of the company for some reason,' claims Snow. '*NME* was counted as a youth title and they were in the hobby division. Anyway, they did the same kind of work as us but were paid more – so the people who worked on the magazine that sold more were paid less, which just didn't make sense. So there was already an enmity between us which was solidified when they went back to work while we were still striking.'

'There were a few blacklegs,' says Roy Carr. 'We all knew who'd scabbed and they were lucky they didn't get their heads caved in.'

Neil Spencer, dispirited by the experience of having to mediate between IPC and the paper's staff, and angry that the small recent circulation gains he'd made had evaporated, left the paper in early 1985 after over a decade on its staff, during which time he'd done much to bring the values of the liberal left into the mainstream. 'The country was getting less racist and less homophobic and *NME* felt like it was at the vanguard of that,' says Snow.

Spencer wasn't the only member of staff from the *NME*'s past finding that the end of their time at the *NME* was approaching. While Roy Carr thrived on his various promotional spin-offs, creating more cassette compilations and tie-in LPs, Derek Johnson departed the paper in 1986, after almost 30 years as a staff member. Charles Shaar Murray had quit the staff in 1980, but carried on writing as a freelancer until 1986. 'I felt culturally and politically adrift in the '80s,' he says. 'By about '86 I wasn't sure whether I was more embarrassed to still be there or they were more embarrassed to still have me there.'

'A lot of the people who worked on the *NME* in the early '80s were very fucked up,' says Ian Penman. 'Unhappy personally and professionally. In the '60s the dream had failed and then with punk it failed again and people like Charlie Murray were just disillusioned. They'd had that star thing in the '70s and been involved with the music and been mates with bands and then it had stopped. New writers were coming in and people didn't seem to know what to do with themselves. There was a feeling that some people had become ghosts at the banquet.'

Mick Farren had fled Britain to New York when Thatcher got elected, but soon stopped freelancing for the *NME*. 'You promise you'll always write to the girl who you left behind but it never happens,' he says. 'And anyway, what was I going to write about? New York was scruffy and experimental, whereas London was the Blitz Club and Boy George.'

By 1981 Nick Kent had quit heroin and started a new group, The Subterraneans, but he was still a magnet for aggro. Following a bad review of the fledgling Adam and the Ants, Adam sarcastically namechecked Kent in the song 'Press Darlings', the B-side of the Ants' 1980 single 'Kings of the Wild Frontier',[155] a song which later ended up on the band's global hit album of the same name. Shortly afterwards the band's guitarist hew Ashman poured strawberry jam over Kent's head in the queue outside Camden music venue the Music Machine.

'When I started at *NME* Kent was still a force to be reckoned with,' says Neil Spencer. 'He'd still churn out copy. But by the time I became editor that had started to wane. He just stopped writing. He'd come in, park himself in the review room, leave empty cans of tomato soup and cigarette butts everywhere, and nod off for hours on end with a bottle of methadone in his hand. People didn't like that. There was a campaign to get rid of him altogether, led by Paul Morley.'

'Nick was regarded as very passé and he didn't adapt at all,' says Barney Hoskyns. 'He dressed in 1983 like he dressed in 1975, probably in exactly the same pair of leather pants. He made no concessions to the passing of time.'

The superstar journalists of the previous decade were the victims of a crime that they had no control over: being too old, regardless of what they had or could still contribute to the huge success of the *NME*. 'There was a lot of ageism about,' says Barney Hoskyns. 'These people were shunned. Charlie was occasionally allowed to write about Hendrix or blues but him and Kent were seen as old hippies or junkies. There was no real honouring of people who'd helped to make the magazine.'

Nicholas Benedict Kent was finally sacked from the *NME* in 1982. He didn't lament the end of his time there. 'Being involved with rock journalism by then was like watching something going down in a quicksand,' Kent says. 'There wasn't a scene or enough inspiring personalities to really get deep into the whole thing. It was like trying to make soup out of old bones.

'I look at the *NME* as a good experience because it gave me a mouthpiece to speak to the world through. And the early years were very exciting. Yes, there was the spiritual bankruptcy of the '70s and there was not a lot of joy about but, hey, you could make up for that lack of joy with a surfeit of pleasure. You could get really high. And I got *really* high.'

Despite the stark historical warnings provided by the death of Pete Erskine and the decline of Nick Kent, some of the younger members of the *NME* staff found themselves acquiring a taste for heroin independent of their forbears' influence. 'Fiona Foulgar was the office matriarch,' says Karen Walter, 'she'd been at *NME* since the early '60s when she was 19. On my first day she gave me the office tour to show me where everything was and we ended up in the kitchen. She said "Do you drink tea or coffee? Well don't use any of the spoons in this kitchen, bring in your own teaspoon from home and lock it in your desk".' Puzzled, Walter opened one of the drawers in the kitchen. She found a pile of IPC teaspoons, each of which was charred and blackened on the underside where some members of staff had been using them to cook up heroin on the communal kitchen stove.

For the early '80s indie kids, heroin was as uncool and redolent of the pre-punk rock dinosaurs as stadium tours, Marshall stacks and fake blood made from yoghurt. While the staff of *NME* considered themselves urbane and intellectual, smack was strictly for hicks and out-of-towners, much like a band from Melbourne who had relocated to London in 1980. The Birthday Party lived in communal squalor in the capital's squatland deadzones and while their fondness for heroin wasn't a pose, exactly, it was certainly a calculated one that showed a kind of artistic solidarity with pre-punk bands at a time when everyone else with a guitar in the pages of *NME* was operating from a rigidly postdiluvian point of view.

'The Birthday Party were extraordinary,' says Barney Hoskyns. 'The lineage was The Stooges or Beefheart, and Iggy was the totemic figurehead in that lineage. But the fact is people didn't take them seriously because they were doing heroin and that was unbelievably uncool. A lot of people were having real problems with cocaine or alcohol, but because they weren't doing heroin it was seen as OK.'

Friendless and alone in London, The Birthday Party formed a community of ex-pat Australian groups including The Go-Betweens and The Triffids. They also cleaved to Barney Hoskyns and Snow. It was inevitable that the pair would be drawn into the drugs scene around the band and their charismatic singer Nick Cave.

'I never shot up,' says Mat Snow. 'I can't stand needles to this day. Really my weaknesses were for beer and pork pies: I was never going to turn into Lou Reed. But The Birthday Party were a lot more hardcore about it. Everything was centred around drugs. We'd all wander around in a pack trying to score from various places, then there'd be evenings where somebody's fixing up in the bathroom and there was lots of lying around and listening to records and talking vaguely.

'There was a certain kind of theatricality about it: it had to be the right record on the turntable and the lighting had to be right. Lots of candles: I remember once Nick Cave set his hair on fire when he nodded out too near a candle.'

Despite the blackened spoons in the kitchen, the actual use of heroin in the office was relatively discreet. 'My drug use was unknown I think,' says Hoskyns. 'I don't think people noticed and I certainly didn't flaunt it. Nick Cave looked like a rock'n'roll junkie and that was very consciously done. Anyone who'd known me would've probably recognised that my health was not what it could be but there wasn't a junkie corner at *NME* at that time. Pete Erskine had died. Kent was on methadone.'

Despite Cave's fearsome onstage presence and intense approach to his art – The Birthday Party released a live record called *Drunk on the Pope's Blood*, while Cave was once spotted on the Tube writing lyrics in his own blood, when a cheap newsagent's Bic biro would happily have sufficed – to Snow, the Australian seemed like ideal flatmate material. When Cave and his girlfriend Anita Lane needed somewhere in London to crash, Snow leased them the spare room in his two-bedroom Brixton flat. Any lingering reservations Snow might've had about the pair's suitability when it came to fulfilling the weekly washing-up rota or paying the gas bill on time proved unfounded: Cave was in the process of commencing his novel *And the Ass Saw the Angel*, and was a something of a model of fastidious domesticity. 'My one most vivid memory of him was that he loved Piccalilli. Used to eat it by the jar,' says Snow. 'But he was working very hard and was discreet about his drug use. He used to moan on at Anita for eating processed food, which I always thought was pretty rich from someone who was shooting heroin.'

When The Birthday Party split up following, among other things, bassist Tracey Pew's imprisonment for drunk driving and theft, Cave assembled a new group, The Bad Seeds, whose debut album *Snow* reviewed extravagantly in *NME*, comparing it to the best work by Leonard Cohen and The Doors. One member of this new group was the German Blixa Bargeld, who had formerly split his time between playing guitar in the last days of The Birthday Party with his own group, Einstürzende Neubauten. Much-favoured at the *NME*, ...Neubauten were notorious for a performance at the ICA in which they circumvented the accepted post-gig routine of hanging around in the dressing room for a bit and then departing in a waiting transit van by using pneumatic drills and jackhammers to tunnel through the stage into the sewers below before panicked staff turned off the venue's electricity.

Reviewing an Einstürzende Neubauten single in *NME*, Mat Snow made casual reference to the fact that it was better than anything on the advance cassette copy of the new Nick Cave and the Bad Seeds album that he'd been sent. Thinking nothing of it, Snow went along to interview his old flatmate for an *NME* feature shortly afterwards.

'We went to the Mute records offices and about two hours after the scheduled time Nick turned up,' Snow says. 'He was really cagey and wouldn't catch my eye or anything, just being horrible to me and the photographer, Bleddyn Butcher, who was one of his mates from Australia. I thought he was just having a bad day, but he started sneering at my questions. So after about half an hour of this I said "Is there something wrong?" And he just looked at me and said "I can't believe you'd do that".'

Snow was perplexed until he heard the song on a free Nick Cave and the Bad Seeds flexidisc given out at gigs. Entitled 'Scum', it was a hilariously vicious disavowal of their former friendship in which Cave fantasised about shooting Snow in the face after calling him 'a miserable shitwringing turd', an 'evil gnome' and recounting an episode when, it seems, Cave had walked in on Snow in the shower in their shared flat. 'He took me in,' Cave sang over a noise like a prison chain gang from a Leonard Bernstein musical, 'he said that I looked pale and thin/I told him he looked fat/His house was roastin hot/In fact it was a fucking slum/Scum! Scum!/Well you're on the shit list/Thrust and twist, twist and screw/You gave me a bad review/I think you fuckin traitor/Chronic masturbator/Shitlicker, user, self-abuser...' and so on for almost five uncomfortable minutes.

'I'm a little bit flattered that someone whose artistic ability I have such respect for would immortalise me like that,' says Snow today. 'He doesn't mince his words, does he?'

14.Youth suicide

'Rock music was dead in the '80s. There were just no good bands...'

Not everyone at the *NME* was quite so impressed by the grime, drama and love of spiced relishes that were mainstays of The Birthday Party's world. As a soul-loving friend of Paul Weller who obsessed over the '60s mod Soho of *Absolute Beginners*,[156] Paolo Hewitt was disdainful of the more gothic end of the indie spectrum. By his own admission Hewitt had spent two miserable years on staff at *NME* before he found a confederate in Stuart Cosgrove.

Cosgrove was a veteran of Northern Soul all-nighters who would routinely take an empty suitcase with him on American press trips, bringing it back filled with obscure soul seven-inches to add to his collection. Together he and Hewitt discovered a shared love of black American music. 'Me and Paolo and the photographer Lol Watson would be going out to The Wag or the 100 Club. We were soulboys and we wore white Levi's jackets, jeans with small turn-ups, brogues, monkey boots, stuff that reflected back to mod.'

The office began to factionalise amid much backbiting and sniping between the soulboys and the art school indie fans. 'The day before I joined the paper I was in an Italian cafe in Soho and Nick Kent walked in,' says Hewitt. 'It was fucking freezing but he just had a leather waistcoat on. He said to me 'watch out for the office politics' and he was spot on. I had this great romantic view of music as this great equaliser, this leveller. At *NME* it didn't do that. There was a lot of intellectual jousting going on.'

Cosgrove was from a housing scheme in central Scotland near Perth, while Hewitt had grown up in a children's home. 'When I started at the *NME* I was very aware of class,' says Hewitt. 'I didn't go to university and I'd speak a bit rough and there were people there who were public-school educated so I always felt inferior.'

'Barney Hoskyns and Mat Snow and people like that had all been to Westminster or big public schools,' says Cosgrove. 'I remember me and Paolo saying "I wonder what it's like, their life? Do they have nannies?" We just had no idea what it was like to occupy that lifestyle.'

While Cosgrove and Hewitt were forming their soul bloc, a new band from Manchester had done much to codify the tastes and audience of the *NME* readers. The Smiths had previous form: for a period singer Stephen Morrissey had fronted the short-lived Manchester punk group Ed Banger and the Nosebleeds[157] who followed their single 'Ain't Bin to No Music School' with a Morrissey composition called '(I Think) I'm Ready for the Electric Chair'. He'd also been a frequent and impassioned correspondent to all of the music papers, sending letters which were all signed Steven Morrissey, 384 Kings Road, Stretford, Manchester, but which combined a wit and passion equal of anything provided by the *NME*'s staff, praising Sparks, the Buzzcocks, Johnny Thunders and The Heartbreakers and The New York Dolls, of whom the singer was president of the UK fan club. 'Indubitably, Buzzcocks will hardly figure strongly – or even weakly – in the *NME* poll,' he wrote, 'and in these dark days when Patti Smith, Loudon Wainwright or even The New York Dolls fail to make an impact on Radio 1 DJs, common sense is therefore not so common. Both this letter and Buzzcocks themselves will probably be filed and forgotten. But for now, they are the best kick-ass rock band in the country. Go and see them first and then you may have the audacity to contradict me, you stupid sluts.'

Morrissey wrote some small live reviews for *Record Mirror* and bombarded the *NME* with letters and unsolicited pieces of writing in the hope that they'd publish his work. 'The *New Musical Express* was a propelling force that answered to no one,' he wrote in a piece for the *Guardian* newspaper's music blog in 2007.[158] 'It led the way by the quality of its writers – Paul Morley, Julie Burchill, Paul DuNoyer, Charles Shaar Murray, Nick Kent, Ian Penman, Miles – who would write more words than the articles demanded, and whose views saved some of us, and who pulled us all away from the electrifying boredom of everything and anything that represented the industry. As a consequence the chanting believers of the *NME* could not bear to miss a single issue; the torrential fluency of its writers left almost no space between words, and the *NME* became a culture in itself, whereas *Melody Maker* or *Sounds* just didn't.'

By the time that The Smiths' third single, 'What Difference Does it Make?', reached the Top 20 in February 1984, the band had become a culture in themselves. The Smiths' record label, Rough Trade, were able to achieve chart success with the backing of the indie infrastructure which had grown up in the years following the punk boom, effecting a change in the way that the whole music business was able to function: independent pressing plants, distributors, PR and marketing companies, booking agents were all sustained by a glut of fanzines covering the indie scene. A chasm developed between the major record labels and their independent counterparts, one that was bridged by the creation of major-label subsidiary labels, able to look and feel like an indie while being plugged into major label marketing muscle. One of these labels was Blanco Y Negro, formed by Rough Trade records' founder Geoff Travis in 1983 in conjunction with WEA records. In January 1985, Blanco Y Negro had signed a group beloved by certain members of the *NME* staff: the Jesus and Mary Chain had been reviewed early on by *NME* freelancer David Quantick, who compared them to a 'giant bee in a ventilation shaft'.[159]

The gig was promoted by a relative newcomer to London's alternative music scene. In 1984, Alan McGee, a red-headed Scotsman, had appeared in the *NME*'s Carnaby Street offices, literally frothing at the mouth as he declared the greatness of the Jesus and Mary Chain, who he was promoting at his club, The Living Room, held in a tiny function room above a pub on Tottenham Court Road. A regular at the club was Danny Kelly, a bespectacled former British Rail complaints clerk and primary school contemporary of John Lydon from Islington, who had started freelancing for the *NME* shortly before.

With Kelly and Quantick championing the new indie sounds and The Smiths-sceptical Paolo Hewitt and Stuart Cosgrove banging the drum for black American soul, battle lines were being drawn. Matters were brought to a head with a Morrissey interview in February 1985 in which he stated that he thought 'reggae is vile', inflaming the sensibilities of the Smedley-clad soulboys. All that *NME* needed for chaos really to break out was a vacuum. It soon arrived in the form of Neil Spencer's replacement as editor.

'Ian Pye wandered into a real hornet's nest,' says Barney Hoskyns. 'He was quite mild and bland, a perfectly nice guy, but there was resentment towards him because he'd come in from *Melody Maker* which was the chief rival and enemy. There were some very bolshie and charismatic people on the staff. Particularly Stuart Cosgrove who hadn't been there that long but had his own little cult following of acolytes.'

Ian Pye was a mild-mannered man who, post-*NME*, went on to make documentaries for the BBC and manage Bristol's Watershed arts complex.

Despite being married to *NME*'s production editor, Jo Isotta, however, he found it hard to fit in at *NME*, partly because of his *Melody Maker* past.

'One day the publisher descended with an announcement about the new editor,' remembers Mat Snow. 'Ian Pye wasn't very highly regarded, if he was thought of at all. His nickname was the Invisible Man. So not only was he a *Melody Maker* man but he wasn't a very highly regarded *Melody Maker* man. Ian didn't have a clue about what we should be doing. But Stuart did and he was really forthright about it in meetings.'

'Ian was very earnest but never mucked in,' says Terry Staunton, a former local newspaper journalist who joined the *NME* staff as news editor in 1986. 'He would rarely join people in the pub. We used to go to the Falkland Arms, which of course Stuart Cosgrove used to refer to as the Malvinas.'

Pye inherited a fractious, dissatisfied paper, riven with in-fighting and losing readers rapidly. In 1980, *NME* had sold well over 200,000 copies a week. By the second part of 1985, this number had almost halved.

At Carnaby Street the office was split into two opposing camps. On the one hand there was the fans of the kind of British indie that was to be typified by the groups included on Roy Carr's belated follow-up to his Rough Trade cassette, C86. Gathering together 22 tracks from established indies like Rough Trade, Cherry Red and Alan McGee's Creation, there was also room for some more homespun concerns: four of the bands on the cassette[160] were signed to Ron Johnson Records, run by a part-time biscuit factory worker from his bedroom in the Derbyshire town of Long Eaton. Specialising in a particular kind of Beefheart-inspired agit-punk that combined unconventional time signatures with art-school japery, Ron Johnson later had modest success with a single by Dutch experimental anarcho-punks the Ex which sold 15,000 copies – although the celebrations in Long Eaton were swiftly curtailed when it was realised that the single was so expensive to manufacture that each copy sold actually cost the label money.[161]

The Ex weren't included on C86, but the cassette and the week of promotional gigs at the ICA featuring some of the acts on the compilation was a much less varied stylistic proposition than C81 had been. Featuring many of the groups who'd performed at Alan McGee's Living Room club, C86 soon became shorthand for a particular strand of indie music: befringed and fey, this was a movement with its intellectual roots in punk that took musical inspiration from the janglier end of 1960s psychedelic pop like The Byrds but omitted any of the kind of musical dexterity or imagination.

The C86 bands stood in stark contrast to the kind of music that

Stuart Cosgrove and Paolo Hewitt wanted to write about. 'Rock music was dead in the '80s,' says Hewitt. 'There were just no good bands. There were some great singles by people like The Colourfield or The La's, but the best music of the decade was coming out of the clubs. People weren't doing that punk thing of getting together in a little garage and wearing leather jackets any more. They were meeting on dance floors. And while rock music was on its arse it was a golden age for black music – the '80s was the decade that produced hip-hop and house, two of the most important musical forms of the century.'

Championing American rap and soul music alongside the early house and techno records from Chicago and Detroit, Stuart Cosgrove and Paolo Hewitt knew they'd seen the future. Meanwhile Danny Kelly, Adrian Thrills and their coterie thought that the currency of *NME* had always been the four-piece white rock band. In one corner: urbane, modern-sounding, danceable and new electronic music. In the other: men in polka-dot shirts and anoraks playing anaemic '60s pastiches. 'Stuart and Paolo thought that the paper should cover anything that was black,' says Hoskyns. 'Then there was the Danny Kelly faction who said that the *NME* was about the white underground, that indie was the bedrock and that the readers didn't really want to know about Run DMC. It was Def Jam records versus C86 and there was no attempt made to blend both and make it all work. So you'd have hip-hop on one page and indie bands on the next and Ian Pye just seemed dazed by the whole thing.'

'Stuart Cosgrove is a human dynamo,' says Hewitt. 'He was in charge of the paper, not Ian. To all intents and purposes Stuart was the editor. Ian would come in to editorial meetings and say "Right, I don't want any arguments, next week we've got Billy Bragg on the cover of the *NME*". And within half an hour Stuart had talked him round and we'd have Schooly D.'

The mid-'80s was a buoyant time for the British music industry. Although vinyl LP sales declined, profits were bolstered by a new format: the compact disc had reached Britain in March 1983.[162] In the indie sector, the concurrent rise of jangly guitar bands and hip-hop meant that sales of vinyl singles rose as the major labels abandoned vinyl to C86 kids and dance heads in favour of CDs. 'I was in love with the idea of indieness because actually Northern Soul was about indie culture. All of those great soul singles were released on indie labels,' says Stuart Cosgrove. 'What I should've done at *NME* was turn around and say that, actually, these wars between indie music and black music are meaningless because the real thing is that they all come from indie cultures. Def Jam was a small indie label. So was Creation. That idea of indieness was what *NME* should've owned. Instead we came into conflict with the people who believed that *NME* should only be writing about white rock music.'

As house music began to arrive in the British charts, the voices clamouring for its inclusion in the pages of the *NME* grew louder. In August 1986, Farley 'Jackmaster' Funk & Jessie Saunders' Chicago house classic 'Love Can't Turn Around' entered the UK Top Ten, courtesy of an extraordinary vocal from flamboyant singer Daryl Pandy whose six octave range was almost overshadowed by an appearance on *Top of the Pops* in which he threw his shoes into the bewildered audience. House had arrived as a legitimate commercial force at the same time as indie music remained an underground concern. Taunted by his house-loving colleagues at the fact that a former Creation act, The Weather Prophets, were unable to achieve chart success despite the backing of a new label, Elevation, a subsidiary of WEA, Danny Kelly sneaked into the office one night after everyone else had left and doctored the *NME* charts, removing the dance record sitting at number 49 and replacing it with The Weather Prophets' single 'She Comes from the Rain'.[163]

Daryl Pandy's barnstorming *Top of the Pops* appearance aside, the house scene was lacking in many newsworthy cover stars. Meanwhile, Alan McGee was phoning the office every week with more and more outrageous Jesus and Mary Chain stories, of drugs busts at customs, backstage fighting. Violence seemed to follow the Mary Chain everywhere: at a gig at the ICA in December 1984, the band were pelted with bottles, leading the *Sun* to anoint them 'the new Sex Pistols'. In April 1985 Jim Reid from the band was beaten up at a Nick Cave and the Bad Seeds gig at Brixton Academy, only a few weeks after a performance at North London Polytechnic[164] had ended in riotous scenes. When they signed to Blanco Y Negro, the rumour doing the rounds in the music business, undoubtedly originated by McGee, was that the Reid brothers had stolen money from Warner Music UK's chairman Rob Dickins' jacket and trashed his office. Dickins was a respected music industry figure who was married to one of *Top of the Pops'* dance troupe Pan's People and joined WEA from Warner Brothers' music publishing arm in 1979. Rob came from a music business dynasty: his father Percy had been Maurice Kinn's right-hand man on the *NME*.

Next to the outrage that followed the Mary Chain, the house scene lacked recognisable stars. 'Ian Pye was just never as strong enough a personality to make sense of it all,' says Terry Staunton. 'These Chicago house acts were usually fairly anonymous-looking guys who'd only made one good record. If you put them on the cover of *NME* it just wouldn't sell because people would see it on the racks in WH Smith and not be able to recognise who was on the front cover. The indie kids suffered from the same problem: no one knew who any of these little shambling bands were.'

1986 had been a weird year as far as *NME* cover stars were concerned: as well as an iconic Morrissey cover which confirmed his new status by lacking any coverlines, there was the Jesus and Mary Chain, a Red Wedge special, and appearances from mainstays like Keith Richards and John Lydon. But there were some slightly more unlikely cover stars. The page three girl Samantha Fox was one. Cilla Black another. The moustachioed Olympic decathlete Daley Thompson and the boxer Barry McGuigan alternated covers with The Shop Assistants and Run DMC.

'We were trying to be a paper that was more than just about music but about youth interest,' explains Mat Snow. 'So you end up with strange things like interviews with Daley Thompson on the front cover. Meanwhile the hip-hop wars raged. But let's face it, you can write about hip-hop all you like but the hardcore *NME* reader was still only interested in The Smiths.'

Under the influence of Stuart Cosgrove, the scope and range of the *NME* grew until music was only one component part of an editorial plan that could include sport, films, clubs, drugs – anything that the paper's readers might be interested in or aware of, even tangentially. It was a forward-thinking idea and one that is common in lads' magazines in the 21st century. In 1986, it was close to commercial suicide. *NME*'s publishers began to get concerned: in February 1986 they recalled the paper from their Carnaby Street outpost and installed them in a cramped office in IPC Magazines' building Commonwealth House.

IPC felt that the *NME* staff were becoming unruly, increasingly difficult to control and diverging from *NME*'s core role: to report about rock music. They were also wary of some of the campaigns that *NME* had recently taken up arms for: first Red Wedge, then the anti-apartheid movement.

On 17 July 1983, the day before Nelson Mandela's 65th birthday, Britain's first major anti-apartheid concert, Africa Sounds, took place at London's Alexandra Palace. In the audience watching Hugh Masekela, The Orchestre Jazira and musicians from across Africa was former Specials founder Jerry Dammers. Dammers was inspired to write a song, 'Free Nelson Mandela', in tribute to the ANC leader, then incarcerated in Pollsmoor Prison after being convicted of conspiring to destroy South African gas and waterworks. Dammers also formed the pressure group Artists Against Apartheid in the spring of 1986.[165] A sympathetic pro-ANC line at *NME* was a potentially dangerous one at a time when the

ANC was still classed as a terrorist organisation by the British Government. 'There was a lot of ill-feeling in the office when people like Paul Simon decided to play in Sun City,' says Stuart Cosgrove, 'and the *NME* was sold in South Africa, which was a matter of some moral repugnance among the staff. IPC's owners, Reed International, had holdings in South Africa, which we considered to be against the ANC's strategy to isolate South Africa from the rest of the world until apartheid was lifted. Through our trades union we established the right of *NME* writers to determine where pieces that they'd written were syndicated to and we made sure that nothing we'd written was ever republished in magazines in South Africa.'

Although *NME*'s South African sales were minimal,[166] the constant lobbying for black American soul and rap artists on the cover meant that the magazine would not be stocked in the country. More generally, IPC were aghast at the way that the paper was becoming what they saw as an increasingly belligerent force.

Meanwhile in the UK the powerful retailer WH Smith, whose shops had been ubiquitous across Britain since a period of expansion in the 1970s and who branched out into music by buying a controlling stake in music retail chain Our Price in 1986, were growing increasingly wary of another *NME* campaign. 'Violence, violence & more VIOLENCE' boasted the coverline on the *NME* issue dated 4 October 1986, above a photograph of a paunchy long-haired man in lurid blue spandex trousers and a fringed buckskin jacket. 'THIS MAN IS SICK!' The man was Blackie Lawless[167] the singer with W.A.S.P. Part of the *Kerrang!*-friendly LA glam metal scene typified by Mötley Crüe, W.A.S.P.'s frontman had been in bands with New York Dolls bassist Arthur 'Killer' Kane and was a childhood friend of Kiss' Ace Frehley, before forming the band Sister in the mid-'70s. Playing underneath a pentagram logo, Sister's gigs would culminate with Lawless setting his boots on fire and eating live worms. Not content with this, Lawless' next band would up the stakes: the highlight of W.A.S.P's live show – which included songs called things like 'Animal (Fuck Like a Beast)' – was a butcher's meat grinder, into which Lawless would tip live rats and pull out hamburger meat, which he would then proceed to throw into the audience. In Reagan's America this kind of behaviour was bound to get you noticed and W.A.S.P's debut album came with a dubious honour: it was the first record in history to have a prominent black and white Parental Advisory logo on the sleeve warning of explicit content. Dubbed the 'Tipper Sticker', the logo was the work of the Parents Music Resource Centre, led by Tipper Gore, wife of Democrat Senator Al Gore.

For the cultural theorist Stuart Cosgrove the story of W.A.S.P. and the PMRC was a media studies piece. 'We analysed what was really going on behind the scenes in the PMRC,' he says. 'The PMRC had been targeting parents, frightening them about the rise of hardcore punk and rap, telling them that their kids would commit suicide if they listened to noise rock – very crude mechanistic stuff. So they decided if they classified the music parents would be able to control what their kids listen to.'

Cosgrove was joined on the story by one of the paper's freelancers and most enduring characters. Like the Sex Pistols before him, Steven Wells wasn't really interested in music. What he was interested in was stirring up as much trouble as possible, about the weekly execution of sacred cows, about getting under the skin of the small-minded and terminally hip. A world-class, championship-level ranter and irritant, Swells, as he became known, started out as a fanzine editor, filling the pages of *Molotov Comics* with pieces on post-punk bands, politics and poetry. As a poet he was invited to support The Jam at Hammersmith Odeon, before sneaking into the pages of the *NME* under an alter ego, that of surrealist female rock writer Susan Williams. Once they found out that they'd been duped, the *NME* kept Wells on to write more about left-leaning bands like The Redskins and Chumbawumba. A fearsome, stroppy presence, Swells believed that the 'Golden Age of British Pop Music'[168] was between 1977 and 1980, 'when punk was pop music'. 'There is a sound where pop meets chaos and rides its fury and when I hear it I fall in love,' he wrote.[169] 'The first time was Paul McCartney, his carcass jerking on some sick speed, screaming himself senseless on "Helter Skelter", the second "Holiday in Cambodia", the third The Beatles' *Live at the Hollywood Bowl*, where pure girly pop is pierced through with a million screams so shrill that you smell the stink of urine, lust and madness.'

Swells wasn't interested in palling around with bands or documenting scenes for posterity. He used *NME* as a platform to take bands to task on behalf of the readers and sometimes the other way around. Infuriating and belligerent and prone to overuse capital letters, he extolled militant socialism, anti-censorship, anti-corporate rock, writing with an intensity that had never been matched. 'If I can leave rock journalism extolling the same virtues of passion, anger, shit-stirring and politicisation that dragged me into it in the first place,' Swells wrote, 'then I'm happy.'[170]

'Swells was a complete and unadulterated maddy,' says Cosgrove, 'but totally brilliant. A complete hoot. For him the story about W.A.S.P. was about the suppression of extreme punk music and censorship. Swells discovered this band from America called Dumping Buckets of Phlegm

Over Bitchy Old Ladies.[171] From the name alone you knew they'd be Swells' favourite group, especially if they were shit.

'The PMRC story was the kind of campaign that only *NME* could own. It allowed us to communicate to alternative Britain. Most of the guys who worked at the paper were from small towns. They were the bright guys at school who were involved in the local music scene and ran fanzines and read *NME* to stay ahead of the curve. And that was *NME*'s heartland: although it was read in the cities, the real strongholds were in small towns.'

Whether alternative Britain was quite as interested in Barry McGuigan and Blackie Lawless as the staff of the *NME* is a matter for debate, but the fact is that the IPC top brass were beginning to worry. If the paper had combined a lack of any clear sense of direction with a predilection for upsetting the most important retail outlets in the country but still been selling, IPC wouldn't have minded. As it was the readership continued to dwindle throughout 1986. Sent to interview the Birmingham-based indie band Felt for a cover in November, Danny Kelly returned to find that the space allocated to him on the front cover for his feature had been given over to a piece examining the causes and circumstances surrounding teenage suicide written by Lucy O'Brien. It was an intelligent and bold piece of writing housed in a brave monochrome cover. It was also the worst-selling issue of *NME* in the magazine's history.

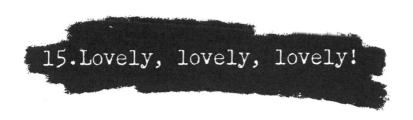

15. Lovely, lovely, lovely!

'They thought that things like house or hip-hop were a three-week fad and everything would soon go back to The Smiths...'

In early 1987 some strange graffiti started to appear on walls and doorways around the *NME* office. Emerging from the office after working late one night, the paper's editor was astonished to see a message of a strikingly violent and personal tone written in capital letters on the side of a building opposite *NME* HQ. 'IAN PYE,' it read, 'MUST DIE'.

At the end of 1986, Pye had made some staff changes in an attempt to modernise the paper and stem the decline in its fortunes. One victim of this reshuffle was *NME*'s long-standing reggae correspondent and sub-editor, Penny Reel. 'Penny Reel was a really nice bloke from Stamford Hill,' says Roy Carr, 'quiet, loved reggae music, stoned a lot.' But the mild-mannered Reel hadn't taken news of his redundancy well. He embarked on a campaign of graffiti and pamphleteering which ended in Pye contacting the police to tell them that his life was being threatened. As far as IPC were concerned the unfortunate incident was just another example of why Ian Pye had to go.

'Ian was on a hiding to nothing,' says Andy McDuff. '*NME* had lost its direction. The punk bubble had burst a long time beforehand and there was a total musical vacuum. Plus you had the success of *The Face* and the glossy magazines, which meant that competition was stronger for readers, but also for good journalists.'

While *NME* was offering 40 pages of black and white newsprint wrapped inside a colour cover, a brand new music magazine was launched in October 1986 by EMAP following the success of *Smash Hits*. *Q* had no place for ink that came off on the readers' fingers or factionalist arguments about music genres: instead it catered for the kind of music fan who'd stopped reading *NME* in the 1970s but was rebuying all of their old vinyl LPs on CD. *Q*'s founding editor was Mark Ellen, who had moved on to edit *Smash Hits*, but recruited his old *NME* colleague Paul DuNoyer to work on the launch of the new monthly glossy. '*Q* had a very retro identity,' says Barney Hoskyns, 'and that was 'everything that you lot at the *NME* have been saying is uncool and crappy we're going to bring back. We're going to make these old dinosaurs acceptable again. We still really love Paul McCartney and Led Zeppelin'. *NME* was so confused and schizoid and unhealthy and *Q* capitalised on that. It wasn't about the style wars. There were no agendas or manifestos. It didn't take things too seriously. And they left *NME* reeling.'

Q jettisoned the ideological jousting of *NME* in favour of a rigid house style which left most of the writing anonymous. 'I was very anti the *NME* when I was at *Q*,' says Mark Ellen. 'The first thing we did was take the journalist out of the piece. The degree to which you were allowed to insert yourself in the piece by then was ludicrous: so you have Paul Morley's 9,000-word piece on Devo where the first 5,000 words are him in the cab on the way to the interview worrying about his sexuality or the state of the world. At *Q* you were banned from using the word I: there was an on the spot £10 cash fine if you handed in a piece written in the first person.'

'At *Q* we devised a style of writing which owed more to P.G. Wodehouse than Lester Bangs,' says Paul DuNoyer. 'We threw out the ideological purity which held that only certain kinds of acts were right for us in favour of the view that everybody's interesting if you can tell their story properly and being old or successful is not a crime in itself, but neither is being young and poor. We tried to go to the opposite extreme of the *NME*'s highly idiosyncratic and individual style. Our feeling was that the majority of potential readers out there had little or no interest in individual rock writers. We felt that era had gone, for better or for worse and had passed into history.'

Somewhat ironically, however, *Q* did provide a place of refuge for some of the *NME*'s old stagers: Charles Shaar Murray was invited to contribute to the magazine from its first issue. Funny but slightly tweedy, *Q* was an instant hit. EMAP's predictions for the success of the new magazine were conservative: they weren't sure if advertisers were ready to commit to a monthly music title. But the profile of the readership – middle-aged and affluent with plenty of disposable cash – proved irresistible.

'We always thought that *Q* would be a sort of monthly colour supplement to the music press,' says DuNoyer. 'We never imagined that it would come to supplant the music weeklies which had been there for all of our lives.'

In the first half of 1987 the sales of *NME* fell below 100,000 for the first time in 31 years. In June, two weeks before the national General Election, the paper's staff had a crisis meeting, although it was not about the decline in readership. Instead the hardcore Red Wedge supporters in the office were lobbying for the next week's cover star: Neil Kinnock, who eventually made his second appearance on the front of the paper under the coverline 'Lovely, Lovely, Lovely!' in an issue that also featured an interview with Ken Livingstone, then standing for election as the Labour MP for the London borough of Brent East.

Unlike Thatcher, who confided in *Smash Hits* that her favourite record was 'How Much Is That Doggy in The Window?',[172] Kinnock had an understanding of rock'n'roll – he'd been a teenage member of the Gene Vincent fanclub – but the *NME* aside, in 1987 the media united against him and the Labour Party in a manner that would not be reversed until the middle 1990s. Despite the significant influence of future New Labour mainstays Peter Mandelson and Philip Gould on the campaign and the efforts of Red Wedge, Thatcher's Conservative Party won the election. Kinnock was a natural performer, but his espousal of multilateral disarmament and pro-Europeanism failed to win back former Labour voters, particularly in the South. But a seed had been sown which would later result in the party's electoral success in the 1990s. 'Peter Mandelson had the office next door to Red Wedge at Labour Party headquarters,' says Billy Bragg, 'and I think that it showed him that the success of the Labour Party would rely on breaking it out of formal meetings and conferences.'

Nevertheless *NME* had backed the loser and IPC were apoplectic at this latest display of political partisanship. 'The Neil Kinnock [cover] was a totally misguided thing to do,' says Andy McDuff. 'Apart from anything else they backed a horse that didn't win. And a lot of the readers found it absurd.'

When the dust settled and the votes were counted, the Conservative Party was returned with a comfortable majority. IPC took stock and called for Ian Pye. He was sacked the week afterwards. For his replacement they needed a safe pair of hands, someone who could start rebuilding the *NME*'s sales, unite the office and ditch the politics. The magazine's publishers searched internally and alighted on someone who had a proven record as a successful music magazine editor, Alan Lewis.

'In '87 I'd been out of music journalism for a while,' Lewis says. 'I'd had a midlife crisis of sorts and after the success of *Sounds* and *Kerrang!* I went and bought a country pub and ran that for a couple of years.' Dissatisfied with life in the countryside, Lewis returned to journalism as the editor of IPC's hugely successful *Smash Hits* copy *Number One*. As far as IPC were concerned, Lewis had the kind of steady hand they wanted on *NME*'s tiller. 'There was an extremely abrasive MD at that time who wanted to tackle the magazine,' he says, 'partly because he regarded the stroppy editorial team as something of a thorn in IPC's side.

'My plan was no more complicated than getting it back to being a weekly music newspaper. At that time *NME* had a very cool image and a lot of clever people working there, many of whom were embarrassed to be there. They wanted to be working at *The Face* and they were trying to change *NME* by mixing up music with fashion and culture but I felt it had drifted away from what people wanted from a regular weekly paper – not least of which was news but also a sense of fun and a knockabout sense of humour.'

The staff of *NME* didn't react well to the news of Lewis' appointment. Always dismissive of *Sounds*, for them he was a crude populist who'd been brought in to be a hatchet man and turn the paper into a lightweight rock rag that was only ever about music. A petition was organised expressing no confidence in the *NME*'s new editor. It was signed by every staff member and most of the paper's freelancers and delivered to Andy McDuff and IPC's managing director. The atmosphere at Lewis' first editorial meeting was accordingly tense. 'It was a total bear garden,' he says. 'Some of the people turned up with their own agendas and were just prepared to knock down whatever ideas I had. Others like Steven Wells were just very prickly characters.

'It was a very intimidating atmosphere in the office. There was this big reporters' room, then the subs-room where the writers weren't encouraged to go and the art room where no one at all was allowed in. The art editor at the time was a guy called Joe Ewart, a very talented guy, but I don't think he even read *NME*. He listened to classical music on Radio 3 all day. Even the editor was encouraged not to enter the art room. It was a real contrast to the days at *Sounds* where we were just a big gang.'

Things came to a head in September 1987, after Lewis had been the editor for three months. He was away on a late summer holiday with his young family, leaving Stuart Cosgrove as de facto editor responsible for putting together the week's issue, set to be a themed special on censorship in rock. The centrepiece of the issue was an article on the controversy surrounding the Californian punk band Dead Kennedys' 1985 album

Frankenchrist, original copies of which had come with a poster insert reproducing the Swiss surrealist painter H.R. Giger's 1973 work *Work 219: Landscape XX*. Also known as the 'Penis Landscape', the painting depicted a series of ten erect members, each penetrating a vagina. For the Dead Kennedys the poster resulted in a notorious obscenity trial that drove them to the brink of bankruptcy. At *NME* the reproduction of the image, sanctioned by Alan Lewis, would've gone unnoticed were it not for complaints from staff at the colour reproduction laboratory where *NME* was produced. It was the perfect opportunity for the management to get rid of those staff members that they'd identified as troublemakers, principally Stuart Cosgrove and Joe Ewart.

'The management at IPC would normally have shrugged it off but they identified the problems with the *NME* with this kind of behaviour and ramped it up into a cause célèbre,' says Lewis. 'Stuart and Joe were held responsible and left soon afterwards.'

Cosgrove and Ewart were paid to leave. In their wake a group of freelancers left voluntarily in protest at what they saw as the pair's unfair treatment, leaving a desperate Alan Lewis to promote long-forgotten indie-pop types The Motorcycle Boy to the front cover of the paper in the absence of any other suitable material.

'Alan was given the job of getting rid of a few troublemakers, of which I was one,' says Stuart Cosgrove. 'I wrote well, I wrote fast, I wrote a lot, I got things done and I was able to articulate the *NME* message clearly but I was seen as being so linked to black music and the anti-apartheid movement that I was scaring the core readers away.'

By the time of his departure, Stuart Cosgrove had proved himself to be a more than capable magazine section editor. Frustrated by the fact that he hadn't been appointed as Ian Pye's successor, the pages that he edited had become almost like a separate magazine: the Media section of *NME* came with the banner 'Hosted by Stuart Cosgrove', often looked totally different to the rest of the paper and allowed him a showcase to explore his own interests: pieces on sport, art, politics and Northern Soul music sat alongside long features on body building, the AIDS crisis or the American military presence in Europe.

'When I left the publisher said to me "All that stuff with South Africa didn't help", but we were supposed to be serving a readership that was in decline while the world was just whizzing past,' Cosgrove says. '*The Face* was the magazine of the decade and *NME* was caught in a vortex of change. The average *NME* reader was interested in pop culture: music, cinema, politics, things like the PMRC. But the publishers wanted it to be a paper that just reviewed music. And they missed so much: the rise of the superstar DJ, the rave scene and the replacement of the gig with the club as the main cultural event. They thought that things like house or hip-hop were a three-week fad and everything would soon go back to The Smiths.'

The Smiths themselves were in trouble by the middle of 1987. In an issue featuring the Scottish pop duo Hue and Cry on the front cover, Danny Kelly had unwittingly caused the band's demise with a piece revealing that guitarist Johnny Marr had left the band. Incensed, both Marr and Morrissey believed that the piece was a plant by the other to discredit them. The week after, it became official when Rough Trade records announced that Marr was being replaced in the group. While it was inevitable that the band would split, to Kelly's chagrin it very much looked like he had caused the rift inside the paper's biggest band to become insurmountable.

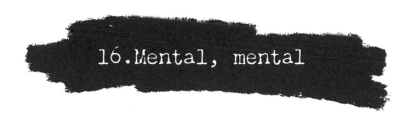

16.Mental, mental

'The people who were writing about house music were viewed as a bit
weird and more interested in the drugs than the music...'

In the spring of 1988, IPC drew *NME* further towards the munificent
corporate bosom, moving the magazine's operations back to the 25th
floor of King's Reach Tower in an office situated in between football title
Shoot and the teenage girls' magazine *Mizz*. Upstairs on the 26th floor,
meanwhile, old rivals *Melody Maker* had been brought back from their
pre-fab gulag. Unlike in 1976, however, there was little resistance to the
move from the *NME*'s staff, not least because after the departure of
Cosgrove and many of the paper's writers, the *NME* didn't really have
much of a staff left to complain about things.

Since the late 1970s, the Thames bankside near Blackfriars Bridge
had been transformed from a derelict post-industrial wasteland into one
of the capital's foremost leisure zones, comprising a mixed-use
development of shops, galleries and housing typified by the old OXO
tower, a former cold meat store rebuilt in the Art Deco period and again
in the late 1980s under the aegis of the Coin Street Community trust.

'Yes, we were being reeled back in by the corporate paymasters,'
says Andrew Collins, who started at *NME* as a designer shortly before
the move, 'but we didn't really mind; we had a bigger office, great views
and computers.'

Alan Lewis used the transition to start to commence rebuilding his
team and fill some of the noticeable white space in the paper's staff list.
Danny Kelly, Paolo Hewitt and Steven Wells remained from the *ancien
regime* and Lewis promoted a C86 fan called Helen Mead to Live editor.
The previous incumbent, a bespectacled 21-year-old former fanzine
writer from Leeds called James Brown, was elevated to the features desk,

causing consternation among some of the older staffers due to his extreme youth and opinionated nature.

'I'd never had a job before I worked at *NME*,' Brown says. 'I'd been a milkman for a while and had a newspaper round when I was at school and that was it. I went from being at school to being on the dole to deciding what was on the front cover of the *NME* every week. I never went to university – I went to Russia with Pop Will Eat Itself instead.'

Brown had come to *NME* from *Sounds* after using a £40 a week government Enterprise Allowance grant to produce a 'zine called *Attack on Bzag!* that covered the politicised Yorkshire indie scene. He duly recruited other fanzine writers in an attempt to change the musical course of the magazine. 'I remember before I started writing for *NME* I'd buy it and just think : "I could do so much better than this". They used to write about the Right to Work marches or CND or pirate radio or have two pages on Carl Lewis and it was a very intelligent and open magazine. But it seemed like a real establishment paper and they didn't know what was going on in the way that me and my mates from the underground press did. A lot of the writers at *NME* when I joined were there because they were friends of people,' he says. 'They didn't have that fan-led appreciation of music and were closer to the record companies.'

Pop Will Eat Itself were emblematic of the kind of band Brown was interested in. A deeply unglamorous act from the Black Country, the group had started out as a breezy indie pop band before discovering hip-hop, investing in a drum machine and producing sampling-heavy rock music distinguished by a kind of rugby club humour and predilection for wearing shorts. Their presence in the *NME* was calculated to unilaterally annoy the paper's serious-minded indie kids and right-on soulboys. But with their love of Def Jam records and sampling culture, the band were also an example of the kind of white rock act for whom debates about the validity of guitars versus turntables were totally irrelevant.

Brown also brought in Bob Stanley and Barbara Ellen from the fanzine circuit, while Helen Mead's boyfriend Steve Lamacq was sports editor on the *Harlow Gazette* who had sold his fanzine, *A Pack Of Lies*, alongside Brown's *Attack on Bzag!* at a GLC-sponsored fanzine fair in London's Brockwell Park. Lewis recruited Lamacq as a sub-editor. From Skelmersdale in Lancashire a sociology lecturer called Stuart Maconie who'd been sending in reviews under the outré pen-name Howlin' Studs Maconies was hired to write features. Slowly a new era was coming into focus.

'Alan Lewis was a lovely bloke,' says Andrew Collins. 'This wry bearded chap who'd been a pub landlord and you could still imagine pulling a pint. James Brown was this whirling dervish, a little boy really. But the feeling was "We've got to save the *NME*". We've got to stop it going down the toilet. The paper was on its knees and could've been closed down because nobody was buying it.'

Like Alan Smith 25 years earlier, Lewis inherited a magazine that had lost its way and was losing readers. He banished politics and put commercial concerns back at the centre of the paper's operations.

'When I worked there I couldn't help look back at the *NME*'s I'd read when I was a teenager and think what a fun time they must've had in the '70s,' says Andrew Collins. 'It was indulgent and it was pretentious and verbose but looking back it was like being dropped into another world. As an art student I loved the way it looked – great chunks of white space everywhere, a real level of artistry. But we were living in a more commercially minded time and had to abandon the indulgence of the early '80s and jolly it up a little bit.'

'The paper's journalism had lost its way,' says Terry Staunton. 'It was all run by record company schedules. So Alan Lewis reintroduced the idea of the front cover story rather than just the front cover artist.'

'Alan had a commercial instinct,' says Andrew Collins. 'One week there was a review of a biography of Kate Bush and Alan went into the photo archive and found this portrait of her by Gered Mankovitz and blew it up and cropped it so that it basically showed off her nipples poking through this leotard she was wearing. This was his instinct. We felt that was a little bit crude and obvious but that was how he'd think.'

Lewis also had a clear view on what the musical direction of the paper should be. Dance music was out. The bedrock of the paper's coverage had always been the four-piece guitar rock band, and that was where it would return. Not everyone at *NME* felt quite the same way.

In the early autumn of 1987, a group of bedraggled punters appeared on London's uptight, dressy West End club scene like lost explorers emerging from the jungle depths. Wild-eyed, with long sun-bleached hair and boots still dusty with sand from Mediterranean beaches, all they could talk about when anyone asked was what they'd seen in Spain.

Founded as a port by Phoenician traders, Ibiza's name was a derivation of that of the Egyptian god of dance, Bes, and the island accordingly had a 200-year history of partying. In the '60s and '70s it'd been a magnet for the hippy aristocracy – Pink Floyd wrote songs about it,[173] while Hendrix, Dylan and Roman Polanski all holidayed there – many of whom stayed on into the 1980s, opening hotels or nightclubs. One of these was Amnesia, an open-air space where DJ Antonio Escohotado mixed together the latest American house records with, curiously, Rough Trade C86-ers The Woodentops, Chris Rea and U2's 'I Still Haven't Found What I'm Looking For'.[174]

As the suntanned British clubbers, beach bums and DJs began to filter back to rain-soaked London they decided to bring a bit of Balearic spirit to the city. The clubs that they started – Shoom, Spectrum and, later, The Trip – were a self-conscious throwback to the high hippy era, employing poster graphics and fluid lettering inspired by the psychedelic art of London and San Francisco. Even the terminology was an echo of the past: when *IT* promoted their first issue launch party at the Roundhouse in October 1966 it was billed as an 'all-night rave', while Spectrum's logo was a facsimile of the Grateful Dead's famous winged eyeball designed by artist Rick Griffin in 1968. The music that these clubs played wasn't all about peace and love, however. In October 1987, one-hit wonders M/A/R/R/S, featuring sometime *NME* writer and DJ Dave Dorrell, released a single which took the Chicago House template and made it rougher and more frenetic: 'Pump Up the Volume' was the first British number one to contain samples, an edgy amalgam of electronic funk, hip-hop scratching and house that was released on indie label 4AD, hitherto famous for their atmospheric guitar rock.

The success of M/A/R/R/S and the acts that followed took the music industry completely by surprise. Certainly no one on the *NME* was paying much attention to acid house, apart from the dedicated clubber Paolo Hewitt, who was joining 2,000 other ravers on Monday nights at Paul Oakenfold and Ian St. Paul's acid house club Spectrum, which opened in April 1988 at Heaven, a gay club underneath Charing Cross station.

Despite Alan Lewis' attempts to make the editorial policy of the *NME* more inclusive and democratic, he was resistant to covering acid house, mainly because he'd learned the lessons of the previous era and was conscious that the scene didn't have the stars necessary to sell magazines. Helen Mead and Jack Barron were converts to the new music, but they were still in a minority. 'Everybody knew what was going on in the clubs except for the people on my neighbouring desks at *NME*,' says Mead. 'Taxi drivers, the girls I'd buy my sandwiches from at lunchtime. But the people that I worked with were totally dismissive. They just did not get it. And there was no attempt to try and get it.'

'Alan had been a *Melody Maker* journalist and had great success with *Sounds*,' says James Brown, 'and he knew that the editorial focus of *NME* under Ian Pye had got too far from home. Alan's formula was simple: if anything went in the charts we'd cover it. We ended up with stuff like T'Pau on the front cover.'

As acid house hit the charts, Lewis had no option but write about what was rapidly becoming a seismic youth culture of its own. Jack Barron was dispatched to The Trip at rock venue and former cinema the Astoria on Charing Cross Road near Denmark Street. As the night ended and clubbers spilled out onto the streets, he described scenes oddly familiar to anyone who'd read the *NME* in 1956. 'A car which is blaring out acid house from a radio has been surrounded by 20 people, who have emerged, sweating and delirious from The Trip,' he wrote. 'Some of the revellers are climbing on to the car roof while others are dancing… in the middle of the road, completely unaware that they are causing a massive traffic jam all the way down the street.'[175]

When the *Sun* jumped on the acid house bandwagon, first by giving away free smiley t-shirts, then within a month condemning the scene, advertising 'Say No to Drugs' badges featuring a *Sun*-branded smiley looking constipated,[176] *NME* had to take notice. Lewis was a shrewd editor who knew that a narrative was developing around acid house that had been played out in the pages of *NME* before – that of tabloid opprobrium versus wild and untamed youth. *NME* had to be involved.

'Alan Lewis had been looking to all these indie guys to save the *NME*,' says Paolo Hewitt. 'I was just Disco Paolo. That's what they called me. "That's Paolo, he goes to *nightclubs*". I didn't care. I was off my tits at the Astoria. But when the Sun did their front cover, Alan Lewis called me in to his office and said "What's this?" and I said "It's what I've been telling you about for the last six month". He hated that because he suddenly realised that Disco Paolo was onto something.'

In July 1988 *NME* contributor Richard Norris appeared on the magazine's first acid house issue. Then, following a summer in which police cracked down on illegal raves nationwide,[177] art editor Justin Langlands posed for a photograph wearing a plastic policeman's helmet and tearing up a picture of a smiley under the headline 'ACID CRACKDOWN'. Suddenly acid house had become outlaw music. 'I DJ in Brighton every Thursday night,' Paul Oakenfold told Hewitt, 'and there have been big things in the local paper. One article said "If your kid is wearing a t-shirt with a smiley face on it, take him straight to the doctor's, he's probably on drugs".'

While the *Sun*'s anti-acid house campaign had been remarkably literal-minded, blaming LSD for the wild scenes that their reporters 'witnessed' at outdoor raves ('school-age children rolled their own

reefers... youngsters screamed "Mental, mental" as lasers lit the sky...'[178]),
a different drug was becoming more common in the *NME* office. In 1981
Ian Penman had been sent to New York to interview David Byrne of
Talking Heads. Meeting a girl in a club, she took him back to her
apartment where she produced a bag of small pharmaceutical capsules.
She kept her stash of ecstasy in the fridge.

First patented by Merck pharmaceutical company in Darmstadt,
Germany, as an attempt to synthesise a new blood clotting drug, by the
1970s MDMA was being used recreationally by middle-class academics
and former hippies as a kind of New Age therapeutic tool.[179] But the
synthesis of ecstasy in industrial scales in the 1980s meant that it became
first a gay party drug, then a kind of yuppie psychedelic, and finally the
drug of choice for the acid house ravers. 'I was on my way to see The
Wedding Present with Alan McGee,' says Helen Mead, 'and Hannah,
Creation's cleaning lady, was there. She was 17 at the time and on the
way to the gig she gave me half an E. She basically single-handedly turned
everybody on to ecstasy.'

Hannah, whose boyfriend was a nervous little man from Manchester
called Noel Gallagher, worked at Creation, where the label was
undergoing something of an ecstasy-fuelled revelation as Alan McGee
and his press officer Jeff Barratt started hosting acid house office parties
at their HQ in Westgate street in Hackney.

'Terry McQuaide managed Flowered Up and was the guy who sorted
out all of the drugs at Creation,' says Mead. 'He would come up to the
NME office with pills until it got to the point where he had to be told
that it wasn't really the done thing to be wandering around the 25th floor
selling ecstasy.'

Not everyone at *NME* indulged. 'I remember Jeff Barratt taking Steve
Lamacq to the Hacienda club,' says Mead, 'and he just had the worst
night of his life. He absolutely hated it.'

'There was a huge dance versus guitars split in the office,' says
Lamacq. 'We'd write things like "Who wants to stand in a field at a rave
miles from anywhere when you can be at a gig with a roof?" '

'The people who were writing about house music were viewed as a bit
weird and more interested in the drugs than the music,' says Jack Barron.
'I used to dole out ecstasy in the office and make my money off it. I saw
it as giving people a sort of spiritual experience. And over the course of a
year more and more people in the music business started getting involved
– so press officers and managers and people who worked at record
companies started taking it. It started off small and promptly spread to
the point where it was OK to listen to house music as well as indie.'

As drugs filtered through into the indie scene and white guitar bands began to attempt to approximate the rhythms of dance music, *NME* felt on surer footing. 'People like Stuart Cosgrove were ahead of their time and spot on about how big house music would become,' says Alan Lewis. 'But they were too far ahead of their time. NME is essentially bought by white middle-class students and that was always our target audience.' Although *NME* covered the acid house scene in some detail, driving around the M25 at 2am looking for an outdoor rave was never most of the staff's idea of a good time. 'Jack Barron and I were completely embroiled in the acid house scene,' says Helen Mead. 'With bands or gigs you would go and be a spectator. With acid house our writing wasn't observational, it was direct experience. Roy Carr always used to tell us the story about how *NME* almost missed out on punk, about how it had remained part of the status quo until Nick Logan decided it was the future. Acid house was the biggest youth movement since punk and affected more change than punk ever did, but *NME* just never got it. It was outside most people's experience. They couldn't understand it.'

17.Kings of the world

'Manchester wasn't interested. Manchester wanted to sit in
dark cellars drinking bitter...'

In 1988, the indie scene was undergoing a major spiritual and financial crisis typified by the constant niggling presence on the *NME*'s indie chart of a label called PWL. Although PWL was competing for space in the chart with 4AD and Creation, it wasn't run out of a bedroom by people who hand-folded singles sleeves. Instead it was the home of producers Stock, Aitken and Waterman, whose mainstay was adapting the European disco and HI-NRG sound to bubblegum pop sung by Australian soap stars and, in one instance, Mandy Smith, teenage bride-to-be of the Rolling Stones' Bill Wyman. By 1988 SAW had scored five number one hit singles and were just entering their commercial pomp. Yet to all intents and purposes they were releasing their records on an independent label. Not everyone was as successful as PWL, however. Problems with distribution and cashflow meant that much of the indie sector that *NME* relied so heavily on for acts was on the verge of collapse.[180]

Salvation came from an unlikely source. In the spring of 1989 a band from Manchester called the Stone Roses released their debut album, initially to lukewarm reviews dismissing them as psychedelic revivalists. By the summer their music, and that of another group from their home town, the Happy Mondays, was inescapable, despite the difference in attitude of each band. 'When I lived in Manchester the Stone Roses were just a dodgy goth band,' says James Brown. 'And Alan wouldn't let the Happy Mondays on the cover of *NME* because he thought that they were just drug dealers.'

The centre of the Manchester scene was The Hacienda, hitherto an ailing superclub founded in a canalside former warehouse on Whitworth

Street West. 'When the Hacienda opened it was a social club for Factory records and their friends,' says Kevin Cummins. 'We'd all been to the big New York clubs and thought it'd be great to have something similar but Manchester wasn't interested. Manchester wanted to sit in dark cellars drinking bitter. The only reason the Hacienda took off is that they started doing "Stella for a quid" nights.' Featuring a stage used alternately for rock gigs[181] and for ravers to dance on, the club provided the perfect venue for the synthesis of indie and dance. By November 1989 when the Stone Roses and Happy Mondays appeared on the same epochal episode of *Top of the Pops*, Manchester had established itself as the alternative music capital of Britain, decked out in fisherman's hats and Joe Bloggs flares. The Mondays even had their own onstage good-times guy – although the spelling was different from the Egyptian god of dancing, Mark 'Bez' Berry became an icon, his eyes rolling back in his head as his long limbs lolled in an ecstasy fervour.

Kevin Cummins moved to London in 1987 to try and pick up more work, but found himself on the train back to Manchester most weekends to cover what was happening there. In March 1990, Granada TV produced an hour-long documentary, 'The Sound of the North', covering the Manchester scene in some detail. 'Manchester is now the music capital of Britain, some say Europe, some say the world,' it boasted, along with footage of James Brown and Stuart Maconie clowning about in the toilets of the city's Dry Bar. Granada also shot inside *NME*'s offices at King's Reach tower, capturing an editorial conference where Cummins and Danny Kelly were reviewing pictures of the Happy Mondays that the photographer had brought back from a photoshoot in Spain.

The photos, taken on the roof of the Hotel Subur Maritim in the Catalan beach town of Sitges during the filming of the video for the band's 'Step On' single, showed Shaun Ryder standing under the building's rooftop Hotel sign. When it was cropped for the cover, all that was left was the huge letter E.

Not all the drugs references in *NME* were as subtle. 'I remember writing a piece on the Happy Mondays at the Hacienda,' says Helen Mead, 'where I just dropped all of the Es out of the copy and took it in to the typesetters. And Alan Lewis was there replacing them all by hand. He thought that my typewriter was broken.'

For Cummins and writer Jack Barron the Sitges shoot was the highpoint of a round-the-world trip in the company of Shaun Ryder, the Mondays and various hangers-on. 'The Mondays had a couple of people who went along with the band everywhere to hold onto the drugs,' says Jack Barron. 'On the flight back from Spain Shaun Ryder was hassling the rest of the band and when he got up to go to the toilet someone decked him. We were met at the airport by police.'

'It was a mad rollercoaster ride around the globe,' says Cummins. 'We were kings of the world. We'd just sit there in meetings and say "Where do you want to go? I've never been to Tokyo" and the next week you'd be on the way to Japan with the Mondays.'

'Jack would go missing for days,' says Stuart Bailie. 'He'd be up for five days with the Mondays. We got to the point where we'd have a sweepstake in the office about how many hours late his copy would be. He was taking drugs every day, but even in an extremely addled state, he'd turn out this amazing flawless copy.'

As the sale of indie records began to rise with the Madchester boom, *NME* hit a new commercial peak. By the second half of 1990 it was back to selling 120,000 copies every week.

While *NME* thrived thanks to its coverage of the Madchester scene alongside the new American post-hardcore groups like the Pixies, Dinosaur Jr., Throwing Muses and Sonic Youth, a new photocopied and hand-stapled fanzine had established itself as what one of its publishers called 'the village paper for the acid house scene'.[182]

Inspired by *The End*, the Liverpudlian terrace 'zine edited by future Farm singer Peter Hooton, a group of suburban ravers from Surrey had started *Boy's Own*, writing about football, music, drugs and style in a laddier, more irreverent echo of what Stuart Cosgrove and his contemporaries had been attempting at *NME* in the 1980s. 'We are aiming at the boy (or girl) who one day stands on the terraces, the next day stands in a sweaty club, and the day after stays in reading Brendan Behan whilst listening to Run DMC,' declared *Boy's Own*'s first editorial. The approach was satirical, knowing[183] and almost impenetrable to anyone not up on the latest acid slang. Helen Mead was friendly with one of the 'zine's publishers, a DJ and former bricklayer from Slough called Andy Weatherall, commissioning him to write some reviews for *NME* under the pseudonym Audrey Witherspoon. In August 1989, a fortnight after the *Marchioness* disaster in which 51 people drowned when a Thames pleasure boat sank in the river a few hundred metres downstream from King's Reach Tower, the staff of the paper had held a summer boat party, at which Mead had also persuaded Weatherall to DJ. This was the final moment that remaining floating voters were converted to dance music. 'We thought that if we couldn't bring *NME* to Andy Weatherall we'd bring Andy Weatherall to *NME*,' says Mead. 'That was when Alan Lewis had his hallelujah moment where he finally realised what was going on with acid house, although mainly due to the inclusion of a Fleetwood Mac song in Andy's set.'

Weatherall's knowledge of rock music was key to the *NME*'s adoption of post-rave club culture. A veteran of punk, he also had connections in the indie scene after meeting Alan McGee and Creation band Primal Scream at a Shoom summer rave outside Brighton

Primal Scream's 85-second track 'Velocity Girl' had opened the C86 cassette, setting the template for the sound with singer Bobby Gillespie's fey vocals and guitar jangling. By the end of the '80s, though, they were looking increasingly beached: still clad in skintight leather jeans while their peers were wearing flares, dedicated to recreating a period of pre-punk classic rock that seemed to date from the Mesozoic Era at a time when indie bands were expected at least to be pretending to live in the future. 'It's 1990,' said Stone Roses singer Ian Brown at the press conference for his band's gig at Spike Island in May 1990 when an American journalist asked him a question about a band whose name was similar to his own. 'The Rolling Who?'[184]

By the time that their self-titled second album was released, Primal Scream's press officer Jeff Barratt was finding it increasingly difficult to find allies at the *NME*, or indeed anywhere in the press, matters not helped by the fact that James Brown and Alan McGee had recently been involved in an altercation at West London venue the Subterania which had ended with Brown punching the Creation Records boss in the mouth. Barratt phoned his friend Helen Mead, pleading with her to find someone – anyone – prepared to travel to Exeter Arts Centre and review the band live. None of her regular freelancers would touch the commission. In desperation, Mead called Weatherall. No one expected him to get on quite so well with the Scream: before long they'd handed him one of the Primal Scream album's ballads, 'I'm Losing More Than I'll Ever Have', to remix for his DJ sets. Weatherall had never made a record before, but added a loping groove from a drum loop from a bootleg of an Edie Brickell record and a snippet of dialogue from the 1966 Peter Fonda and Nancy Sinatra biker exploitation film *The Wild Angels*. Retitled 'Loaded', Weatherall debuted the new track at a gig at the Sub Club underneath the Subterania in November 1989. Before long it had been added to Radio 1's daytime schedule, reinventing Primal Scream as unlikely chart staples[185] and inventing a new genre: baggy.

Although some of its staffers had been at the heart of the acid house scene, Alan Lewis was right: raves were too far beyond the magazine's comfort zone really to be covered with much authority, leaving the 'zines and glossy style mags like *i-D* to it. But a sound based around indie bands with classic influences, a clubland mentality and the outlaw status afforded by ecstasy consumption was tailor-made for the paper. Suddenly Weatherall became the hottest remixer in the country as groups strove to recreate Primal Scream's success by alloying shuffling funky drummer beats to chiming guitars. Another Scottish C86 act, The Soup Dragons, had a top five hit in 1990 with a baggy cover of the Rolling Stones' 'I'm Free', following Candy Flip's version of The Beatles' 'Strawberry Fields Forever' into the charts, along with records by The Farm, Flowered Up, The Mock Turtles, Northside and The Paris Angels. Many of these groups featured their own onstage dancer in the manner of Bez – Flowered Up had Barry Mooncult, a bald double glazier who loped around in a giant tatty latex daisy collar – and most of them at least made an attempt to affect the wide pupils and slack jaw brought on by ecstasy consumption.

The success of these groups, many of whom were backed by major labels, meant that indie became shorthand for a style of music rather than a kind of independent DIY ethos. But as guitar music began to infiltrate the top ten again, *NME* was in the position of being able to co-opt dance and hip-hop culture into its own vision, rather than attempting to write about them from the point of view of an insider: when Public Enemy finally appeared on the front of the magazine[186] it was alongside The Pixies and Welsh indie act The Darling Buds, billed as 'The greatest rock'n'roll band in the world'. The hip-hop wars had been fought and hip-hop had lost.

Meanwhile, the tastes of the paper were increasingly being shaped by two staffers who were distinguishing themselves for their unstinting dedication to the sweaty, cider-soaked indie scene: Steve Lamacq had been promoted to *NME* news editor from the subs' room following an unfortunate habit of including spelling mistakes in headlines, recruiting another fanzine veteran, Simon Williams, along the way. Between them they had a reputation as being the indiest men alive: Lamacq once took a week's holiday off from his job going on tour with bands for *NME* to go on tour with a band, Hull's Kingmaker. 'Everyone on *NME* at that time wanted Danny Kelly's approval,' says Lamacq. 'And you won it with a good piece of writing or with a great news story or by discovering a great band. So me and Simon set ourselves up as unofficial A&R men. Danny used to see us as the blokes in the corner who used to write about these weird new bands but all of a sudden we became the kingmakers.'

During the summer of 1991, a clique of mostly drunken and scruffy indie acts developed around a basement club on Oxford Street called Syndrome and a few pubs in North London within staggering distance of each other. The owners of the Falcon[187] in Camden hosted nightly gigs in their back room and gave Williams and Lamacq a weekly *NME-*

sponsored slot. For the first time in what was almost its 40-year history, *NME* reversed the trend where record companies would bring the paper's writers new groups in an attempt to get them some column inches. Now it was earning a reputation as the place where the labels could read about which bands they should be signing each week. 'Danny Kelly would call Steve in to his office and say "Which one of your bands are we putting on the cover this week?" ' says Andrew Collins, 'and we'd have these great bands that Steve had found that no one else had heard of like Teenage Fanclub and The Frank and Walters.'

The bands who congregated at Syndrome or the Falcon were more likely to be middle-class and art-school educated than the Madchester acts, but Chapterhouse, Lush, Moose, Revolver, Swervedriver or My Bloody Valentine became mainstays of the paper through their association with the *NME* journalists they bumped into around Camden. 'Thursday night was always Syndrome,' says Lamacq. 'That was the club where everyone went: Lush, stray members of Ride or Blur. I started going there when I was news editor and I'd just go there until I found a story. I'd literally just get someone drunk on IPC expenses until they told me something that they shouldn't have done, then sneak off to the toilets and write it all down on the back of my hand. I'd always wake up on Friday mornings with all these weird messages in pen on my arms and have to piece the story together.'

18. The New Morrissey Express

**'It was like a Cobra meeting for the government, like being
on a real newspaper...'**

As the '80s progressed, relations between media owners and the unions reached their nadir. In February 1986 industrial action by the National Graphical Association, NUJ and Electrical, Electronic, Telecommunications and Plumbing Union ended in skirmishes between strikers and police after a demonstration against the opening of a new electronic printing plant by Rupert Murdoch's News International in Wapping. The new Wapping plant marked the end of an era: instead of legions of compositors, machine-room workers and linotype operators working in often filthy and dangerous industrial conditions, journalists could now set their own type directly by computer. A year later a union-organised march on Wapping rapidly descended into one of the most violent episodes in British industrial history[188] as riot police clashed with demonstrators. At *NME*, union activism was a little less militant. 'Swells would make us have these little NUJ meetings in the park,' says Helen Mead. 'I'd have a notebook and have to take minutes. No one came.'

Under Alan Lewis' editorship, the *NME* had established itself as a successful and very market-focused consumer magazine, far removed from its politicised earlier incarnation. But the legacy of political action was something that journalists on the paper in the early '90s felt they'd inherited from their predecessors. 'Nobody was under any illusions that the *NME* was a radical revolutionary newspaper,' says Andrew Collins. 'We knew that we weren't Parsons and Burchill, and you couldn't throw a typewriter out of the window at King's Reach Tower because the windows wouldn't open. But nevertheless we were all left-wing people who'd grown up in the '80s with those Billy Bragg-style *NME* politics.

I voted Labour in 1987 because of the Neil Kinnock cover.'

Alarmed at events in Wapping and the loss of magazine sales due to industrial action throughout the '80s, in the autumn of 1988 IPC management took steps to decrease the NUJ's influence within the company by attempting to bring in private contracts with senior editorial staff, effectively denying them the opportunity to join a union. When the militants *manqué* at *NME* found out what was going on, they committed to industrial action. More of a show of solidarity with *NME*'s past than an actual meaningful protest, the picket line outside King's Reach was a pretty forlorn affair. Befitting a group of music journalists, most of the picketers would arrive around lunchtime and knock off early to go to the Stamford Arms. 'The NUJ had hardly anyone out on strike,' says Andrew Collins. 'The only magazines that came out were *NME* and *New Scientist*, because the bloke who ran the NUJ chapel worked there. In some ways it was pathetic but in other ways it made us feel solidarity. Billy Bragg stood with us on the picket line one morning, which was brilliant. James Brown and Steve Lamacq were supposed to be going to New York to report on the CMJ music festival but had to cancel it because they were on strike. They were furious.'

'The sort of work that I was doing after Red Wedge collapsed in 1987 was predominately in support of the trades unions,' says Billy Bragg. 'It seemed as though the unions represented the kind of society that I wanted to live in and the *NME* had always supported me so when they went out on strike the least I could do was go down and support their industrial action and sing them a couple of songs.'

While the staff were outside in the cold, the new computer technology that had been installed by IPC meant that Danny Kelly and Alan Lewis were able to put together a whole issue of the paper single-handedly. Previously the paper had been assembled using the kind of linotype technology patented in the 19th century, applying hot metal alloys through a kind of stencil to produce each individual line of text in a way that had hardly changed since Gutenburg. Now this technology was, finally, obsolete and meant that the strike was a futile gesture: IPC issued the staff of *NME* and *New Scientist* with an ultimatum, declaring that if they didn't return to work they'd lose their jobs. In 1993, the NUJ was finally derecognised by IPC, reflecting a general decline in union influence in publishing nationwide.[189]

The lasting legacy of the strike as far as *NME* was concerned was that Danny Kelly, who was not a member of the NUJ and was thus free to pass through the picket line, such as it was, had been seen by IPC to have been committed to producing the magazine while his colleagues were outside agitating. When Alan Lewis was promoted to editor-in-chief in February 1991, after winning industry body the PPA's prestigious Editor of the Year award for reversing the *NME*'s sales decline, Kelly was appointed his successor, to the chagrin of other members of staff. 'They thought I was leading the strike because I got Billy Bragg to come down and have his picture taken with us,' says James Brown. 'That fucked me. That meant I'd never be editor of *NME*. They didn't even give me an interview.'

**New Moz Express: Morrissey poses with Vera Lynn
for the 40th anniversary of NME, March 1992**

Under Kelly's direction, the paper became known colloquially as the New Morrissey Express: every time they put the former Smiths frontman on the cover, sales spiked inevitably. 'Our relationship with Morrissey was rooted in Kevin Cummins' relationship with him which was unbelievably close,' says Andrew Collins. Cummins knew Morrissey socially from Manchester and had shot The Smiths' first gig[190] through his habit of documenting every band that he saw play in the city.

'Morrissey was perfect for *NME* because he was intelligent and articulate,' says Collins. 'But it started to get ridiculous. We did things like put Morrissey on the cover when he was touring Japan and got him to hand-write some picture captions for some of Kevin's photos. And that was the cover story. It was like a fan magazine.'

For *NME*'s 40th anniversary edition, there was only one possible choice of cover star: the man who'd been entwined with the paper's history since the 1970s, first as a reader, then a frustrated correspondent, then a commercial mainstay. Morrissey was shot by Kevin Cummins holding up an early copy of *NME* put together by Maurice Kinn, Ray Sonin and Percy Dickins in a shabby room on Denmark Street before rock'n'roll and its attendant culture had even been conceived. Forget acid house and baggy, Morrissey was the *NME*, something which made what happened in August 1992 all the more strange.

On a sunny weekend in North London's Finsbury Park, Madness reformed to play their first gigs since they'd split up acrimoniously in September 1986. Assembling a supporting bill of local acts, the two-day Madstock festival included turns from Flowered Up, Camden swamp-rockers Gallon Drunk and Ian Dury and the Blockheads. Only one act performing wasn't a Londoner: Morrissey was fresh from a successful US tour during which he sold out the 17,000-seat Hollywood Bowl in 23 minutes, breaking a longstanding record set by The Beatles, but his band were due to go onstage immediately prior to the Nutty Boys' appearance. The day had already been a strange one: the crowd included several far-right skinheads who'd spent the morning attacking an anti-Gulf War Troops Out march in nearby Islington and who passed the time before Madness' arrival onstage by fighting and pelting the support acts with coins and bottles. Morrissey suffered the same fate, pulling short his set when an orange juice carton thrown from the crowd hit him in the face. 'There was something weird about the whole event,' says Andrew Collins. 'The crowd was full of people who I used to read about going to Specials gigs. It was a pretty scary atmosphere.' Most of the *NME* contingent contented themselves with lurking in the backstage bar while Morrissey played, so it was a small surprise on Monday morning when the paper's sole black writer, Dele Fadele, arrived at the office, fuming. 'Dele was an amazing guy,' says Collins, 'a fabled African prince who lived in a squat. He came in to work absolutely impassioned and offended by what he'd seen at Finsbury Park.'

As Fadele described it to the rest of the staff, Morrissey had appeared onstage in a gold lamé shirt, waving a Union Jack thrown onto the stage in front of a huge picture of two skinhead girls taken by *NME* photographer Derek Ridgers in 1980[191]. It was a provocative move in front of Madness' crowd, which had always been dogged by an unaccountable association with the far right. But the fact that Morrissey's set also included the songs 'Bengali in Platforms' ('Bengali, Bengali/Oh, shelve your Western plans/And understand/That life is hard enough when you belong here') and a new track, 'The National Front Disco', seemed calculated to inflame the sensibilities of both the right-wing and liberal members of the crowd, for entirely different reasons.

In retrospect Morrissey's dalliance with skinhead imagery was just another manifestation of the singer's fascination for rough boys rather than any evidence of fascist tendencies: when the first-wave skinheads of the late 1960s mutated into suedeheads and smoothies, the one place where the look was perpetuated until its revival in the late '70s was in the pages of specialist gay magazines.[192] As the author Will Self noted in the *Observer*'s *Life* magazine, '[Morrissey would] be run out of the British National Party in seconds if they caught him swishing about like this'.[193]

But that year there was nothing cute about messing about with such loaded imagery. 1992 was the year that Combat 18, the white supremacist group implicated in the deaths of several non-white Britons, was formed. It was also the year that the Anti-Nazi League was revived after nine years' absence, specifically to counter the resurgence of the fascist British National Party. The *NME* had contacts with the ANL, later organising a float featuring Billy Bragg for the League's Carnival Against the Nazis[194] and covering the election of BNP councillor Derek Beackon to the Millwall ward of East London borough Tower Hamlets in September 1993. When the paper's staff heard about what Morrissey was up to, they were aghast.

An emergency summit meeting was held at King's Reach tower. 'Stuart Maconie and David Quantick had set up this kitsch Kylie shrine in the office,' says Stuart Bailie, 'and the cover of the next week's magazine was supposed to be a very arch piece by Maconie about Kylie.' "I enter into her perfumed presence, all that kind of stuff. But then Dele came in completely perturbed about what he'd seen at Finsbury Park, so it immediately became Morrissey versus Kylie.'

Conscious of Morrissey's centrality to the magazine's continued boom, Smiths fan Danny Kelly had initially intended to run a glowing review of the singer's Finsbury Park performance in the paper, while Stuart Maconie urged moderation, arguing that the Union Jack was the flag that had saved Britain from fascism, rather than representing it. But Fadele's passion infected the whole office.

Music journalists aren't really proper journalists in the Woodward and Bernstein sense. Given the opportunity to comprehensively and exclusively cover a news event, however trivial, the staff of the *NME* reacted with zeal.

'It was like a Cobra meeting for the government,' says Collins, 'like being on a real newspaper. *NME* never really did news, because there wasn't really much news to actually put in apart from tour dates. But we were in a unique place to cover this.'

Approaches to Morrissey for an interview were declined and the following week's *NME* instead featured a five-page examination of his lyrics and interviews, scouring all for clues as to his possible racism, as well as an impassioned piece by Dele Fadele. The conclusion? While crediting Morrissey with the ability to employ irony in his art, the staff of the *NME* had to conclude reluctantly that their hero was, at best, a misguided Little Englander.

'There was a couple of years where the magazine felt safe and smug. It was puns ahoy as Danny, Stuart and Andrew Collins would sit in a room and laugh at each other's jokes all day,' says Stuart Bailie. 'With the Morrissey thing we were trying to relight the spirit of the *NME*.'

Part of the violent reaction to Morrissey's appearance was heartfelt. But part of the trick of a weekly newspaper is magicking news from nothing, brewing up storms in teacups. Not that the hardcore Morrissey fans saw it that way: almost as soon as the magazine came out, the office was deluged with abusive letters. 'When I worked at *NME* we'd constantly be getting letters screaming about stuff we'd written,' says Barbara Ellen. 'We didn't mind in the slightest. *NME* people were used to being treated rather terribly by the readers.'

Morrissey himself had always had a playful relationship with the paper, once arriving at an interview with Danny Kelly armed with his own tape recorder to safeguard against misrepresentation.[195] This time, though, he was less impressed. 'My lawyers are poised,' he said in a statement issued by his press officer. '*NME* have been trying to end my career for... years and year after year they fail. This year they will also fail.'

He didn't consent to speak to *NME* again for 12 years.

19.Cambridge for losers

'I remember being in the pub with all of them just sitting there with their heads in their hands, acting as if World War Three had been declared...'

On one day in April 1991, the number of weekly music papers in Britain halved. While *Kerrang!*'s sales grew with the rise of thrash metal, *Sounds* was struggling to find readers and advertisers who could be tempted away from *NME* or *Melody Maker*: there was simply no longer a demand for more than two weeklies. *Daily Express* publishers United Newspapers, then in the process of scaling back their consumer magazines operations to concentrate on business and trade papers, closed *Sounds* and *Record Mirror* and sold *Kerrang!* to EMAP, where it joined another metal fortnightly, *RAW*.

Keith Cameron was one of the *Sounds* journalists left jobless by the magazine's closure. '*Sounds* was based in the *Daily Express* building at Ludgate House by Blackfriars, so *NME* was nearby,' he says. 'Occasionally my colleague Dave Cavanagh would get drunk in the bar downstairs at Ludgate House and then go down to the Stamford Arms where *NME* drank to try and bad vibe them all out.'

Advised by his friend Steve Lamacq to meet *NME* editor Danny Kelly with a view to lining up some freelance work, Cameron went for a meeting at King's Reach Tower. 'Danny was sceptical about what a man from *Sounds* could bring to the *NME*,' says Cameron. '*Sounds* was easily the worst-selling of the weekly music papers at that time and *NME* was so fixated on its rivalry with *Melody Maker* that it didn't really seem to register.'

As the competition shrivelled and faded, and *NME* and *Melody Maker* became the last weeklies left, the enmity between the two magazines intensified. 'IPC published loads of women's magazines and they all hated each other too,' says Andy McDuff, who was publisher of both *NME* and *Melody Maker* between 1987 and 1988. 'I remember the first year that IPC held their editorial awards they put the *NME* and *Melody Maker* tables next to each other and a drunken fight broke out between them. It just developed into a drunken mass brawl.'

The public appetite for specialist weekly music titles had begun to dwindle in the mid-1980s when the tastes and interests of the music press began to infiltrate the wider culture. By the early 1990s a whole generation of teenage *NME* readers had grown up and moved on to commissioning jobs on Fleet Street or in television and magazines. Information which had previously been only available through the music press was now appearing across the media, while a former punk like Tony Parsons was writing a column for the ultra-establishment *Daily Telegraph*. The territory which *Melody Maker* and *NME* were fighting over was shrinking, while competition for advertising grew more intense. To the initiated there was a difference between the two magazines' editorial policies: *Melody Maker* was more serious and reflective and covered obscure American noise bands, while *NME* was irreverent, more colourful and more likely to feature bands consisting of men in shorts jumping up and down. But in a desperate bid to define the difference between the two magazines, *Melody Maker* assistant editor Steve Sutherland wrote a live review of a new band, Suede, supporting Kingmaker, which he transformed into an attack on his colleagues working on the magazine on the floor below. 'He basically said that Suede are everything that the *Melody Maker* are about – glamorous exciting, new – and Kingmaker are everything that the *NME* stands for – stolid, indie, boring,' says Andrew Collins.

Drunken fisticuffs were one thing, but to the staff of the *NME* this was quite beyond the pale, not least because there was still simmering resentment around the fact that *Melody Maker* hadn't joined *NME* on the picket lines in the strike of 1988. 'That strike really drove a wedge between us and *Melody Maker*,' says Collins. 'Their editor Allan Jones saw his chance – *NME* wasn't on sale that week because we were all out on strike and he knew he'd sell more papers than us.'

Somewhat ironically, Suede had actually met through a classified advert placed by their singer Brett Anderson in *NME*. 'The "Musicians Wanted" section in *NME* was much smaller than in *Melody Maker*,' says the band's first guitarist, Bernard Butler. 'When I saw the advert that Brett put in I thought it was interesting that he'd chosen *NME* to advertise in rather than *Melody Maker*, because the classifieds section was so small. That was intriguing to me – he'd obviously chosen *NME* because it was important to him. The ad said '"Influences: The Smiths, The Pet Shop Boys and Lloyd Cole and The Commotions." I loved all of those bands, even though I thought it was strange that he was advertising for a guitarist but put down The Pet Shop Boys as an influence. The ad also said "No Musos" which was a really weird thing to write on a Musicians Wanted page.'

It was the terminology of Sutherland's writing that really stuck in the *NME* staff's craw, though: to him, the difference between *Melody Maker* and the *NME* was the same as that between 'dogshit… and diamonds'.

The enmity between the staff of the *NME* and Sutherland solidified, which was uncomfortable for all concerned when they bumped into each other in the IPC canteen and downright embarrassing on the day in October 1992 that it was announced that Steve Sutherland was to be the paper's new editor.

When Danny Kelly surprised everyone by announcing that he was leaving after 18 months as editor to move to EMAP and edit *Q*, Alan Lewis invited Sutherland out to the Stamford Arms for a pint. 'The thing with *NME* under Danny was that, like all magazines, it had reached its golden age,' says Sutherland. 'From the outside it seemed a little bit like a boys' club of people writing for one another. But I think that IPC felt as though they'd slightly lost touch with what the average music fan on the street wanted to read.'

A large proportion of the working week under Kelly's editorship was spent in his office producing the paper's notorious punning headlines. 'We were, unlike *Melody Maker*, a funny and clever paper,' says David Quantick. 'We'd have things like the best-ever strapline under the front cover logo for the Inspiral Carpets – "Underlay! Underlay!"'

'Alan Lewis asked me what I want to do and I burbled on for a few hours over several pints about how it'd be great to do a boxing magazine,' says Sutherland. 'Then a week later Danny resigned and it all fell into place. They wanted to get back in touch a bit with the readers and I think that they knew pretty darn well that if they brought me in they could have a bit of a clear out of the staff because I'd done this terrible thing, the stupid immature review of Suede supporting Kingmaker, which went down terribly with the *NME*.'

'IPC obviously thought "this place needs freshening up and we're going to annoy people into leaving by getting Steve Sutherland in",' says a new recruit to the paper's freelance roster, a petrol station attendant from Beverley in East Yorkshire called Johnny Sharp who wrote under his school nickname Johnny Cigarettes. 'I remember being in the pub with all of them just sitting there with their heads in their hands, acting as if World War Three had been declared. My thought was "'It's only a fucking newspaper. It's not Rwanda is it?"'

Sutherland was greeted on his first day in his new job by a copy of his diamonds and dogshit review, blown up to A3 size and pinned on the door to his office. It was followed by a series of anonymous abusive faxes, while his first editorial meeting rapidly descended into a shouting match. 'When I arrived the plan for that week's front cover was to do something with Kylie Minogue and if anything was emblematic of what was wrong with *NME* it was the idea that they could embrace Kylie Minogue, who no one cared about at that time,' he says. 'I took over in the same week that Sinead O'Connor had played a gig in America and she'd torn up a picture of the Pope and been booed not only by the audience but by many of the other performers on the bill. I was excited by this because it seemed weird and I had a nose for news and decided that we were going to do Sinead. And they said "We don't do things like this at *NME*" and I said "We do now". And it sold very well.'

Faced with the prospect of working for an editor that they hated, many of the staff, including Stuart Maconie, Andrew Collins and Live editor Mary Anne Hobbs, tendered their resignation. 'We'd been on strike and I got the impression that some of the people who came out on strike were deemed to be troublemakers by the publishers,' says Lamacq, 'and this was a chance for them to bring the *NME* staff into line. So on the Tuesday when Alan Lewis came down to the office and said he was going to make an announcement about the new editor we all knew who it was going to be. I typed my resignation letter and went down the pub.'

Luckily for those who found their position on the paper untenable after the arrival of Steve Sutherland, by the early 1990s *NME*'s reputation and influence was such that being a journalist on the paper could actually be the first step in a legitimate career in the media. Stuart Maconie and Andrew Collins in particular were increasingly in demand by radio and television producers to appear as talking heads, while Mary Anne Hobbs became one of the first presenters on a new indie radio station launched in 1992. Intended as a sort of aural counterpart to *NME* in the same way that John Peel's show had once been, Xfm was launched with the financial backing of The Cure's manager Chris Parry and broadcast for four weeks a year on an old pirate radio frequency within the London area only. Meanwhile David Quantick, who had written for satirical puppet show *Spitting Image* at the same time as penning reviews of Wreckless Eric or Frank Chickens for *NME*, was joining the writing team of Radio 4's groundbreaking spoof current affairs magazine show *On The Hour*. 'I call the old *NME* 'Cambridge for losers',' he says, 'not because it was full of pretentious failed students – although it often was – but because of the way people who went to Oxbridge still dominate the media in an unfair and class-based way. *NME* was a doorway into journalism and other things for people who wouldn't have been able to do it otherwise. Untrained writers, unqualified journalists, men and women who were passionate about music like Steve Lamacq or brilliant writers like Danny Kelly or just uncontainable anywhere else like Swells or Dele Fadele – none of these people were going to get jobs at Radio 4 or the *Guardian* any other way.'

It was also a boom time for magazines. Alongside the short-lived and terribly-named Indicator, the book-with-CD package *Volume*, or *Deadline*, which featured interviews with The Senseless Things and Carter the Unstoppable Sex Machine alongside strips drawn by future Gorillaz artist Jamie Hewlett, indie fans could now buy the glossy monthly Select, relaunched by *Q* editor Mark Ellen after being bought by EMAP from United Magazines in 1991. In the immediate post-house, baggy period, *Select* was able to do justice to the colourful psychedelic imagery that abounded in promo videos and on record sleeves – daisies, fisheye lenses, coloured light cells and kaleidoscopic effects – that the *NME* could never do. The era of full-colour newspapers had arrived on Fleet Street in 1986 with the launch of Eddie Shah's ill-fated middle-market tabloid Today, printed using pioneering computer photosetting technologies. In 1992, though, *NME* was still partly printed in black and white and where colour was used it occasionally made the text illegible in an unconscious throwback to the days of the underground press. Under Alan Lewis, an increased focus had been placed on the visual aspect of the magazine, as photographers were invited for the first time to attend weekly editorial meetings. 'The *NME* had always had a really strong visual identity,' says Kevin Cummins, 'but they wanted to give it a more journalistic feel where pictures and words were a whole rather than just what had happened before which was you'd have a 3,000-word feature with a black and white photo of three blokes looking in different directions and one bloke wearing a hat.'

The result was some of the strongest and most memorable cover images in *NME*'s history – like The Stone Roses daubed in paint[196] – but *NME* struggled to compete with *Select*'s glossy full-colour magazine approach. '*Q* was a huge success,' says Mark Ellen, 'so EMAP decided that they wanted to launch a new magazine really quickly and produce an anti-*Q* for people who hated what *Q* stood for. We came up with what was like a monthly colour supplement to *NME*. They'd just appointed a new editor there, Steve Sutherland, and for whatever reason loads of people left. So pretty quickly we were able to get hold of some monumental talents who all felt poorly treated by IPC: Stuart Maconie, Steve Lamacq, Andrew Collins, David Quantick. That saved us, really. That and the fact that we had a sort of psychedelic poster section in the middle of the magazine with lots of famous people in colour looking wonderful – it was an idea taken from *Smash Hits* – in out-of-focus shots and taken through fisheye lenses and our readers just loved it because they were colour and glossy and exactly what the *NME* wasn't.'

The warm glow of ecstasy was felt in the coldest places. In the wettest and greyest corner of America, the Pacific Northwest, a group of friends involved in the independent label Sub Pop would regularly drive out into the woods nearby and hold days-long MDMA parties. The music most of the bands on the label played was either crude garage rock or an unrelentingly heavy derivation of 1970s metal and *NME* had been running in a slow third place behind Melody Maker and Sounds in its coverage of grunge – one of the label's minor acts, Nirvana, were first written about in *Melody Maker* in 1989, almost a full two years before they appeared in *NME*. Keith Cameron met Nirvana on their first European tour supporting Tad in October 1989 and after *Sounds* closed, his friend Steve Lamacq advised him to become *NME*'s grunge expert. When Nirvana became the biggest group in the world after selling a million copies of their second album, *Nevermind*, within six weeks of its release in the autumn of 1991, *NME* was well placed to cover the band as they struggled openly with the pressures of the transition from a cult-level indie act to being public property. Nirvana were wary of the rock business and guarded their privacy warily – one American journalist resorted to literally stowing away on their tourbus in order to get a story – and when Mary Ann Hobbs interviewed the band immediately prior to their appearance on Channel 4's excruciating late-night youth TV programme *The Word*, she found singer Kurt Cobain curled in the foetal position in the corner of *NME* photographer A.J. Barratt's studio and being coaxed by his PR into reluctantly giving an interview.[197] Within six months rumours began to filter back to the *NME* office that Cobain was struggling with an addiction to heroin. Sent to Spain to interview Nirvana on their European stadium tour in the summer of 1992, Keith Cameron was shocked to find out those rumours were true. The rest of the band, meanwhile, were struggling with Cobain's new wife. 'She seems almost universally disliked,' Cameron wrote.[198] "'The Wicked Witch Of The West"' is one crew member's assessment, while someone else refers to Kurt being a nice guy "BC – before Courtney."'

'I remember when I got back from the trip Danny Kelly saying "If you're going to write what you've just told me you'll be ostracised",' says Cameron. "'You'll never be able to write about them again"'. And it was tempting not to, because the band's management were thinking of getting a book written about the band and I was one of the people who they'd approached. But I felt sufficiently concerned about the individuals in question that there was no alternative to write about what I'd seen. I genuinely believed that if Nirvana became successful it'd make them happy. In many ways it was the exact opposite.'

Cameron was faced with a stark choice: either maintaining his place in Nirvana's trust by ignoring Cobain's drug problems when it came to writing the feature, or attempting to help the singer by detailing the full extent of his addiction. He chose the latter option. 'Soon after the article came out, the band headlined the Reading festival,' he says. 'I was told – and this says a lot about the dysfunctional nature of the team around the band – by one of their managers that the piece was brilliant. Then shortly afterwards the band's other manager told me separately that I would never write about the band again. Dave Grohl saw me and told me that he thought the piece was very brave. But Kurt had a problem with it because I'd insulted his wife. Courtney was in hospital giving birth but Eric Erlandson from her band, Hole, was there. I was having a conversation with Kurt about things and Eric just drenched me with his vodka and lime.'

In August 1989 London club owners The Mean Fiddler took over the running of the annual Reading Festival. A continuation of the National Jazz and Blues Festival, in the 1970s and '80s Reading had been transformed into an inglorious three-day celebration of heavy rock which began to struggle in the face of competition from the Monsters of Rock event held at Castle Donington in Leicestershire. Mean Fiddler invented the modern festival era by revamping Reading as a haven for *NME*-reading middle-class student indie fans who wanted to see New Order, The House of Love and The Sugarcubes together on the same bill. But the new Reading also marked the start of a huge expansion in British festival-going. With their roots in the 1970s festival movement, the huge outdoor acid house raves and spontaneous free parties were legislated against in the 1994 Criminal Justice and Public Order Act, which also increased police powers to stop and search suspected persons. The Act followed a decade-long clampdown by police and landowners on unlicensed festivals that commenced with the violent suppression[199] of a vehicle convoy of so-called New Age travellers on their way to the Stonehenge Free Festival that had been held every summer solstice since 1972. The era of the unlicensed free party was replaced by the gradual commercialisation of music festivals which reached a peak in the mid-1990s when the BBC took over the broadcasting of Michael Eavis' Glastonbury festival from Channel 4, bringing what had once been an obscure event for hippies into millions of households. Although it had covered the passage of the Criminal Justice Bill through parliament, *NME* benefited from the increased exposure that Glastonbury began to receive, becoming one of the festival's sponsorship partners. 'In 1991 the Reading festival had really upped their game,' says '90s *NME* publisher Robert Tame. 'And we were approached by the Glastonbury festival organisers to help us find bands for the second stage, partly because Simon Williams and Steve Lamacq had been putting on these NME gigs in Camden that had a really good reputation as being the place to see new bands first. So we called it the *NME* stage and put up these huge scrims with the *NME* logo on either side of it. That was the point where the *NME* began to be recognised as more than just a newspaper.'

An entrepreneurial type who later founded the Fine Burger Co. chain of fast food restaurants, Robert Tame presided over a period where *NME* began to consolidate its brand outside of the pages of the paper, hiring a PR company, Anglo Plugging, to oversee the expansion of the magazine into other media, while a deal was done with the BBC to promote the magazine on Mark Goodier's Radio 1 show *The Evening Session*, which Steve Lamacq took over in 1993 after a stint presenting on Xfm.

The Evening Session also broadcast the first of the revived *NME* Awards, held in January 1994. In 1991 the annual Brit Awards had made some concessions to the vibrancy of the independent sector, nominating the Happy Mondays, Stone Roses and The Charlatans for awards. By 1993, it was back to business as usual: an odd and self-indulgent celebration of major label blandness, presided over by the chairman of the BPI, Rob Dickins. 'The Brit Awards were in a terribly sorry state,' says Terry Staunton. 'All the major labels block voting for each other's artists. There was this bizarre dance duo called The London Boys who were nominated in two or three categories. Kate Bush was among the nominations even though she hadn't made a single record that year. Things got spiky at a press conference when I asked Rob Dickins why these people were being nominated for awards. In the following week's

Music Week Rob Dickins gave this interview saying "If it wasn't for my dad he wouldn't have a job in the first place".'

Riled at the fact that the Brits was so out of touch, Staunton and Steve Sutherland decided to stage their own ceremony, The Brats. While the 1993 Brit Awards were hosted by *Rocky Horror Picture Show* writer Richard O'Brien at the cavernous Alexandra Palace, the inaugural Brats in January 1994 took place in less auspicious surroundings: a pub basement on Tottenham Court Road near where the old UFO club had once been.

'Vic Reeves and Bob Mortimer presented the awards,' says Staunton. 'Me and David Quantick were told by Steve Sutherland to take them out for a meal before the ceremony but to make sure that they didn't get pissed. He gave us carte blanche to buy them a big showbusiness lunch, which ended up being a round of cod and chips and cups of tea in a chippy round the corner. The bill came to £14 but I doctored the receipt so that I could claim £44 on expenses.'

The awards were distinguished by the presence of Suede, who won three gongs, including that for Best New Band and who had been added to the bill of the 1993 Brit Awards at the last minute after Staunton's public row with Rob Dickins. Within 18 months, Suede and the bands that followed them would be inescapable. *NME* was entering another golden age.

20.Don't forget about the rock

'We knew that one of the greats of our time had passed on – we were the NME and we had to do him justice...'

In 1992 music was in a dire state. The charts were ruled by the kind of novelty dance hits typified by Slipstream's top 20 single 'We Are Raving', which refitted the evergreen Rod Stewart song for a section of the record buying public hitherto previously uncatered for: the dangerously insane. In the wake of grunge followed a group of American bands – Blind Melon, Soundgarden, Pearl Jam – who swapped Nirvana's wit, independence and mischievous spirit for parodic levels of self-regard and tunelessness. The mood among the *NME* staff was one of a culture in crisis. 'We didn't have anything to write about,' says Steve Sutherland. 'We had to do things like interview Brian Jones through a medium to find out if he'd been murdered. One week we sat down and said "The Stone Roses have been recording their second album for three years and it's getting painful. Let's go and find them." So we sent a writer up to Manchester and found where they were rehearsing. That was the front cover of the paper. It was a desperate time for music.'

The legacy of the paper's 40-year history didn't help. Following the departure of most of the staff with Sutherland's appointment, a new generation of writers arrived on the *NME*. They'd all grown up reading the paper and wanted to be taking drugs with Led Zeppelin or being attacked by the Sex Pistols. Instead they were being sent to review Family Gotown or Jacob's Mouse at JB's in Dudley.

One of the new intake was a fanzine writer from Enfield called Paul Moody who got his first freelance commission by sending in a photograph of himself, along with a letter complaining about the standard of the writing and bands covered in the paper. 'I felt the mag needed to be more like the wild days of Mick Farren, who I idolized,' he says. 'I was living in Brighton and knew there was something almighty stirring. Lots of people were thinking the same way. Bobby Gillespie was living down there, great clubs, it was a cool scene. And yet the *NME* gossip column was talking about Ned's Atomic Dustbin drinking snakebite at The Bull And Gate. It was all wrong.'

Moody, Johnny Cigarettes and a new freelancer poached from *Melody Maker* called John Harris would sit around in the *NME* office disconsolately leafing through back issues of the paper from the 1970s and marvelling at the lack of glamour and verve circulating in the current crop of bands.

'We were totally weighed down by the paper's past,' says Johnny Cigarettes. 'But then again so much of the old stuff we read was absolute bollocks. Hugely mythologised. I remember reading a review of The Faces' "Ooh La La" by Charles Shaar Murray and the payoff line to his review was "Ooh La La indeed". Just honkingly awful. We loved this idea of Mick Farren always having this huge afro – we thought that was incredibly cool – and him posing for his photo in the paper holding a fucking flicknife. We just imagined all of the journalists on the paper in the '70s to be these eternally strung-out characters.'

This interest in the past of *NME* was part of a wider campaign to bring rock music back into the mainstream. In January 1992 the Leeds-based electronic duo LFO appeared on the front cover of the magazine amid a pile of broken guitars. The message was clear: techno was the future and rock music was the preserve of either indie no-hopers or Q-approved stadium acts.

'When I started at the *NME*, rock music was considered to be totally dead,' says Paul Moody. 'It was the last days of grunge and the consensus view in the office was that guitar music was totally over. At the time it was only me and John Harris who believed we could get rock back into the mainstream again. We stuck a huge picture of Keith Richards on the office door one night with some quote about "Don't Forget about the Rock" underneath.'

Attending the inaugural In The City music showcase in Manchester, Harris and Moody lauded a group of punk-inspired British bands who were the opposite of the dreary introspection of the major label grunge era. In typical *NME* style these groups were instantly grouped together in a newly created scene: The New Wave of New Wave. 'In the first issue of January 1994 we set out a feature explaining that the new way of doing things would be Punk and New Wave influenced guitar bands such as Elastica, S*M*A*S*H and These Animal Men,' says Moody. 'We wanted to make sure that the indie wardrobe of baggy t-shirts and shorts was out and that dressing up for gigs was in.'

The New Wave of New Wave didn't last long, but it did return a particular aesthetic to indie music. As teenagers who'd grown up during the late '70s mod revival, the younger *NME* journalists wanted to recreate the era's energy, love of amphetamines and dress sense. 'After Steve Sutherland joined it provoke a huge exodus of people,' says Stuart Bailie. 'There was a new generation of writers like Paul Moody and John Harris and Ted Kessler who had an agenda to promote bands with an attitude and a bit of style about them.'

Following the opening of Flip in the late '70s, second-hand shops nationwide began to take an industrial approach to importing old clothes from thrift shops in America, buying them by the tonne and shipping them to the UK as ballast on freight ships. Bands on a budget could ransack corduroy flares, garish 1970s polyester shirts with huge collars, old Levi's denim jackets, three-button Ivy League mod suits or tatty Adidas tracksuit tops, reassembling into something approaching a coherent style, as 'second-hand' began to be referred to as 'vintage'. Meanwhile, in Camden bands and journalists began to frequent a pub, The Good Mixer, previously favoured by Morrissey, members of Gallon Drunk and the residents of the nearby Arlington House hostel for homeless men. 'All the bands were new and all the journalists were new,' says Ted Kessler, who joined the paper as a writer in 1991, 'and you had a situation where all of the journalists were the same age as the bands, who were the same age as the fans. We all grew up liking The Jam and so did people like Noel Gallagher and so did Damon Albarn and there was a connection.'

'The first two years that I worked at *NME* it was more fun than being in a band,' says Kessler. 'I can't imagine how being in a band was more fun. There was a generation of people there, John Harris, Johnny Cigs, Paul Moody, who were all just so excited about being there. We'd get in to work at ten thirty and our lunches would start at quarter to one when we'd go to the pub. We'd go back to the office about three, properly pissed, delete a few ansaphone messages and then go to a pub in town where we'd stay from six until ten and then go to a gig at the Astoria.'

In April 1993, Suede singer Brett Anderson appeared on the front cover of *Select* posing in front of a Union Jack backdrop under the headline 'Yanks Go Home!' for a piece commissioned by the magazine's new features editor, Andrew Collins. Inside the magazine Stuart Maconie expanded on his feelings about the importance of the Union Jack, in between interviewing a group of very English-sounding groups including

Pulp, Denim, The Auteurs and St. Etienne, the band featuring former *NME* writer Bob Stanley. This disparate bunch of groups, all of whom shared a love of the music of the 1960s and 1970s, had a name: Britpop.

Cementing the re-emergence of the homegrown music scene's importance was the death of Kurt Cobain in April 1994, two weeks before Blur released their breakthrough album *Parklife*. His death came just over a month after he overdosed on champagne and the sedative Rohypnol and slipped into a coma during a European tour stop in Suite 541 of Rome's Excelsior Hotel. 'When you dream about working for *NME* you always aspire to being the one who documents amazing historical moments,' says Stuart Bailie. 'After the Rome thing, *NME*'s designer Mark Pechart found this photo from a Nirvana photoshoot they'd done around the time of their first album. All the pictures on the contact sheet were of Kurt laughing and smiling but there was this one shot of him wearing eyeliner and looking directly at the camera. Mark took the photo and put it in a brown envelope to use when Kurt died.'

Only three weeks later Kurt took his own life. 'We'd had a big meeting to talk about which artists would merit a front cover if they died,' says Terry Staunton. 'We drew up a list which had Paul McCartney at the top of it. The idea was that we'd be prepared if the worst happened. And lo and behold Kurt died a few weeks later and we weren't prepared at all. We knew that one of the greats of our time had passed on we were the *NME* and we had to do him justice. The paper was all laid out and ready to go when the news began to filter through. This was the days before we had mobile phones or the internet so I was in the office until gone midnight trying to get hold of some sheriff in Seattle just trying to scrape together whatever information we could.'

Two weeks later the *NME* Kurt tribute issue appeared, with photographer Martin Goodacre's shot of the singer reproduced in black and white on the front. Within days the picture was being bootlegged on shirts in Camden market.

'*Melody Maker* had the "in" with Nirvana because Keith Cameron had fallen out with the band,' says Steve Sutherland. 'Everett True from the *Maker* was part of the coterie that were sniffing around Kurt, the yes men who didn't try and save his life. But we destroyed them with our front cover. It looked great and we felt like we'd really done it justice. Then the week after *Parklife* was reviewed and suddenly you had Britpop going full pelt.'

While Suede's debut album received a moderately half-hearted review, *Parklife* was hailed as an instant classic, something that intensified the rivalry between the two bands. 'Our first album got a deliberately lukewarm review in *NME* because they'd been writing about us for six months' solid,' says Bernard Butler. 'They chose someone to write a bad review of the album to make a story out of it, rather than give it nine out of ten or something.' It was an odd conclusion to a period of fulsome praise for the band in the pages of *NME*. 'I found all of the hype embarrassing,' says Butler. 'You'd go to a gig and all of your peers would hate you because they thought you'd had an easy ride, that the press were slavering over us right from the start. And all the press meant that we quickly became divided by it as a band. Brett was good at doing interviews and enjoyed it but we felt like we were being ignored. I remember being really excited about one of our first *NME* interviews, with Stuart Maconie. I was talking about how much I liked New Order and he just sighed and asked us about T-Rex and Bowie, because his piece was going to be about how we were a glam band. It was really frustrating. And I just started saying "You know what? I'm not into this". I'd rather go to the park or something than sit there being asked about all of this really dull stuff.'

The split in Suede proved terminal: when it came to writing songs for their second album, 1994's *Dog Man Star*, Bernard Butler and Brett Anderson were only communicating via post. Meanwhile one of Suede's early patrons, Morrissey, still harboured a grudge about his treatment at the hands of the *NME*, writing the song 'Speedway' on 1994's *Vauxhall and I* album ('and all those lies/written lies, twisted lies') about the paper. Other *NME* stalwarts found their careers rejuvenated by Britpop: Paul Weller became, in the words of Paul Moody, 'a mod talisman draped over fashion mag centrefolds'[200] following tributes from Britpop bands who'd grown up reading about The Jam in *NME*.

One of those groups was Blur. Formerly a chaotic indie band lumped in with baggy, Blur's chart ascendancy commenced in March 1994 when their single 'Girls & Boys' reached the top five, despite the fact that they seemed never to leave the pub. 'They were always out at Syndrome or The Dublin Castle in Camden,' says Simon Williams, 'drinking too much and having a blast. They insisted that the early positive *NME* reviews that people like me and Steve Lamacq wrote had prevented EMI from dropping them.'

Relations with other Britpop mainstays were less cordial. Since his time dating Creation's cleaner, Noel Gallagher had formed his own group, Oasis, spotted one night after blagging their way onto a bill in May 1993 at Glasgow's King Tut's Wah Wah Hut. For the staff of *NME*, Oasis' early demos were simply too retro. In January 1994, a weedy early demo version of 'Cigarettes and Alcohol' appeared on a Creation Records sampler cassette sellotaped to the front of that week's magazine. Derided as chancers by most of the staff, the band's first review by Johnny Cigarettes derided them as Madchester throwbacks, the 'long overdue product from the bankrupt scally also-rans factory'.[201]

In April 1994, John Harris was dispatched to interview the Gallagher brothers in Glasgow. Finally interviewing them late at night in a room at the Forte Crest Hotel, the resulting conversation was a hilarious document of a row between the two brothers that ended with Liam explaining how he felt about his brother: 'I fucking hate him. And I hope one day... I can smash fuck out of him, with a fucking Rickenbacker, right on his nose, and then he does the same to me.' Returning to the *NME* with his interview, Harris' tape became a fixture on the office stereo. It proved so popular that the unedited recording of the interview was released as a single by Simon Williams on his new record label, Fierce Panda, reaching number 52 in the charts in November 1995.

'A long overdue product from the bankrupt scally also-rans factory...' Liam and Noel Gallagher show their distaste for the paper, May 1994

When it came to taking out press ads for Oasis' debut album, Definitely Maybe, Creation's MD Tim Abbott bypassed the *NME* entirely. Instead he took out space in the football magazines *Shoot* and *When Saturday Comes*, alongside adverts in the style magazines and dance papers.[202] It was a canny move by Abbott, who understood that the patronage of the *NME* was only really useful for getting a band recognised in the early stages of their career. Instead he made a point of getting to know tabloid journalists, like a columnist on the *Sun* called Andy Coulson.[203] Abbott's strategy paid off: *Definitely Maybe* became the fastest-selling debut album that the UK had ever seen. It also meant that from now onwards, *NME* would be considered as an indie ghetto, a dead end for any act serious about getting into the charts.

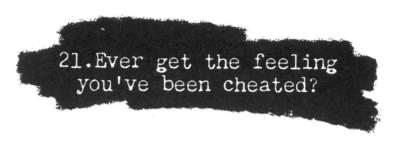

21.Ever get the feeling you've been cheated?

'This is the time of your life. Forget Burchill, forget Parsons, forget all that fucking stuff because this is now and it's happening...'

In July 1993, BBC Radio 1 appointed a new controller to replace Johnny Beerling, who had joined the station as producer of former Radio Caroline DJ Tony Blackburn's show in 1967. When Matthew Bannister arrived at the nation's most listened-to station, he was reminded of the BBC's public service values by recently appointed BBC Director-General John Birt. Radio 1, Birt believed, had to differentiate itself from its commercial rivals by broadcasting more documentaries, improving its current affairs coverage and championing new British music.

Tony Blackburn had left Radio 1 in 1981, but during his fourteen years on the station had patented an image of the DJ as a permanently tanned and medallion-wearing showbiz swinger who seemed less interested in the music that he was playing than his chances of one day presenting a television gameshow. In August 1993, the veteran DJ Dave Lee Travis was sacked after condemning Bannister's new regime live on air during his weekend mid-morning show. Many of his colleagues were replaced or moved on soon after, leaving Bannister to open up the tyranny of the station playlist, allowing specialist music DJs to play more of the music that they wanted. The result was that Radio 1, listened to by over 15 million people each week, began to play more guitar-based British rock of the kind that had previously been the preserve of John Peel's late-night show.

At the same time that Bannister was overhauling Radio 1, EMAP published the first issue of its new magazine *MOJO*,[204] edited by Paul DuNoyer with managing editor Mark Ellen. *MOJO* was a perceptive and well-timed recognition that the growth of CD catalogue reissues was creating a culture where novelty was no longer the primary currency of rock'n'roll, but that for many music fans all music is new, whether it was recorded yesterday or 50 years ago. In that sense *MOJO* was the ultimate Britpop magazine, chiming with a musical movement that repurposed the musical styles of the 1960s and 1970s to its own ends. Somewhat ironically considering *Q*'s demolition of the unique *NME* voice in its quest to be a levelheaded consumer guide, DuNoyer employed some of his former colleagues, including Charles Shaar Murray and Nick Kent, in an attempt to pull in readers who'd grown up reading their pieces in *NME* in the '70s. 'For *MOJO* I wanted to do something that was as glossy as *Q* but recaptured the individual voices that I'd enjoyed from *NME*,' DuNoyer says. 'These things tend to go in cycles. With *MOJO* I was hoping to recapture some of the flavour of the *NME*, but not confined to writing about the present. We saw the past and present as existing in a continuum.'

In the 1970s, *NME* had a virtual monopoly on coverage of rock music. But by the middle 1990s this was no longer the case, as Radio 1, *MOJO* and everyone from Channel 4's new youth show *TFI Friday* to the daily newspapers picked up on Blur and Oasis or got overexcited about second wave Britpop bands called things like Powder, Thurman and Pimlico.

National interest in Britpop peaked on Monday 14 August 1995, when the nationally syndicated commercial news station ITV's *News at Ten* ended with an item about the chart battle between Oasis' 'Roll With It' and Blur's 'Country House', high-profile new singles released on the same day. 'Even The Beatles and the Rolling Stones each timed the release schedules of their singles so that the other could enjoy a number-one,' wrote the *Independent*, noting that 'there is not much love lost between Colchester's Blur and Oasis, from Burnage in Manchester... NME has quoted Noel Gallagher of Oasis as saying: 'Blur are a bunch of middle-class wankers trying to play hard ball with a bunch of working-class heroes. There will be only one winner.'[205]

'I'd been up to see Heavy Stereo in Wolverhampton,' says Stuart Bailie, and all of the Creation promotional team were there going on about how they were going to slaughter Blur. It soon became clear in an editorial meeting that this was an event: Celts versus Angles, working class versus middle class. Within a few hours of the magazine hitting the newsstand we were on the ten o'clock news.'

With a cover designed by Mark Perchart from an old Muhammad Ali boxing poster which pitted Damon Albarn against Liam Gallagher in

'The British Heavyweight Championship', that week's issue of *NME* became the focal point for the global media, who rapidly picked up on the feud between the two bands. The chart battle was covered everywhere from the tabloids to the serious news monthlies, invariably quoting *NME* journalists.

'In 1995 I stood up in an editorial meeting and made a speech,' says Steve Sutherland, 'where I said "This is the time of your life. Forget Burchill, forget Parsons, forget all that fucking stuff because this is now and it's happening". We owned Britpop. Everything we touched was genius. We started to really put on sales. The tabloids didn't get it until we did the Blur versus Oasis thing. Both those bands were big but after that they just rocketed.'

Despite *NME*'s omnipresence, though, it was another magazine that ended up defining the era. Following his departure from *NME*, James Brown had briefly managed *Fabulous*, punk revivalists fronted by journalist Simon Dudfield and featuring *NME* photographer Martin Goodacre on guitar. Fabulous were a knowing attempt to create some Sex Pistols-style controversy, stealing the carpet from EMI records' reception, gatecrashing a Manic Street Preachers showcase gig at the Diorama Theatre near Regent's Park and driving around London in a communal band car, an Austin Maxi decorated by Screamadelica artist Paul Cannell and bearing the words ARREST ME painted in huge letters on the boot. *Fabulous* only released one record,[206] but, perhaps unsurprisingly, it became NME's Single Of The Week. Brown had then turned down an offer by The Beastie Boys to move to America and work on the launch of their *Grand Royal* magazine before he received a call from Alan Lewis inviting him to an interview for the editorship of *NME* following Danny Kelly's departure. 'In the interview they said to me"If you don't get this would you like to start your own magazine?" he says, 'and they asked me what it'd be like and I said "Like *Arena* edited by Hunter S. Thompson'. I didn't get the *NME* editor's job but a year later we started work on *loaded*.'

loaded was named after the Primal Scream song and created alongside another music journalist, Mick Bunnage, who had worked for *Record Mirror* and *Sounds*. Quite apart from the Primal Scream connection, the dummy copy of its first issue featured a Paul Weller interview on the front cover, which Alan Lewis removed, afraid that buyers would mistake it for a new music magazine. 'With *loaded* we built on our experiences at *NME*,' Lewis says. 'We tried to copy the *NME* ethos of mixing a lot of humour and attitude and I think that a lot of the early readers of *loaded* were either *NME* readers or former *NME* readers. For the first five years *loaded* wasn't about girls: on those early covers we'd have Harry Hill or a rock star or a footballer.'

'Britpop got out of control very quickly,' says Paul Moody, 'and James Brown and *loaded* was very important in spreading the message that rock'n'roll and hedonism was back.'

'The main benefit of *loaded* for *NME* was that anything I did, James Brown would do two thousand times worse,' says Steve Sutherland. 'IPC editors could get away with murder after *loaded*. So we did stuff like hire a helicopter to take people to Glastonbury. We could run a much more rock'n'roll paper than we otherwise would've been able to. But after Britpop we were not an indie magazine any more. We were a mainstream magazine and we were on the telly all the time and *NME*'s reputation was very high.'

The commercial success of Britpop proved infectious to the staff of the *NME* as sales of the magazine rose to 117,000 in the second half of 1995 following coverage of the Blur and Oasis chart battle. 'I was in the Stamford Arms with Steve Sutherland one night,' says Roy Carr, 'and he turned to me and said "I'm the most important person in the British music industry" at which I fell about laughing. Him and Robert Tame were doing lots of coke and champagne.'

It wasn't long before the sense of self-confidence turned to defeat. Despite the fact that female musicians were accepted as part of the Britpop cabal, and *NME* covers featuring artists like PJ Harvey, The Beastie Boys, Tricky and The Manic Street Preachers sold consistently well during the 1990s, it was a self-consciously laddish and orthodox movement that had little time for the oddballs or outsiders that had previously populated the independent sector. In his early interviews, Albarn, a former drama student whose father Keith had managed The Soft Machine, had espoused a fondness for the novels of Herman Hesse and French playwright Antonin Artaud's confrontational surrealist Theatre of Cruelty. Interviewing Albarn following the success of 'Country House', Steve Sutherland found that his band were – in a deliberate echo of the days of the Ad-Lib and the Cromwellian – 'kings of Swinging London',[207] while Albarn had transformed himself into a football-loving lad-about-town. 'I know it's a very flippant thing to say,' he told Sutherland, 'but if Kurt Cobain had played football he'd probably be alive today.'

Meanwhile Oasis had gone on to be the biggest group in Britain. In August 1996 they played two concerts in the grounds of Knebworth House in Hertfordshire. Over 2.6 million people applied for the 300,000 tickets. The band had moved far beyond a need to speak to *NME*, which was left to covering the strictly second-string Britpop bands.

'We did a Charlatans cover in the middle of Britpop and it sold 98,000 and alarm bells went off because sales had gone under 100,000 for the first time in years,' says Ted Kessler. 'Then there was the second Sleeper album that got sent into the office which was so clearly bad but everyone was pretending that it was this very important record. I remember thinking at the time that the next wave just wasn't going to be as good commercially as the first wave.'

It was the beginning of an inglorious time for *NME* as the staff struggled to find new bands – Campag Velocet, Gay Dad, Ultrasound – to get excited about. Even the election of Britain's first rock'n'roll premier in May 1997 wasn't enough: after giving their unwavering support to the Labour Party during eighteen years in opposition, it took less than twelve months before the *NME* turned on Blair, running a photograph of the former Ugly Rumours singer with a headline taken from John Lydon's onstage pronouncement at the last-ever Sex Pistols gig in San Francisco in 1978: 'Ever Get the Feeling You've Been Cheated?'

Epilogue

At the height of the Cold War in 1963, a Pentagon military research department called the Advanced Research Projects Agency initiated a project to investigate creating a communications network that could survive any kind of cataclysmic Soviet nuclear attack. Their solution was the creation of an integrated network that would link a handful of America's room-sized computer processors. 'In a few years,' wrote one of the Agency's members in 1968, 'men will be able to communicate more effectively through a machine than face to face.'[208] It took over two decades for this prophesy to become practicable, after the British computer scientist Tim Berners-Lee drew up proposals for a project dubbed the WorldWideWeb which allowed for a universal network of hypertext documents that could be searched through browsers. Marrying his web to the existing system of interconnected computers called the Internet, Berners-Lee laid the foundations for a revolution in information distribution.

IPC was quick to react to the possibilities of the new medium, thanks to their coverage of the developing technology in *New Scientist* magazine. Shortly after the launch of Newscientist.com in 1996, the company decided that *NME* would be the next of their titles to get a website. The only problem was that no one really knew what a website actually was.

'I couldn't even imagine what the internet was and no one could describe it,' says Steve Sutherland. 'But we decided that we had to have one of these things. We realised that news could be delivered faster online than in the paper. When I took over *NME* it was billed as 'the world's biggest selling rock'n'roll newspaper'. Suddenly you could see that overnight you could no longer be a newspaper. So we had to work out what the magazine was going to become.'

The timing wasn't particularly auspicious for the paper to be having a crisis of identity. With the end of Britpop the staff of the paper realised that the readers that they'd gained in 1995 and 1996 weren't prepared to stick around for the long haul. 'That post-Britpop period was disastrous,' says Ted Kessler. 'The thing about *NME* is that you've got 51 covers every year. Even in a really fertile period for music you have trouble filling them all. So when you're going through a period where there are only four bands that are active and two of them will only really talk to you twice a year you're in trouble. We wanted to get rid of older readers and try to get in this new readership which didn't really exist. We did a redesign where we finally went to full colour and that redesign alone lost us 30,000 readers. And once you fuck those people off they never come back.'

Things were even worse over at the *Melody Maker*. In 1997 longstanding editor Allan Jones left to edit IPC's new monthly *Uncut*. Under new editor Mark Sutherland the paper attempted to dedicate itself to coverage of the nu-metal scene which was producing a huge boom in sales for *Kerrang!*. 'A perennial question was always what the difference was between *NME* and *Melody Maker*, both from an advertiser point of view and a consumer point of view,' says Robert Tame, the publisher responsible for both. 'We'd tried to position *Melody Maker* as a new band paper, as well as being the paper for musicians, while *NME* was more about the heritage of its interviews and slightly bigger stars.' A move to a glossy format was unsuccessful and in 2000 *Melody Maker* suffered a final great ignominy: it went the way of *Accordion Times* and was incorporated into *NME* after 74 years on newsstands.

Although *NME* had been one of the first print music titles to create a website, the success of *Music Week's* digital spinoff Dotmusic and ex-*NME* editor Danny Kelly's music site Music365 meant that IPC felt bold enough to invest further in NME.com, at the possible expense of sales of the paper. 'We either had to be murdered or commit suicide,' says Steve Sutherland. 'We knew we had some heritage and some recognition in the market and if we delivered news people were likely to come to NME.com rather than some website that had just been created that they'd never heard of. At the end of the day we launched a website because we had to. We didn't know if we were cannibalising our product and to a certain extent no one still does.'

In 2011 even the most recent events in this book belong to another world. The idea of a science fiction comic called *2000AD* seems hopelessly quaint. Some of the heroes of the *NME* – Kurt Cobain and Richey Edwards, but also Joe Strummer and Malcolm McLaren – are no longer with us. Some, like Nick Cave or Keith Richards, have lived far longer than anyone would've ever predicted. Many of the bands that once featured on the front cover of the paper – I'm looking at you, Judas Jump, Baby Amphetamine and Terris – are dimly remembered, if at all. Children discovering flexidiscs or cassette tapes at car boot sales or in junk shops would view them as impossibly anachronistic archaeological artefacts. The existence of one weekly paper devoted almost solely to music, let alone three or four, is a throwback to a time when a man caught not wearing a hat outdoors was viewed with suspicion, if not outright hostility.

But, despite persistent predictions about its imminent sale or closure, *NME* survives, albeit at the centre of a nexus of spin-offs including a curious Russian version which launched in 2001, the website, a television and radio station and a multi million pound televised awards ceremony sponsored by a brand of hair wax. During my time on the paper In the noughties, *NME*'s circulation rose again, tethered to the success of acts like The White Stripes, The Strokes, Franz Ferdinand and the Arctic Monkeys. But *NME* has given up its position as the authoritative voice of underground culture, precisely because, post-Britpop, that underground culture is no longer underground. The only place that music culture is still capable of creating a healthy generation gap is in metal – *Kerrang!* and *Metal Hammer* comfortably sell more copies than *NME* and have done for 15 years. The *NME*'s concerns, things which were once the sole preserve of the hippies – centre-left politics, the preservation of the environment, nuclear disarmament, music festivals, sexual equality, animal rights – are now the mainstream. The ideas that the *NME* expressed and the language it used to express them are ubiquitous. Former *NME* writers are all over the media. Some of them are even household names. The paper's approach to simultaneously documenting and lampooning rock'n'roll is reproduced everywhere from glossy monthlies to otherwise serious daily broadsheets.

Thanks to its website, *NME*'s presence has become more global. But the paper itself is a curious relic of a past era, like Oxo cubes or Belisha beacons. The days of live rock photography as an art form are vanishing due to megapixel smartphone cameras at gigs and the convention, started by big American rock bands in the late '80s in an attempt to deter bootleg merchandisers, for bands to only allow photographers to shoot the first three songs of their set – the ones where nothing dramatic or photoworthy ever really happens. I know *NME* photographers who now shoot much of their work using an iPhone and post it to Tumblr or Instagram before it appears in the paper. In the past press officers existed to facilitate relations between the artist and the media. Now their job is to shut them down. New bands hire brand consultants and social media strategists before they get a manager. There are fewer outlets for long-form journalism or expansive features interrogating an artist's point of view or motivations. The days of the star journalist are gone, replaced, potentially, with the star blogger. Much music journalism seems to consist of second-guessing the tastes of the reader by making *Which? Magazine*-style consumer recommendations – although with the instantaneous access to pretty much any recorded music ever made at any point in human civilisation provided by the internet, even this form of writing seems irrelevant. The *NME* is one of the few places left where you can still get all of this stuff. What it'll look like at the end of the next 60 years is impossible to know. But I'm betting it'll be as mischievous, opinionated, funny, infuriating, capricious and passionate as ever.

Endnotes

1 Maurice Kinn died of cancer in August 2000. Gorman, pp. 18–19.

2 About £22,000 in 2011 using the retail price index.

3 New York's Tin Pan Alley occupied a stretch of West 28th Street in Manhattan where music publishers gathered from the 1880s onwards. The name is thought to refer to the sound of cheap upright pianos being played simultaneously.

4 Gorman, Ibid.

5 A nickname for several broadcasters on Nazi propaganda programme *Germany Calling*, most closely associated with William Joyce.

6 The *New Musical Express* was selling almost 15,000 copies more a week than its rival.

7 *New Musical Express*, 14 September 1956.

8 Melly, p. 29.

9 *The Times*, 15 September 1956.

10 *New Musical Express*, 21 September 1956.

11 Nuttall, p. 37.

12 Andy Gray replaced Ray Sonin when the latter immigrated to Canada in 1957. Sonin attempted to launch a Canadian music paper called *World Music*, before starting a 33-year career as a DJs on Toronto's CFRB radio station, broadcasting until his death in 1991.

13 Griffiths, p. 329.

14 Sandbrook, p. 97.

15 *New Musical Express*, 2 August 1963.

16 *New Musical Express*, 10 April 1964.

17 All circulation figures are taken from publishing industry body the Audit Bureau of Circulation's biannual reports and represent the total average net circulation per issue within a six-month period.

18 *New Musical Express*, 1 May 1964.

19 Quoted in Cross, p. 167.

20 *New Musical Express*, 12 November 1965.

21 Quoted in Fletcher, p. 153.

22 *New Musical Express*, 12 March 1965.

23 *New Musical Express*, 3 July 1964.

24 *New Musical Express*, 26 June 1964.

25 Sandbrook, p. 112.

26 *New Musical Express*, 18 June 1965.

27 Beckett, p. 16.

28 *New Musical Express*, 25 June 1965.

29 *New Musical Express*, 23 May 1964.

30 *New Musical Express*, 15 October 1965.

31 *New Musical Express*, 26 November 1966.

32 Keith Altham interviewed Burdon at his flat for the *New Musical Express* Summer Special in 1966: 'He says he got it there so they only have to carry him upstairs! He was joking, of course'.

33 *New Musical Express*, 1 April 1967.

34 *New Musical Express*, 20 May 1967.

35 Sandbrook, p. 250.

36 Although it is equally possible that the author, noted ballet critic Richard Buckle, was being sardonic in the *Sunday Times*, 29 December 1964.

37 Quoted in Brooker, 1992, p. 221.

38 *New Musical Express*, 29 July 1966.

39 Lindberg, p. 170.

40 Quoted in Wale, p. 11.

41 Melly, p. 239.

42 *New Musical Express*, 14 January 1967.

43 *New Musical Express*, 10 August 1968.

44 *New Musical Express*, 19 October 1968.

45 *New Musical Express,* 14 September 1968.

46 In February 1967 police arrested Mick Jagger and Keith Richards for possession of amphetamines and allowing cannabis to be smoked on his property, respectively.

47 Quoted in Wale, p. 11.

48 Quoted in DeRogatis, p. 75. Bangs also described *Creem* as 'the counter-counterculture'.

49 *New Musical Express*, 13 December 1969.

50 Critchley, p. 36.

51 Quoted in Gorman, p. 165.

52 *The New Musical Express*'s ABC result for the second half of 1971 was 136, 092.

53 Quoted in Wale, p. 11.

54 York, p. 11.

55 *New Musical Express*, 5 September 1969.

56 *New Musical Express*, 15 November 1969.

57 Young, p. 493.

58 Beckett, p. 226.

59 *New Musical Express*, 15 January 1972.

60 *The Times*, 15 January 1972.

61 Beckett, p. 315.

62 Johnson, Wolfe, p. 50.

63 York, p. 29.

64 Decharné, p. 276.

65 'Nick never took notes,' claims Roy Carr, 'so he'd just write whatever he wanted about people.'

66 According to a profile piece written by Chris Salewicz entitled 'The Almost Legendary Nick Kent', *NME*, 10 January 1981.

67 Quoted in DeRogatis, p. 168.

68 *New Musical Express*, 8 May 1976.

69 *New Musical Express*, 8 February 1975.

70 *New Musical Express*, 6 July 1974.

71 *New Musical Express*, 21 December 1974.

72 Quoted in Gorman, p. 192.

73 Following a lengthy period of clinical depression, Ian MacDonald killed himself in August 2003.

74 According to an interview with the journalist Karl Whitney in 2009.

75 Kent, p. 37.

76 Elms, p. 95.

77 Bradbury, p. 81.

78 *New Musical Express*, 19 January 1974.

79 *New Musical Express*, 1 August 1975.

80 In November 1959, Jones also launched her own monthly newspaper, aimed at the immigrant community, *The West Indian Gazette And Afro-Asian Caribbean News.*

81 Hebdige, p. 24.

82 *New Musical Express*, 10 July 1976.

83 Beckett, p.15.

84 London's population dropped by 600,000 between 1961 and 1971. Beckett, p.15.

85 *New Musical Express*, 29 October 1977.

86 A quotation from 'Desolation Row', the closing track of Bob Dylan's 1965 album *Highway 61 Revisited, New Musical Express*, 19 June 1976

87 New Musical Express, 26 July 1975.

88 Ibid.

89 Or The Tally Ho in Kentish Town, The Rochester Castle in Stoke Newington, The Greyhound in Fulham and numerous other venues.

90 New Musical Express, 17 September 1977.

91 New Musical Express, 21 February 1976.

92 New Musical Express, 7 May 1977.

93 New Musical Express, 17 November 1976.

94 New Musical Express, 22 May 1976.

95 New Musical Express, 3 July 1976.

96 In 1978 Coon took over as manager of The Clash after they sacked original manager Bernie Rhodes.

97 Better Badges later compiled a weekly badge top ten in *NME*.

98 Sideburns was responsible for the famous illustration of a guitar fretboard which read 'This is a chord. This is another. This is a third. Now form a band'.

99 Savage, p.148.

100 The Smiths also picked a Jim French photograph of a male nude for the cover front cover of their 1983 single 'Hand In Glove'.

101 The shirt remains much-bootlegged, even though McLaren was prosecuted for obscenity in August 1975 because of it.

102 The pseudonym of gay Finnish artist Touko Laaksonen, who specialised in stylised illustrations of men with huge muscles and tight trousers showing off massive phalluses.

103 Burchill, p.104.

104 Brian Epstein, then manager of the record department at a branch of his father's music shops, contributed a regular new releases column to the paper.

105 One particularly opportunistic Allen title, *Dragon Skins,* combined skinhead violence with the fad for Kung-Fu movies led by the crossover success of Bruce Lee's 1973 film *Enter the Dragon.*

106 Kent, p. 297.

107 York, p.23.

108 Logan was cautious enough to let the readers have their way when it came to the 'Creep of the Year' category, also inhabited by the Pistols.

109 Coe, p.155.

110 York, p.28.

111 When IPC moved out of King's Reach Tower in 2007, the building was finally diagnosed with Sick Building Syndrome caused by a deficient air conditioning system and provoking 'headaches; eye, nose, and throat irritation; dry coughing; dry or itchy skin; dizziness and nausea;

concentration problems and fatigue' among those spending long periods in the building. LSE, 2006.

112 Deneslow, Robin, the *Guardian*, 12 May 1976.

113 *New Musical Express*, 23 April 1977.

114 *New Musical Express*, 2 April 1977.

115 Savage, p. 365.

116 *New Musical Express*, 3 July 1976.

117 *New Musical Express*, 24 April 1976 .

118 Seddon

119 Shortly before being arrested for possession of heroin in February 1977, Keith Richards checked in to Toronto's Harbour Castle Hotel under the name K. Redland. *New Musical Express*, 18 November 1978.

120 Released in 1980.

121 *New Musical Express*, 4 February 1978.

122 *New Musical Express*, 17 December 1977.

123 Quoted in a profile piece written by Chris Salewicz entitled 'The Almost Legendary Nick Kent', *NME*, 10 January 1981.

124 The operation seized LSD with a street value of £7.6 million and inspired The Clash's song 'Julie's in the Drug Squad'.

125 Words that he has since passed off as a joke.

126 Quoted in Beckett, p. 449.

127 They married in 1979.

128 *NME*, 16 June 1979.

129 Bubbles, who suffered from bipolar disorder, committed suicide in November 1983.

130 Bubbles' masthead logo survived only minor design tweaks until it was replaced entirely in April 2010.

131 The illustration was signed 'ALAN MOORE. WITH APOLOGIES TO AUB THE DAUB'. Moore contributed illustrations of Siouxsie Sioux and Elvis Costello to the paper before joining *Sounds* as a regular comic strip artist.

132 Where Mick Jagger famously stopped in for a pint of mild following the press conference after his arrest for possession of cannabis in 1967.

133 Beckett, p. 576.

134 *The Times*, 4 June 1980.

135 Felix Dennis, famously given a more lenient sentence by the *Oz* trial judge because he was 'the least intelligent' of the defendants, founded one of the country's most successful magazine publishing businesses in 1973 with *Kung Fu Monthly* and, later, *Personal Computer World* and *Mac User* magazines.

136 Cummins' iconic image made the cover of *NME* twice: once in

1979 and again for a 30th anniversary special in July 2009.

137 *NME*, 16 February 1980.

138 Reviewing The League Unlimited Orchestra's *Love And Dancing*, *NME*, 3 July 1982.

139 *NME*, 17 January 1981.

140 *NME*, 12 May 1979.

141 Greenberg, p. 156.

142 Richard Cook, *NME*, 20 March 1982.

143 *Smash Hits*, 11 December 1980.

144 None of the bands on the bill at the Harmborough Tavern – The Business, The 4-Skins and The Last Resort – were explicitly far-right, although some audience members had spray-painted racist slogans on walls around Southall before the concert began.

145 The *Evening Standard*, 1 May 1980.

146 *The Times*, 31 July 1984.

147 The *NME* registered an ABC result of 230,939 for this period, higher than anything the paper had sold in the 1970s.

148 *NME*, 17 January 1981.

149 Other contenders were Red Steady Go, More to the Point and Moving Hearts and Minds. Bragg and Collins, p. 168.

150 *NME*, 18 March 1978.

151 American Trades Union activist Karen Silkwood died in mysterious circumstances in 1974 while investigating claims of industrial negligence at the nuclear fuel production facility where she worked.

152 Bragg, Collins, p. 150.

153 Following Margaret Thatcher's speech to the 1922 Committee in July 1984 describing the striking miners as 'the enemy within', Neil Spencer commissioned a set of badges that read 'The *NME* within'.

154 *The Times*, 30 June 1984.

155 'If Passion ends in fashion, Nick Kent is the best-dressed man in town'.

156 *Absolute Beginners* was written by Colin MacInnes at the age of 44 in 1959. In 1986 a film version was released, directed by *The Great Rock'n'Roll Swindle*'s director Julien Temple. Paul Weller chose the book when he appeared on Radio 4's *Desert Island Discs* in September 2007, along with records by the Small Faces, James Brown and Nick Drake.

157 Reviewing the Nosebleeds live for *NME*, Paul Morley mistakenly referred to their singer as Stephen Morrison. *NME*, 26 May 1979.

158 Morrissey, 2007.

159 Cavanagh, p. 89.

160 The Shrubs, Big Flame, A Witness and Stump.

161 The label's founder Dave Parsons ended up being declared bankrupt and losing his house as a result.

162 *Billboard*, 24 November 1984.

163 Cavanagh, p. 224.

164 On 15 March 1985.

165 Robert Keating, 'Anatomy of a Cause Concert', *Spin* magazine, September 1988.

166 '20 or 30 copies a week at the most,' according to Andy McDuff, who took over as *NME* and *Melody Maker* publisher in 1987.

167 Born Steven Duren.

168 *NME*, 18 November 1989.

169 Steven Wells died in June 2009 after a three-year battle with Hodgkin's lymphoma.

170 *NME*, 5 January 1991.

171 Actually the title of a song by cult musician and writer John Trubee, most famous for his song-poem 'Peace & Love', the key refrain of which was 'a blind man's penis is erect because he is blind'.

172 *Smash Hits*, 25 March 1987.

173 'Ibiza Bar', from the band's soundtrack album *More*, 1969.

174 Sean O'Hagan, 'Acid House', *Spin* magazine, January 1989.

175 Cavanagh, p. 243.

176 'Here's your chance to help stamp out the evils of drugs – by wearing a *Sun* badge. Send a sturdy stamped addressed envelope to DRUGS, The Sun…'

177 The *Sun*, 28 August 1989.

178 The *Sun*, 18 November 1988.

179 Collin, p. 32.

180 Cavanagh, p. 223.

181 Including one during which Einstürzende Neubauten drilled through the club's walls.

182 Andy Weatherall in Brewster, Broughton, p. 2.

183 In one issue they updated the old *Sideburns* punk illustration for the '90s: 'here's a sampler… here's two decks… now go form a band!'

184 *NME*, 9 June 1990.

185 'Has there ever been a more unlikely Pop Messiah than Bobby Gillespie?' wrote *NME* in a review of Primal Scream's Brixton Academy headline gig in 1992. 'A gangly streak of piss with a face like a plastic spoon; a man who couldn't carry a tune if you gave him a wheelbarrow with stabilizers.' *NME*, 4 April 1992.

186 *NME*, 8 October 1988.

187 Closed in 2002.

188 The *Financial Times*, 26 January 1987.

189 Gopsill, p. 140.

190 At the Manchester Ritz on 4 October 1982.

191 The pictures were originally commissioned for a piece on the skinhead revival that appeared in *Rolling Stone* and formed the basis for an exhibition called 'Skinheads' at Chelsea's Chenil Studio Gallery in October 1980.

192 York, p. 12.

193 Will Self, 'The King of Bedsit Angst Grows Up,' *Life* magazine, 3 December 1995.

194 Held on 28 May 1994.

195 'He takes a tape recorder from… [a]… valise and sets it going next to mine – a little monument to misrepresentation – and drinks arrive. Mine is a large glass of orange juice, his is an ornate silver samovar filled with hot chocolate,' *NME*, 8 June 1985.

196 *NME*, 18 November 1989.

197 *NME*, 23 November 1991.

198 *NME*, 29 August 1992.

199 On 1 June 1985.

200 *NME*, 25 September 1993.

201 *NME*, 11 December 1993.

202 Cavanagh, p. 447–8.

203 Ibid.

204 In October 1993.

205 'Big-hitters slug it out in battle of the bands', the *Independent*, 14 August 1995.

206 'Destined to be Free', on Jeff Barratt's Heavenly label.

207 *NME*, 16 September 1995.

208 Quoted in Wu, p. 174.

Bibliography

Abrams, M., 1959, *The Teenage Consumer*, London Press Exchange, London.

Aizlewood, J., 1994, *Love is the Drug*, Penguin, London.

Anson, R., 2000, 'Birth of an MTV Nation', *Vanity Fair*, November 2000.

Beckett, A., 2009, *When the Lights Went Out*, Faber and Faber, London.

Bradbury, M., 1980, *The History Man*, Arrow, London.

Bragg, B., Collins, A. 2007, *Still Suitable for Miners*, Virgin, London.

Brewster, B., Broughton, F., (eds) 2009, *Boy's Own: the Complete Fanzines 1986–9*, DJhistory.com, London.

Brooker, C., 1992, *The Neophiliacs*, Pimlico, London.

Brooker, C., 1980, *The Seventies*, Penguin, London.

Burchill, J., Parsons, T. 1987, *The Boy Looked at Johnny*, Faber and Faber, London.

Burchill, J., 1999, *I Knew I Was Right*, Arrow, London.

Cavanagh, D., 2000, *The Creation Records Story*, Virgin, London.

Chouvy, P., 2009, *Opium: Uncovering the Politics of the Poppy*, I. B. Tauris, London.

Coe, J., 2002, *The Rotter's Club*, Penguin, London.

Collin, M., 2009, *Altered State: The Story of Ecstasy Culture and Acid House*, Serpent's Tail, London.

Collins, A., 2007, *That's Me in the Corner*, Time Out, London.

Critchley, R., (ed.) 1975, *The British Household in the Seventies*, IPC, London.

Cross, C., 2005, *The Beatles: Day-by-Day, Song-by-Song, Record-by-Record*, iUniverse, Lincoln.

Decharné, M., 2005, *King's Road*, Weidenfeld and Nicolson, London.

DeRogatis, J., 2000, *Let It Blurt: The Life and Times of Lester Bangs*, Bloomsbury, London.

DuNoyer, P., 2009, *In the City*, Virgin Books, London.

Elms, R., 2005, *What We Wore*, Picador, London.

Farren, M., 2002, *Give the Anarchist a Cigarette*, Pimlico, London.

Fletcher, T., 1998, *Dear Boy: The Life of Keith Moon*, Omnibus Press, London.

Fountain, N., 1988, *Undergound*: The London Alternative Press 1966–1974, Comedia, London.

Gilbert, P., 2004, *Passion is a Fashion: The Real Story of The Clash*, Aurum, London.

Gopsill, T., Neale, G. 2007, *Journalists: 100 Years of the NUJ*. Profile, London.

Gorman, P., 2001, *In Their Own Write*, Sanctuary, London.

Gorman, P., 2008, *Reasons to be Cheerful: the Life and Work of Barney Bubbles*, Adelita, London.

Greenberg, S., 2009, 'Where is Graceland: 1980s Pop Culture through Music', in *Living in the Eighties*, eds G. Troy and V. Cannato, OUP, Oxford.

Griffiths, D., 2006, *Fleet Street*, British Library Press, London.

Harris, J., 2003, *The Last Party*, 4th Estate, London.

Hebdige, D., 2001, *Subculture: The Meaning of Style,* Routledge, London.

Hill, S., 2008, 'Lost in the Seventies: The Secret History of *Smash Hits*', available from www.1970sproject.co.uk

Johnson, E., Wolfe, T. (eds) 1975, *The New Journalism*, Picador, London.

Jones, S. (ed.)., 2002, *Pop Music and the Press*, Temple University Press, Philadelphia.

Kent, N., 2010, *Apathy for the Devil*, Faber and Faber, London.

Lazell, B., 1997, *Indie Hits 1980–1989*, Cherry Red, London.

Lindberg, U., 2005, *Rock Criticism from the Beginning*, Peter Lang, New York.

LSE, 2006, *Bankside 123*, LSE Cities Studio, London.

MacDonald, I., 1995, *Revolution in the Head*, Pimlico, London.

MacInnes, C., 1961, *Absolute Beginners*, Ace, London.

MacInnes, C., 1966, *England, Half English*, Penguin, London.

Maconie, S. 1999, *Blur: 3862 Days*, Virgin, London.

Maconie, S., 2003, *Cider with Roadies*, Ebury Press, London.

Mankowitz, W., 1960, *Expresso Bongo*, Evans Brothers, London.

McNamara, J., 2010, *The 21st Century Media (R)Evolution*, Peter Lang, New York.

Melly, G., 1989, *Revolt Into Style*, OUP, Oxford.

Miles, B., 2003, *In the Sixties*, Pimlico, London.

Moody, P., 2010, 'Staple Diet', 26 February, *Don't Panic*, available from http://ww.dontpaniconline.com/magazine/music/staple-diet

Moore, A., 2007, 'Unearthing', in *London: City of Disappearances*, ed I. Sinclair, Penguin, London.

Morrissey, S., 2007, 'I abhor racism, and apologise – for speaking to *NME*', 4 December, the *Guardian* [Online], available from http://www.guardian.co.uk/music/musicblog/2007/dec/04/morrisseyresp onds

Murray, C., 1991, *Shots from the Hip*, Penguin, London.

Nelson, E., 1989, *The British Counter-Culture 1966–1973*, Macmillan, London.

Nuttall, J., 1968, *Bomb Culture*, MacGibbon and Kee, London.

Pevsner, N., 1962, *London: The Cities of London and Westminster*, Penguin, London.

Rawlings, T., (ed.) 2000, *Sniffin' Glue: The Essential Punk Accessory*, Sanctuary House, London.

Reed, J., 2010, *The King of Carnaby Street*, Haus, London.

Salewicz, C., 2006, *Redemption Song: The Definitive Biography of Joe Strummer*, HarperCollins, London.

Sandbrook, D., 2006, *White Heat*, Little, Brown, London.

Savage, J., 1991, *England's Dreaming*, Faber and Faber, London.

Seddon, T., 2008, 'Drugs, the informal economy and globalization', *International Journal of Social Economics*, vol. 35, no.10, pp. 717–28.

Travis, A., 2001, *Bound and Gagged: A Secret History of Obscenity in Britain*, Profile, London.

Turner, A., 2008, *Halfway to Paradise: The Birth of British Rock*, V&A Publishing, London.

Wale, M., 1972, *Voxpop: Profiles of the Pop Process*, Harrap, London.

Whitney, K., 2009, 'Like Diluting an Essence', 3 May, *3:AM* Magazine, available from http://www.3ammagazine.com/3am/like-diluting-an-essence/

Wright, H., 2006, *London High*, Frances Lincoln, London.

Wu, T., 2010, *The Master Switch*, Atlantic, London.

York, P., 1980, *Style Wars*, Sidgwick and Jackson, London.

Young, R., 2010, *Electric Eden*, Faber and Faber, London.

Acknowledgements

Many thanks to everyone who agreed to be interviewed for this book, and for being so generous with their time and memories:

Keith Altham, Stuart Bailie, Danny Baker, Jack Barron, Don Black, Billy Bragg, James Brown, Julie Burchill, Bernard Butler, Keith Cameron, Roy Carr, Andrew Collins, Stuart Cosgrove, Kevin Cummins, Paul DuNoyer, Barbara Ellen, Mark Ellen, Mick Farren, Paolo Hewitt, Danny Holloway, Barney Hoskyns, Chrissie Hynde, James Johnson, Nick Kent, Ted Kessler, Steve Lamacq, Alan Lewis, Andy McDuff, Helen Mead, Paul Moody, Charles Shaar Murray, Tony Norman, Richard Norris, Lucy O'Brien, Tony Parsons, Ian Penman, David Quantick, Chris Salewicz, Jon Savage, Johnny Sharp, Alan Smith, Mat Snow, Neil Spencer, Terry Staunton, Steve Sutherland, Robert Tame, Karen Walter, Don Watson, Simon Williams, Michael Winner.

For contacts, information, advice and encouragement thanks to:

Marian Paterson and Alan Woodhouse at *NME*, Fiona Buswell and Anna Pallai at Faber and Faber, Monica Chouhan for help with picture research and Barry Dickins, Steve Double, Martin Goodacre, Tim Jonze, Adam Kinn, Alex Needham, Pennie Smith, Joe Stevens, Chris Wiegand and Andy Willsher.

Thanks to my sister for never complaining when I stole her copies of *Smash Hits*, *Number One* and *NME* and thanks most of all to Malcolm Croft and everyone at Portico Books.

Visit **www.historyofnme.com** to share your memories of reading *NME*, read the full transcripts of the interviews featured in this book and listen to playlists of music by the bands that shaped the paper.

Index

Picture Credits

p15, p22, p27 © Adam Kinn
p30 © Cummings Archives/Redferns
p36 © Dezo Hoffmann/Rex Features
p44 © LFI/Photoshot
p62, 76, 90, 109, 111, 119, 129, 136, 140 © Joe Stevens
p73 © Keith Morris/Redferns
p124 © Pennie Smith
p127 © Rex Features
p150 © Janette Beckman/Redferns
p190, p208 © Kevin Cummins/Getty Images